PARCELLS

Sports Publishing Inc.
www.SportsPublishingInc.com

Other Great *Daily News* Books

Jets: Broadway's 30-Year Guarantee
Big Town/Big Time: A New York Epic 1898-1998
Yogi Berra: An American Original
Yankees '98: Best Ever
The Amazin' Mets: The Miracle of '69
Joe DiMaggio: An American Icon
New York Giants: 75 Years of Football Memories
New York Rangers: Millennium Memories
Knicks: New York's 1970 NBA Champions
Big Town Biography: Lives and Times of the
Century's Classic New Yorkers

DAILY ▣ NEWS

Developmental Editor: Terrence C. Miltner
Production Supervisor: Susan M. McKinney
Book Design and Layout: Erin J. Sands
Dustjacket Design: Scot Muncaster
Photo Editors: Eric Meskauskas and Angela Troisi
Proofreader: David Hamburg

ISBN: 1-58261-146-7
Library of Congress Number: 99-65517

Printed in the United States.

www.SportsPublishingInc.com

TABLE OF CONTENTS

ACKNOWLEDGMENTS

As Bill Parcells worked his way to the top of the coaching ranks, he brought excellence and championships to every team he coached. The *Daily News* has been there to record the big games and the bigger victories of this Hall of Fame-bound coach.

This book would not have happened if not for the overwhelming support of Ed Fay (VP/Director of Editorial Administration) and Les Goodstein (Executive Vice President/Associate Publisher) of the *Daily News*.

Others who were instrumental in making this project such a success include Lenore Schlossberg, John Polizano, Eric Meskauskas, Mike Lipack, Angela Troisi, Vincent Panzarino, Faigi Rosenthal, Peter Edelman, Alan DeLaQueriere and Scott Browne. From the sports department, I specifically want to acknowledge the support of editor Leon Carter.

Space limitations preclude me from thanking every writer and photographer whose work appears in this book. However, wherever available, I have preserved the writers' bylines and the photographers' credits to ensure proper attribution for their work.

Finally, I am grateful for the support and hard work of my colleagues at Sports Publishing Inc. My thanks go to Susan McKinney, Erin Sands, Scott Muncaster, David Hamburg, Terry Hayden and Crystal Gummere for all of their hard work on the production of the book, and to Joseph Bannon Jr., Jeff Ellish, Victoria Marini and Joanna Wright for their guidance and feedback on this project.

Terrence C. Miltner
Developmental Editor

CHAPTER 1

ON THE RISE

Bill Parcells, in the light sports jacket in the center, stands on the Hastings College sideline with then-head coach Dean Pryor.

*F*rom his first job in 1964 with Hastings College in Nebraska, a young football coach named Bill Parcells followed a winding road to the top of the football world. After stops as an assistant coach at Wichita State, Army, Florida State, Vanderbilt and Texas Tech, Parcells earned his first chance as a head football coach at the Air Force Academy in Colorado Springs, Colorado. But after only one season at Air Force, he accepted an offer to be an assistant coach in the NFL with the New York Giants. It was one move too many and he walked away from coaching when his family balked at another move.

It all worked out. After a year in private business and rooting for the Denver Broncos, Parcells was back in the game and back in the NFL as an assistant with the New England Patriots. From there it was on to his hometown team, the New York Giants, and in 1982 he became the Giants' defensive coordinator.

Assistant coach Bill Parcells (far left) with Hastings head coach Dean Pryor, Don Boyett and Dr. Lynn Farrell.

Bill Parcells' College Coaching Career

1964	Hastings College (NE)	Defensive Assistant
1965	Wichita State	Defensive Line Coach
1966-1969	Army	Assistant Coach
1970-1972	Florida State	Assistant Coach
1973-1974	Vanderbilt	Defensive Coordinator
1975-1977	Texas Tech	Defensive Coordinator
1978	Air Force Academy	Head Coach

Parcells Busy as Line Coach at West Point

Associated Press

F ootball may seem way out of season to most sports fans, but a former River Dell High standout from Oradell is hard at work on the gridiron.

Duane (Bill) Parcells is the defensive interior line coach at West Point, and spring football practice opened for Army's team on April 6.

The Cadets will wind up practice on Saturday night, May 4, when the annual spring game will be played in Michie Stadium. That's when Coach Tom Cahill and his staff will display the probable 1968 Army team.

Cahill coached Parcells at River Dell High en route to his present position at West Point, where he was honored as college football's "Coach of the Year" in 1966. Last season, Parcells rejoined his old mentor.

"My association with Coach Cahill began at River Dell where I played two years under him," Bill said.

"After leaving River Dell in 1959, I went to Colgate one year and transferred to Wichita State, but remained in contact with him. When he was named coach at West Point and asked me if I was interested, I leaped at the chance because I had plans for a coaching career."

Parcells, who is married and lives at West Point with his wife and two small daughters, has spent a busy winter helping Coach Cahill set up for spring drills, reviewing personnel and representing the academy at various functions.

Bill played quarterback at River Dell, but was switched to the line at Wichita State and competed in the College All-Star Game at Soldier Field in Chicago in 1963.

The Cahill-Parcells combination helped start the fine football tradition that present coach Matty Certosimo has continued at River Dell High, a perennial power.

Parcells is a familiar name at River Dell and Army. Bill's brother Don starred in the backfield at both schools, playing three seasons at fullback for the Cadets. He graduated in 1965.

Don Parcells suffered 10 shrapnel wounds in his leg in Vietnam combat but has recovered completely. He has been serving as an instructor at Fort Sill in Oklahoma where he lives with his wife and infant son.

Mr. and Mrs. Charles H. Parcells are proud that another son is coming up the ranks. Douglas Parcells, 14, showed good potential as a fullback on offense and a defensive tackle for River Dell Junior High.

As the tradition of winning football has grown at River Dell, the name Parcells has been synonymous with the decade of gridiron excellence.

AP/Wide World Photos

Bill Parcells as an Army assistant coach.

Giants Tap Parcells as LB Coach

By Norm Miller

For the fourth assistant on the Giants' new coaching staff, Ray Perkins yesterday went for a New Jersey-bred guy who decided that after 18 years of working the college of the hinterlands, it was time to take his shot at the pros, especially when it meant getting back to the old neighborhood where he grew up.

Bill Parcells, born in Englewood and raised in Hasbrouck Heights and Oradell, had resigned as head coach of the Air Force Academy on Wednesday to accept the job as Giant assistant in charge of linebackers.

Like Parcells, the three Perkins aides named on Wednesday also were from outside the old Giants family. They were Ralph Hawkins (defensive coordinator), Pat Hodgson (receivers) and Ernie Adams (special offensive assistant).

Why would a career football man quit a college head coaching position to become an assistant in the NFL at age 37?

Sentiment and opportunity.

"It's been dancing around in my head for several years," Parcells said yesterday over the phone from Colorado Springs. "A number of my friends had gone into the NFL and done well. I figured this was the right time to make my move.

"This was not my first pro opportunity," he went on. "I had a chance years ago. I started thinking that maybe such an opportunity won't come around again. I had the gut feeling that this was the right move for me."

The opportunity to return to New Jersey also was a factor.

"I'll be happy to get back there." Parcells said. "My immediate family is still living in adjacent counties. This will be my first chance in 18 years to be near them."

Parcells graduated in 1959 from River Dell High School in Oradell, where he played quarterback. After accepting a scholarship to Wichita State—during the era of platoonless football—he played guard and tight end on offense and end linebacker on defense.

"It took them only 10 minutes (at Wichita State) to figure out I couldn't throw the football," he chuckled about his switch from QB.

Before landing his first head coaching assignment at Air Force Academy a year ago, Parcells held a number of assistants jobs: at Hastings (Nebraska); at his Wichita State alma mater; at West Point, under Tom Cahill, his high school coach; and then at Florida State, Vanderbilt and Texas Tech.

DAILY NEWS

After a year as the head coach at the Air Force Academy, Bill Parcells was in the pros. But he was out of football shortly after that.

CHAPTER 2

BECOMING THE BIGGEST GIANT

New Giants head coach Bill Parcells talks to his team.

*R*ay Perkins brought Bill Parcells back into football after Parcells' hiatus in 1979: First, he recommended Parcells to the New England Patriots and then he brought him to the New York Giants. By 1982, Parcells had been elevated to the Giants' defensive coordinator position and Perkins opened the door for Parcells to take over the team when he resigned to become the head football coach at Alabama, Perkins' alma mater.

When Parcells got the nod from Giants ownership to build on the framework that Perkins had assembled, everyone was happy. Parcells had his dream job, ownership had avoided a major coaching controversy and the players had a coach they knew and liked. All the pieces seemed in place for the Giants' return to glory.

Dream Job for Parcells

By Jack Wilkinson

The thought first crossed his mind a while ago. "You bet," Bill Parcells said. "Probably at that '58 playoff game with Baltimore." Parcells was sitting in Yankee Stadium that day ("And the game before that, too, when Summerall kicked the field goal to beat Cleveland"), a 17-year-old Giant fan from New Jersey rooting for his team, and fantasizing. Fantasizing about becoming head coach of the Giants one day. For Bill Parcells, one day came yesterday.

"I think the New York Giants are for Bill Parcells what the University of Alabama is for Ray Perkins," Parcells said yesterday, after the defensive coordinator was named to succeed Perkins as head coach of the Giants. "I'm from Bergen County (Englewood). I grew up a Giant fan. I'm one of the luckiest guys in the world, doing exactly what I want to do. Very few people can do that."

Or this: Parcells becomes just the 12th head coach in Giant history. He will assume those responsibilities once the season ends, once Perkins leaves. For now, Parcells, 41, will concentrate on Sunday's game in Washington, on his job as defensive coordinator and linebacker coach, which he's held since coming to the Giants from New England before the '81 season.

"I owe everything to Ray Perkins," Parcells said. "I'm still working for Ray Perkins. If it wasn't for him, and his willingness to take a chance on me, I'd never be in a position to be coach of the Giants."

Actually, Parcells was first hired by the Giants in February of 1979, before Perkins' first season, and worked three months before resigning. "I just had a personal situation I felt needed attention and I attended to it," Parcells said. He had just left Air Force after one season as head coach, but his wife was hesitant to leave Colorado. She liked living there and didn't want to take their three children out of school in mid-year. Parcells resigned from the Giants job and went into private business in Colorado.

But the following February he became linebacker coach for the Patriots and their head coach, Ron Erhardt. Now Erhardt will work for Parcells: fired after last season, Erhardt now coaches the Giant tight ends, and could become Parcells' offensive coordinator. Under Erhardt, the Patriots scored a club-record 441 points in 1980.

Parcells, though, will be in charge. But he'll remember what Perkins brought to the Giants. "Work ethic, pride, staying power, improvement," Parcells said. "I would like to build upon what foundation Ray and George (Young, the GM) have made. I feel fortunate I don't have to start over. I feel fortunate to inherit the by-products of what other people have done."

Born in Englewood, Parcells was an outstanding player at River Dell High in Oradell. He was an All-Missouri Valley linebacker at Wichita State from 1961-63, but shunned the pros to begin coaching at Hastings College in Nebraska in '64. He handled the defensive line at Wichita State in '65, then spent 1966-69 as the linebacker coach at Army. He became, and remains, good friends with Bobby Knight, the coach of the Cadet basketball team.

After stops as an assistant at Florida State (1970-72), Vanderbilt ('73) and Texas Tech (1975-77), Parcells went to Air Force. Eventually, he came home to New Jersey. Now, he's truly home.

"I wasn't really aware of Ray's situation until Monday," said Parcells, who, like all the assistants, knew Perkins had interviewed in Alabama on Sunday. "And I wasn't certain of that then." He was well aware by 6:30 Monday evening, when Young began interviewing Parcells after Perkins decided to leave. "George was interested in finding out what my views were, my approach, my philosophy on things," Parcells said. "He'd never had the opportunity to ask me."

Young liked what he heard: although a contract still must be drawn up and signed, Young and Parcells agreed with a handshake. "I would have done this for free," Parcells said.

What Parcells hopes the coaching change doesn't do is distract the Giants or hurt their playoff chances. "There's always that possibility," he admitted. "But I don't really think so. We got some class guys and it's their team." Soon, it will be Bill Parcells' team.

Young Kept the Flame Burning

By Phil Pepe

As keeper of the Giant flame, the important thing for George Young is to always be prepared. The flame must not be allowed to burn out, or even flicker. George Young cannot allow himself to be taken by surprise, he cannot afford to make snap judgments. The selection of Bill Parcells to succeed Ray Perkins as head coach of the Giants was a quick decision. It was not a snap judgment. George Young does not operate that way.

George Young has known for about a year that Bill Parcells had the qualities he desired in a head coach. It was knowledge he filed in the folder in his mind under the heading, "Coaches." He didn't know until last Thursday that he would have to pull out that folder and use it.

Thursday was the day Ray Perkins told George Young the University of Alabama had asked to talk to him about replacing Bear Bryant as head coach, and Perkins asked Young for permission to talk about the job that has been his lifelong dream. George Young granted Perkins permission and immediately called up his file on coaches.

"Later in the day," Young recalls, "Bill Parcells walked by my office and I yelled to him and asked him to come in. We talked for two hours."

In that two-hour conversation, George Young had the advantage of knowing he might have to find himself a new coach and the added advantage that Bill Parcells had no idea he was being interviewed as Perkins' successor.

"I wasn't interviewing him," Young corrected, " I was evaluating. In this job, you're always evaluating people. When I go to a college game or another pro game and I talk to people, I'm evaluating."

When they had finished their two-hour talk, George Young knew that if Ray Perkins left, Bill Parcells was the man he wanted as Perkins' replacement. It wasn't until Monday that Perkins told Young he had accepted the Alabama job and the Giant GM knew he had to move quickly.

"I was in Tulsa at the time, attending a scouting meeting," Young recalled. "I knew the man I wanted, that wasn't a problem. The problem wasn't who, it was when and how."

George Young called Bill Parcells at home that night and told him to get all his work done the following day, then see him when he was finished. Parcells was on the job at 6 a.m. Tuesday morning, preparing for Sunday's Redskin game. By 6 p.m., he was in George Young's office. They spoke for about four hours and when he left, Bill Parcells was the Giants' new head coach, a job about which he had fantasized since he attended the Giants-Colts playoff game in 1958 when he was just 17 years old.

"My main objective was to try to do it as soon in the week as possible," says Young, "to minimize the distraction for the Redskin game as much as possible. I felt it was important to get it done as soon as possible rather than dance around and have it hanging over my head and the heads of the players. You've got to be fair with your players. They live in a world of anxiety and I didn't want to add to that anxiety. By doing it now, we have eliminated that anxiety. This is a guy they know and like and they know they're not going to have to start from ground zero with a new coach."

Continuity was an important factor and it is a tribute to Ray Perkins, to the job he has done here, to the groundwork he has laid, that it was decided to replace Perkins with a member of his staff, a person Perkins hand-picked to be his defensive coordinator. But continuity was only possible because George Young had the man he wanted right on his staff.

"The one thing I asked myself," he said, "is would I make the same decision in January as I would now? The answer was yes, so why wait? I didn't want to run the risk of losing him. Somehow people always think a stranger is a better guy. In Baltimore, we had a guy named Chuck Noll sitting on our staff and we let him get away."

George Young was not going to make the same mistake the Colts made. Bill Parcells was his man and the fact that he was born and raised in New Jersey is, according to Young, "a bonus. It helps only because he's the right man."

Just as Ray Perkins, without New York-New Jersey ties, was the right man four years ago. Then, George Young was looking for a disciplinarian.

"I knew I needed a tough guy who could go nose to nose with the players," Young says. "I wanted a guy with no wounds, a guy who hadn't failed someplace else. I wanted an audacious guy and a young guy. I didn't want a 50-year-old guy, like me. I wanted a surgeon. Then, I was looking for a point guy, now I was looking for the continuity guy. It wasn't a quick decision. I don't have my neck stuck out."

When you are prepared, you never do.

Giant Players Sad but Wish Perk Luck

By Jenny Kellner

There was no bitterness and little surprise among the Giants yesterday morning after coach Ray Perkins announced he was leaving at the end of the year to replace Bear Bryant at Alabama.

But that didn't mean they were happy about it.

"I'm sad and happy at the same time" said linebacker Brad Van Pelt, who has seen four coaching changes since he came to the Giants in 1973. "I'm sad to be losing him when we're on the verge of really turning things around. I got the first drift of it on the news last night, but it's not a real surprise. His name has been tossed around as Bear's replacement for some time. But I'm happy for Ray because this is a dream come true for him."

One bright spot in a hectic day was the announcement early yesterday that defensive coordinator Bill Parcells, former head coach at Air Force, would take over for Perkins at the end of the year. It was a decision the players cheered.

"I hope success doesn't spoil him," said linebacker Harry Carson. "He's easy going, he's well liked. He likes to have fun, but he knows how to be serious. And he'll probably smile more than Ray."

Parcells, nicknamed "Tuna" by the players because of his resemblance to TV's Charley the Tuna, was kidded by players as he gave his first interview as the Giants' new head coach.

"All right, Tuna," cracked linebacker Brian Kelley. "Way to move in, Tuna. I mean sir Tuna."

Although everyone agreed that the timing of Perkins' announcement could have been better, Van Pelt, perhaps better than anyone else, can understand how Perkins made the decision.

"I have been in the same position," said Van Pelt, who lives in Owasso, Mich. "I've always wanted to play for the Detroit Lions, although that's lessened recently. But you never know when the opportunity is going to present itself."

Certainly Giants' general manager George Young eased things a bit when, right after Perkins' statement, he told the players that Parcells would replace Perkins.

"But it really doesn't matter, because Coach Perkins is leaving a good framework here," said Carson, who, with the other Giants preferred to keep Perkins' speech to them private. "The timing is a little off, but the world will still be turning. All I want is to start 1983 off on a winning note, hopefully playing the Jets in the Super Bowl. I want to finish this year as a winner, and help Coach Perkins in his dream for a Super Bowl ring before he gets his first national championship."

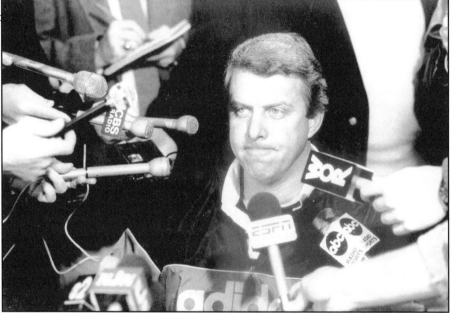

Once he took over as head coach, all eyes, and microphones, were on Parcells.

There'll Be Giant Changes

But Parcells won't rush new regime

By Jack Wilkinson

U nder Bill Parcells, there'll be some changes made. "I think life's too short to walk around with your teeth gritted all the time," said Parcells, who replaced Ray Perkins yesterday as head coach of the Giants. "At least for me. I like to joke. I like to laugh.

"My philosophy's still the same: if we can get it done like that, OK. If we're not getting it done, I don't think I'm gonna be very loose. I think it centers around people being able to concentrate when it's time to concentrate. Business is business."

There is much business to tend to. Yesterday, Parcells talked to his team. "Nothing heavy," he said. "About 20 minutes." About Perkins' contributions, off-season conditioning, rehabilitation, discipline and his philosophy.

"Course they're pretty familiar with that," said Parcells, who just finished his second, and last, season as defensive coordinator. "I have to be the head coach of the whole team. But I'm gonna try to keep a pretty close hand on the defense. My role's changing, but I hope my personality isn't. If it did, I'd be pretentious. That's the last thing I want. I'm Bill Parcells. Our players know me. You can usually tell what I'm thinking by the expression on my face."

Later this week, you will be able to tell more about Parcells' Giants. Today, he'll meet with many players, particularly vets and those undergoing rehabilitation. Tomorrow, it's the coaches. "I don't view them as my coaching staff," Parcells said. "I view them as coach Perkins' staff."

Although no one has mentioned leaving, Parcells said, "I think there is a good chance there will be some changes on the staff. Who, how many, would be conjecture at this point. There's been some conjecture about offensive coordinator (Ron Erhardt has the title, but Perk ran the offense). I haven't contacted anybody."

In picking coaches, Parcells said, "I don't want clones in the Bill Parcells image. I want what anybody wants in business: bright, motivated types, young, knowledgeable in their fields of expertise. Guys who can get players to do what they want them to."

Parcells likes to let players "use their strengths in your basic scheme. The worst thing you can have, particularly on defense, is a guy out there in a mental straitjacket: Do I step with this foot? Do I line up six inches away?"

Of his QB, Parcells said, "I don't want to open that can of worms. Just call me evasive." He called the situation "competitive" between Scott Brunner, Phil Simms and Jeff Rutledge.

Coach Bill Parcells puts players through their paces during a workout.

Parcells Rehires Former Boss Erhardt

By Bill Madden

I n what was actually a very easy decision, new Giants head coach Bill Parcells yesterday announced the retention of his former boss, Ron Erhardt, as offensive coordinator.

Parcells, who has been interviewing all the holdover Giants assistants while slowly forming his staff for next year, was certainly expected to retain Erhardt. Before coming to the Giants last year, Parcells served as an assistant at New England when Erhardt was the Patriots new coach.

"There was never any doubt in my mind about him (Erhardt) coming back," Parcells said yesterday, "but I just wanted to know what his feelings were. I wanted to be sure we were on the same page."

It was reasonable to assume that Erhardt, having already been a head coach, might have felt slighted about being passed over for the job as Ray Perkins' successor by one of his own former assistants. Parcells conceded that he wanted to be certain Erhardt wouldn't be uncomfortable. "But that was really a very minor point in our talks," Parcells said. "Primarily we talked about his feelings on the offense. There's no question that I plan to give him a lot of leeway."

Under Erhardt's direction last year, the Giants offense improved from last in the conference in '81 (270.4 yards per game) to ninth (303.2).

Earlier this month, Parcells announced the retention of Pat Hodgson as receivers coach, Bill Belichick as linebackers coach and Romeo Crennel as special teams coach. "We're not anywhere near complete," Parcells said.

CHAPTER 3

REBUILDING
THE GIANTS

As Lawrence Taylor became more of a defensive threat, the Giants became more of a playoff contender.

A new head coach usually enjoys a honeymoon period with the fans, ownership and the media. But after a 3-12-1 inaugural season, not only was Bill Parcells' honeymoon over, but it looked like he and the Giants might be headed for divorce.

Despite the Giants' off-season flirtations with Miami's Howard Schnellenberger, Parcells managed to keep his job. Parcells' team made the playoffs in 1984. In 1985, the Giants made it all the way to the NFC championship game against the vaunted Chicago Bears. Even though the Giants lost to the eventual champions of Super Bowl XX, the progress shown by Parcells' squad would bode well for the 1986 season.

Dedication Has Paid off for Parcells

By Bill Verigan

The grin was as wide as an open door. Nothing could be hidden behind it.

"I'm an 8-year-old again with my own baseball glove and bat," blurted Bill Parcells. But it's even better than that, much better. He is a 41-year-old coach with his own New York Giants.

Even as a kid, he had dreamed of coaching the Giants. Other kids dreamed of throwing a winning pass or breaking loose for a deciding touchdown with the title on the line, but Parcells dreamed of being the coach. He clung to that dream until it came true.

"I've been very, very lucky," he said.

He had luck, he had talent, but most of all he had dedication. Parcells believes he developed that last trait in the gym at River Dell High School just across the Hudson in New Jersey. Mickey Corcoran was his coach and his inspiration.

"He was the basketball coach, and more than anybody else, he was the one who made me into the kind of player I wanted to be back then and the kind of player I want to coach now," said Parcells. "You had to do the job and do it with enthusiasm, or else you had to look for another job. He would kick you right out of the gym a lot of times. I only found out a lot later that he was doing it all with the blessing of my father. They were in collusion."

"His father told me if he needs a kick in the backside give it to him," Corcoran recalled. "He didn't need one often. He was always slow, very slow," he said, "but he was also the best athlete in school. He was a quarterback and linebacker in football, a forward on the basketball team and just about every-thing in baseball."

Bill Parcells was the kind of overachiever he wants on the Giants. If the over achiever has talent, so much the better, but he can't stand a player who fails to reach his potential.

Many of his players have learned that lesson. At their first meeting, Parcells told Curtis McGriff, "You can never play for me." When McGriff asked why, the coach told him he was fat. "I'll lose weight," said McGriff. So Parcells set a limit, and McGriff has never exceeded it.

That's Parcells' kind of player. "Some players have to be told once, some have to be told twice," he said. Nobody gets a third chance.

Maybe Parcells' own limitations as an athlete helped lead him to coaching. He began playing football at Wichita State on a tryout basis. "I had one semester to make the team or go home," he said. "I made it and started for three years."

Eleven players were drafted off that team in 1964, and Parcells was good enough to be selected in the third round by the Detroit Lions. But he quickly realized that he would never excel in the pros. "I was just an in-between size," he said. "I was about 238, and the best players were a lot bigger so I became a coach."

Thus began an odyssey that took him to seven different colleges. He grew and made friends at every stop. At Florida State, he got to know Dan Henning, who once said Parcells would be the best coach on any staff. He also got close to Bobby Knight at Army. Knight's son, Timmy, now one of the Giants' ball boys, told Parcells, "You coach just like my father." Parcells could think of no greater compliment. (The presence of Knight's son and two of Vince Lombardi's grandsons among the Giant ball boys reveals a lot about the kind of coach Parcells would like to be.)

Parcells' college odyssey appeared to be over when he was invited by Ray Perkins to be a defensive coach for the Giants in 1979. He accepted, and his old dream seemed to be coming true. Instead, Parcells woke up and walked away from the job.

At the time he was the head coach at the Air Force Academy, and his wife and three daughters were reluctant to make another move. His wife was happy in Colorado.

"There comes a time in life when you have to make a difficult decision," he said. "That decision was my gut check. I'd been in coaching for a long time. I'd been in sports most of my life. Now, just as I was reaching my professional goals, I had to leave.

"When I told the Giants I had decided to take a job outside of football, I knew I might never get another chance to coach. It was difficult, but it also put football in perspective for me. I got to see that football is not the only thing on earth."

But he sorely missed it, and his family understood when in 1980 he accepted a job with New England. Perkins helped him get that job, then created an opening on the Giants' staff the following year for Parcells as defensive coordinator.

It was strictly against the Giants' policy. GM George Young said, "It's a rule of thumb here that we don't rehire a guy once he quits. But Bill was an exception. We know he had been sincere in leaving, and we wanted him to return."

When Perkins resigned to return to Alabama, the natural successor was Parcells. There have been obvious changes, but Parcells stresses how much has remained the same.

"The approach to the game has not changed appreciably," Parcells said. "Ray brought in the kind of players who cause you to win, and that's an advantage for me. And we have much of the same philosophy." The players and assistants see a change, though. They talk about their rapport with Parcells. They are having more fun than they had under Perkins, but they realize that the real fun comes from winning.

"This is the honeymoon before the first game is played," Parcells said. "You only get to stick around in this game if you keep winning. So far I've been lucky. I've only had two losing seasons, and I don't want any more."

Friendly 'Enemies' for a Day

By Bill Verigan

The friendship between Bill Parcells and Dan Henning began a decade ago when they were assistant coaches at Florida State.

It survived when they wound up on opposite sides of the country, and when first Henning, then Parcells, briefly left coaching. It has even survived racquetball arguments.

Henning is a coach whom Parcells could always find room for on his staff, and the same is probably true on the other side of the friendship. When the Giants hired Parcells for the first time as an assistant, Henning made a point of calling GM George Young to say, "Parcells will be the best coach on your staff."

However, that friendship is about to be tested. They're both in their first year as head coaches in the NFL and Parcells' Giants are playing Henning's Falcons tomorrow in Atlanta.

The phone calls between New Jersey and Atlanta were put on hold a week ago. For the first time in a long time, the two of them will be in the same town at the same time and fail to get together for dinner.

Henning has stopped talking completely about their friendship. "There are a lot of things I could say, but I don't want to," Henning said.

Parcells has not gone that far. He said yesterday that Henning "is just a good person. I love the guy. If I needed an offensive coordinator, he'd be the first guy I'd go to. There'd never be anyone else."

"Our careers have been parallel in many ways," Parcells said. "We became friends at Florida State. We were both from the same area. He's from New York City, and I'm from New Jersey. We both had Irish fathers. We've both been down and out, both out of coaching. He was involved with the security department for the World Trade Center when he was out in the early '70s, and I was involved in business. We know what the other man has gone through."

Hard Year on, off Field for Parcells

By Bill Verigan

Bill Parcells could never have imagined what this season was going to be like with the Giants. These are sad days in many ways for the coach. What happens on the field is only a game. The losses this season are sad, but they aren't tragic.

Even the injuries, which are so debilitating and so frequent on this team, eventually heal. A few of the 24 men who have passed through the Giants' injured reserve list might have their careers ended prematurely, but a team survives on the belief that there is always next week, next season.

Unfortunately, tragedy also pursued this team and the man who coaches it off the field this season. Bob Ledbetter, the man chosen by Parcells to coach the running backs, died of a brain hemorrhage. Parcells' father, Charles, underwent triple bypass surgery. Few fathers and sons are closer, and there was the anxiety of those weeks his father spent in the hospital, from tests to recovery. Then, before his father was released, Parcells' mother, Ida, became ill. She is presently hospitalized.

Parcells never mentions such matters unless he is asked. He always stresses that they in no way have affected the time and effort he has devoted to the team. Coaches always try to live in two worlds. When disappointments happen on the job, they find their pleasure at home.

If he has lost some of his quips, it's only understandable during a season like this.

"I think I have this game in perspective," Parcells said yesterday after the Giants' record dropped to 3-9-1 with a 27-12 loss to the Los Angeles Raiders. "It's very, very important, and it's my job, but I understand what station it occupies in the realm of the world. It's important for me, but it's not the only thing."

As a coach, he suffers disappointment on Sundays, then looks with optimism at the week ahead. Instead of dwelling on his team's latest loss yesterday, he preferred to look at the positive contribution that a couple of rookies—Byron Williams and Kevin Belcher—had made in the game.

If ever a team was jinxed, it is the Giants. That was the word around the league before this season.

Troy Archer, who would be anchoring the defense along with Lawrence Taylor and Harry Carson, died in a car crash in 1978. Linebacker Dan Lloyd got cancer in 1979. Then center Keith Eck had a heart attack on his way to camp. And running back Doug Kator was struck by cancer.

Those are the losses off the field. The Giants also lead the league in injuries this year. They have come out of only two games without a serious injury.

Phil Simms, the quarterback who personifies the frustration of this team, ruptured the thumb on his throwing hand in the very game he took over. General manager George Young thought Simms would be the quarterback for the 1980s when he was drafted in the first round in 1979, but a new injury has struck him every year.

When the Giants went with Jeff Rutledge, he dislocated a kneecap. The only quarterback to remain healthy is Scott Brunner, but he's not impervious. He limped off the field on two bad ankles Sunday, and Parcells said he also has contusions of the elbow and ankle. However, Brunner will probably start the remaining three games, according to the coach. Such injuries don't have any impact on this team.

Starters lost for long periods or the entire season include Carson, Rob Carpenter, Jim Burt, Bill Neill, Curtis McGriff, George Martin, Terry Jackson and Floyd Eddings. The Giants are not talented enough or deep enough to suffer such losses without a devastating effect. Without such losses, the Giants at least had a chance to reach mediocrity.

Men who play for the Giants for any prolonged period become philosophers, like Carson.

"Your career will be over or the season will be over too soon," said the linebacker, who is in his eighth year. "I just enjoy it while it's there. I look at those people who don't have a chance to play. Maybe you don't play well sometimes, but at least you have a chance to play. That's enough motivation."

It's Time for Giants' Young to Take Noose off Parcells

By Bill Verigan

The Giants named an assistant general manager yesterday. That means George Young is coming back, because GMs aren't allowed to hire assistants if they are about to get the boot.

Young's five-year plan for reconstructing the Giants ended with a 3-12-1 record. That's not progress. It was the worst record for a Giant team since 1974 (2-12). But his five-year plan will become a six- or seven- or eight-year plan.

Young has been granted more time by the Maras, but Bill Parcells and his coaching staff are still wondering whether they will return. Now that he is sure of his fate, perhaps Young will provide the same courtesy to his coaching staff.

Every week, the Maras, Young and Ray Walsh get together to thrash out their differences and make plans. Parcells probably figures in those plans, but they have not let him know, despite the two seasons remaining on his contract.

There are reasons to doubt the coach will be back. The GM, who promoted Parcells a year ago, has fed the uncertainty of the coaching situation. He has refused to comment on Parcells' status for next year and apparently investigated the availability of an old crony, Howard Schnellenberger of the University of Miami.

Parcells was never Young's man. Ray Perkins was Young's man and Parcells was thrust upon the GM by the abrupt resignation of Perkins. Parcells was promoted for the sake of continuity.

By keeping the pressure on Parcells, perhaps Young has taken some of the pressure off himself. It's time Young started to feel the squeeze.

Parcells played with what Young gave him. That wasn't easy. Young hasn't come up with a proven quarterback. He still insists that Phil Simms is the

Giants' quarterback for the '80s, but the decade might end before Simms completes a healthy season. In five years, Young still hasn't come up with an offensive lineman worth mentioning.

Parcells made some blatant rookie mistakes, but few coaches have success during their first season with a team. Unlike Young, Parcells admits he made mistakes. But Young seems to be turning Parcells into a scapegoat by refusing to reveal the future of the coaching staff.

Indecision affects a football team. Players must have confidence in the coach and believe he is in control. The Jets under Walt Michaels were 0-3 in 1981 and on the verge of complete collapse. The Jets' management probably saved the season by announcing that Michaels was in no danger of being fired.

Some of the Giants' players are fed up with management's lethargic approach to putting together a winner. That's why veterans like Harry Carson and Brad Van Pelt want to be traded. Lawrence Taylor's differences are not with Parcells, either, but the man above.

Young once procrastinated with Taylor, and it has turned out to be costly. Now, he is procrastinating with the coaches. Young's next announcement should be a firm assurance that Parcells is returning.

Bill Parcells with Giants G.M. George Young.

Parcells Ducks Fame Just Like the Noose

By Bill Verigan

Nearly a year has passed since the rumor surfaced. The Giants were dropping another game in a 3-12-1 season when a bunch of hooded informed sources were ready to slip a noose around Bill Parcells' neck and hire Howard Schnellenberger as his replacement.

It didn't happen. But, as with many rumors, there might have been a hint of truth involved. It died hard.

Now, a year later, the rumor lies somewhere in an unmarked grave. Parcells is a likely candidate for NFC Coach of the Year. There are a bunch of guys over in the AFC who could qualify, but go ahead and try to name anyone better in the NFC.

Parcells said he could think of several. The mention of receiving such an award himself makes the hair bristle on Parcells' neck. At first he acts embarrassed, then he gets mad.

"We've got seven victories," he said. "It's a long way to the wire. There are four games and 22 days left."

Forget about awards. "I wanta win because I wanta win, the same as these players," he said. "The real cherished moments are those small moments of interaction when you share an accomplishment with the team, the interaction with the players."

The Giants are likely to be favored in their last four games, starting with the Chiefs on Sunday at Giants Stadium. but Parcells said he never knows the betting line. He doesn't believe in it any more than he believes in luck.

"Luck has nothing to do with anything that happens in football," he said. "Whenever I hear anybody in the game use that word I become suspicious that I'm talking to a guy who doesn't know anything about the game."

Parcells' Playoffs

By Bill Verigan

The Giants are in the playoffs.

Roll that around your tongue a few times. The Giants are in the playoffs . . . the Giants are in the playoffs . . . the Giants are in the playoffs. Sounds good, doesn't it?

The Giants are in the playoffs because Don Shula played it as only Don Shula knows how—to win—the way George Young knew he would.

"If you think he's not going to try," George Young was saying Saturday, "you don't know the nature of the man. You've got to put yourself in that man's head. I've known him since 1953. He gets upset when he loses pre-season games."

The Giants are in the playoffs because of Dan Marino's brilliant passing and Mark Clayton's legerdemain at catching a football and running with it after he catches it. But do not say the Giants backed into the playoffs. They are in the playoffs because they won more games than anybody in the tough NFC East except the champion Redskins, because they beat the Cowboys twice and had a better conference record than the Cardinals and those are the rules for playoff qualification in the NFL.

You would not have given them much of a chance after their spiritless defeat by the Saints Saturday, but you would have given them much less of a chance last December, after they won only three games, or last July or August, after they tore it up, sent a lot of veterans packing and decided to go with a whole lot of kids.

We are talking major overhaul here, wholesale changes, urban renewal of a decadent football team and one man deserves the most credit for getting the Giants in the playoffs, for his courage and his convictions. The man is Bill Parcells and he is the single most important factor in the Giants' success. Phil Simms says so. So does Dave Jennings.

"We played hard and stuck together and it all started with what Bill instilled in us in training camp," said Phil Simms.

Bill Parcells is your average guy, the guy you might run into at the neighborhood bar and talk sports with over a couple of beers.

And yet there is a dedication there and a mental toughness and a sense of purpose and direction. He had a plan and an idea and he implemented that plan with the help of George Young. Bill Parcells' plan was to rid the Giants of some of the older players, the contented fat cats who had come to accept losing as their lot. He wanted younger players, hungrier players. That's why there were four rookies, two first-year players and three second-year players in the Giants' starting lineup in their final regular season game Saturday.

"The biggest reason for our success is the job Bill Parcells did as our coach," said Dave Jennings, who has been a Giant longer than any other on this current squad. "He didn't change a lot of things and he stayed on us mentally to get us to cut down on our mistakes and our penalties. He kept us together when people got down on us. I think he deserves most of the credit for what we've done this year, but he wouldn't think so. Bill doesn't care about accolades."

He has refused to enter into discussion about being named NFL Coach of the Year, even bristling at the mere mention of the idea. What Bill Parcells cares about is performance and results, not accolades. What he cares about are facts. The Giants are in the playoffs as a wild card against the Rams. That is a fact Bill Parcells can deal with. The only thing he cares about now is beating the Rams and moving on to the next plateau.

Another Big One for Bill

By Bill Verigan

For most of the Giants, this thing against the Rams Sunday is the biggest game of their lives. This is a size 13 triple E football game. With some careful consideration you might even come to the conclusion that it is a bigger game than the 1964 Mineral Water Bowl.

All things are relative and Bill Parcells remembers the 1964 Mineral Water Bowl as a very big game, life and death to a 23-year-old rookie assistant coach of the Hastings (Nebraska) College Broncos.

The game was played in Excelsior Springs, Mo., against Fort Hays State in 15-degree weather and with a snow fence circling the field. It was light years away from the NFL playoffs, but just as important to Bill Parcells then as the Rams are now. His Bronco defense did a job that day, holding Fort Hays scoreless in a 6-0 victory that was the launching pad for a coaching career.

The stakes weren't very high in terms of financial reward. The Mineral Water Bowl offered no money to participating schools, hardly even a thank-you.

Still, it was big stuff for a 23-year-old coach and now, two decades later, come the Rams. The trappings are different, much more is at stake, but it is no bigger in its way than the 1964 Mineral Water Bowl was in its. In preparation, in the necessity of blocking and tackling, it is no different.

It does not matter now how the Giants got here, it only matters that they got here. There is no such thing, Parcells says, as backing into the playoffs. There are rules and qualifications and the Giants met them.

"We won enough games to make it, that's all that counts," says Parcells, who doesn't believe that being here changes anything about his approach to the game.

"I don't think you can do anything drastic in a game like this. All a coach can do is give his team the best chance to win. A coach can only ruin his team at this point. I can ruin this team faster than anyone. You've got what you've got and you do what you can do and if that's good enough, fine."

A week ago, the Giants' playoff chances looked dead, but they got a lease on life from the Redskins and the Dolphins, but that does not mean they are in a no-lose situation Sunday.

"We're not in this for the fun of it," says the coach. "This is serious business. We have a job to do and we're going out there to do that job."

"Nobody gives you any medals for trying hard," Parcells says. "You're supposed to try hard. Only the results count. The bottom line. If a guy isn't ready to play in a game like this, he'd better find another line of work. And if there is anybody out there who needs a pep talk, he's not going to be here long."

Bill Parcells has no false illusions about himself or his team. That is not a great team he is coaching, but it is not a great team he is coaching against Sunday. How many great teams are there in the NFL? San Francisco, maybe. The Dolphins on offense, the Raiders on defense. Parcells feels the Giants can compete with any of them. Styles often dictate results and Parcells thinks his team has the style to win Sunday. He is confident the Giants will beat the Rams. "My expectations," he says, "are greater than anyone else's. But we could get blown out, 50-6, you never know."

If there is confidence in the Giant locker room, there certainly is not overconfidence. If anything, that emotion may be an intangible that favors the Giants.

"Nobody thinks we can do anything," says Parcells. "That's perfect. I love it. It just makes things better."

Nothing could be better than the Giants in the playoffs, still playing when 16 other teams are not, still eligible to win the Super Bowl.

If the Mineral Water Bowl was a big game to a 23-year-old rookie coach, Sunday's wild-card game is big to a 43-year-old second-year NFL coach. But Sunday's game is not necessarily the biggest of Bill Parcells' career. That one, he hopes, has yet to be played.

Bill Parcells hugs Giants guard Chris Godfrey after the Giants defeated the Los Angeles Rams, 16-13, in the NFC wild card game. The following week, the Giants fell, 21-10, to the 49ers.

The Not-So-Gentle Giant

By Fred Schruers

At noon every weekday in the New York Giants' fall training camp in Pleasantville, N.Y., head coach Bill Parcells appears for his meeting with the press. Like many of his players, the handful of reporters call him by his first name, but he is not a man without recourse to a useful psychic distance. He tends to keep a poker face and speak in a quiet, husky monotone, yet the gradations of his mood are plainly sensed. Just a little bonhomie on Parcell's part can light up a room; just a trace of anger can put off a frightening gleam.

Parcells' office in the bunkerlike confines of Giants Stadium is decorated with toy elephants. And appropriately, there is an elephantine stolidity to this 6-foot-3 220-pounder; indeed, when he wears his bell-shaped headphones and gray coaching garb, and stands spraddle-legged to put his hands on his knees and peer into the colorful riot on the field, he presents a jumbo-like image that's almost endearing. But this doesn't mean you can transgress Parcells' turf; he knows that a healthy bull elephant, tusks intact, has no effective predator. "Hey," he says, remembering the cornered feeling he fought off during an abysmal 1983 season, "they go after the weak ones."

"They" could include the 70-odd thousand spectators on a bad day in Giants Stadium, 45 more in uniform looking for a sign of frailty, plus the team execs he works for. Nor are the few people sitting in the press room he now enters clawless. But, unlike his predecessor Ray Perkins, Parcells betrays little fear of sportswriters. He takes his place as one among leaf-eaters, ready for a little muted trumpeting in the forest.

"Just for my edification, Bill . . ."

"What's 'edification' mean? I only went to Wichita State. I didn't go to Georgetown."

Most of those present knew that Parcells indeed went to that southern Kansas institution, but only after dropping out of Colgate because he didn't like

In 1985, Parcells' Giants beat Chuck Noll's Pittsburgh Steelers to finish the season 10-6.

the sports program ("I said, 'These guys just aren't serious about this stuff'") and was twice an all-conference linebacker. And not one of them would lay serious money that Parcells doesn't know what 'edification' means.

"Just to help me out, then, Bill—how's [rookie running back Lee] Rouson looking on special teams?"

"Good," replies Parcells, "A good guy for covering kicks. That, um . . ."

"Enhances?"

"Yeah, we had that one my third year. 'Enhances' his chances of making the team."

"Are you having fun this year, Bill?"

Parcells gives the writer a wake-up-and-chew-the-Astroturf look, then settles almost thankfully into the Hamlet rendition coaches so love. "It hasn't been fun for me at all, really. There was a point in this camp when I made a list of guys I definitely want. And it was only 29, 30 names. I'll tell ya, I'm a little worried about our defense. We haven't got that attack mentality we had last year. Don't get me wrong—I don't think they're gonna honk it up in there and run the ball down our throats—they're not gonna honk it up and drive us down to the Hackensack River. It's just a feeling . . ."

Parcells pauses in this mournful monologue to watch pens racing across notepaper. He looks so studiously downcast that you know he's inwardly delighted. He has sent a warning to his defense.

Parcells, 44, grew up in Bergen County. Although his father was perhaps the best-known schoolboy athlete in the history of Hackensack High before going on to college-football stardom, "he never tried to influence me toward or away from athletics. The only thing he ever said was when I was about 13, after he'd seen me in a game. I was a wise guy, wasn't doing my best, and he said, 'If you're gonna go down there and do that, you might as well give up the game.' And that really hurt. I remember that like it was yesterday."

The lesson took. Tom Godfrey, now the athletic director at Northern Highlands High School, recalls a Babe Ruth League game in which his teammate, the young Parcells, was catching. Bobby Myslik, now the athletic director at Princeton and then the most feared slugger in the league, came to bat. "So Bill calls time, takes off his gear, goes out to play left field. Myslik hits the ball about four miles, Bill catches it, comes back and puts on the gear. He was about 14, but he was just like a coach. He knew what had to be done."

Soon the rangy Parcells was playing quarterback for River Dell High under Tom Cahill, who would eventually hire him to coach defense at Army. River Dell needed a score and had seen their fullback rebuked twice by Fair Lawn High School's goal-line defense. Parcells saw no need to change the play; he simply switched positions and battered into the end zone himself.

In high school he met Mickey Corcoran, who would become "like a second father." Corcoran had played ball for Englewood's St. Cecilia High under a young coach named Vince Lombardi, then coached at the Horace Mann School in Riverdale before moving back to his home county to be River Dell's first varsity basketball coach. From the moment Parcells stepped onto a court with him, the two have never lost touch. "I talk to Mickey almost every week," says Parcells. "He's still coaching me. I can ask a question like 'Am I doing something stupid here? What do you see?' and get a straight answer. He tells me, 'Boy, your team doesn't tackle very good.' Things like that. He's the coach and always has been."

"I had never seen an athlete quite like Bill," recalls Corcoran. "From Jump Street he had an extremely inquisitive mind. He was a very emotional player. Not a rah-rah; he led by example. A great improviser on the court. Sometimes I'd take kids to see local games—Army, Fordham, Columbia—and he always went. He studied the intrigue of maneuvering and manipulating. He became a master of detail, but the key thing he's learned is to understand people and control emotions in a charged situation."

In 1980 Parcells turned up as linebacker coach with the New England Patriots—a job the understanding Perkins helped him get. In 1981, with no misgivings over his earlier false start, the Giants brought him back to coach the defense. The team went to 9-7 that year, with Parcells' mastery of a 3-4 defense, spearheaded by Lawrence Taylor, bringing them from 25th to third in yards-per-play obdurateness.

The 1982 season would be a haywire year—the NFL players went on strike, Rob Carpenter held out—but at Ray Perkins' alma mater, Alabama, an ailing Bear Bryant was looking for someone to pass the torch to. It was an offer

Perkins couldn't refuse. In hurried sessions with the club owners, George Young stood firmly for elevating Parcells, partly for the sake of continuity ("We were still in a race for the playoff"), but mostly because he liked his rapport with the players: "It was giving somebody who had coached half the team an opportunity to coach the rest."

Many felt that what the punchless Giants needed was a head coach schooled in offense. Young demurs: "Three of the present-day coaches who will surely be Hall of Famers are Don Shula, Tom Landry and Chuck Noll—all defensive men." Unfortunately, all of Parcells' expertise could not shield him from what 1983 held in store—the deaths of his two parents, of assistant coach Bob Ledbetter, and a rash of injuries that left Harry Carson, Phil Simms and Rob Carpenter sidelined. The Giants went 3-12-1 and the fans howled angrily. Very few knew the personal anguish Parcells was undergoing. "It was a big mess," he says. "Don't think it didn't cross my mind to throw up my hands and say, 'Who needs this?' But hey, they attack the weak ones. So I said, 'Well, I'm gonna start fighting.'"

"He came away scarred," says George Young, "but after the season I was most impressed with his evaluation of what had taken place, and with his plan to remedy it." Parcells says the key was convincing the players "that we were gonna win. And they believed me, 'cause I didn't panic.

"Right before last season started a friend of mine gave me a piece of advice. He said, 'You're driving a train. It's in a dark tunnel. You don't know where you're going, and you don't see any light at the end, and behind you riding in the train are your players; your owners; your general manager; your personnel director; the fans; and the press—and they're all screamin' at ya, wanting to know what the hell is going on. You don't have time to turn around. Just drive the train, and either get it out of the tunnel or wreck the sonuvabitch.' That was pretty good advice."

The Giants went 9-7, including crucial back-to-back victories over the divisional rough guys, the Redskins and Cowboys, and an inspired surge to snuff out the Rams in a wild-card playoff game at Anaheim. In the end they lost to San Francisco, but Bill Parcells was named NFC East Coach of the Year. Legendary Raiders coach John Madden sums up what distinguished him: "I've always felt this was a game of people, not charts and figures, and that's how Bill Parcells coaches."

Now it's the season of 14- and 15-hour days for Parcells. He's up by 5:30 most mornings, making the half-hour drive from Upper Saddle River to the stadium. Win or lose, he tries not to bring the games home. "I don't have anything concerning football in my house. My wife doesn't understand a lot about football, but I know she feels the pressure of winning when it's on this visible a level. I know I'm a very subdued individual when we've lost, and it affects her and I'm sad that it does. My youngsters in school are from time to time the recipients of verbal abuse because of the way the team's playing, and that's not fair.

"When you win, like we did in Dallas last year, those are the good rides home. Those kids are so happy and proud of themselves. It's an exhilaration, but for me it doesn't last very long. Sometimes only two or three hours, sometimes only till I walk back in that tunnel."

Parcells rises and moves back around his desk to sit heavily, musing as if he didn't have company. A half-mile beyond the drapes at his back is the Hackensack River he's determined his team won't get pushed into. Asked for some sort of prediction on the Eagles game, he says: "They're gonna give us a lot of trouble. I don't have to tell the older players it's gonna be tough down in Philadelphia."

Suddenly, Parcells doesn't look very elephantine: "You know," he says, "a lot of time you can see the fatigue set in. I heard Merlin Olsen say something once, that the guys are like wounded bears then, and I thought that was interesting, because you see it in your team; the fatigue is there, it's hot, they're trying to function under pressure and fight that fatigue, mental fatigue too . . .

"You can see it. They're like bears playing on instinct."

Giants coach Bill Parcells leaves the playing field in Chicago after the Giants lost, 21-0, to the Bears in the 1985-86 NFC championship game.

CHAPTER 4

TO THE TOP

Giants' 1986-87 Season

During the 1986-87 season, Bill Parcells found a lot of reasons to smile.

*T*he pieces finally came together in 1986. The defense was monstrous, the offense potent, and the coach was all wet.

After big wins, the tradition of Parcells' Gatorade baths gave way to superstition as the Giants kept winning in 1986. But the baths weren't going to cool the fire in Bill Parcells' belly. He stayed on his players, and by the time the Giants left for Pasadena to play Denver in Super Bowl XXI, Parcells' team was ready for football's ultimate challenge. In fact, the outcome was a foregone conclusion. The Giants won handily, Parcells got his championship bath, and all of New York felt the Giants were on the brink of a dynasty.

Parcells Fumes over Trade Talk

By C.U. Smith Muniz

O n the eve of the Giants' first preseason game against the Atlanta Falcons, coach Bill Parcells had this state of the union message yesterday.

"I'm not happy with anybody right now," he said.

Most of all, Parcells was angry with a yet unidentified reporter, who allegedly told running back Joe Morris the coach was talking about trading him. Morris is in his option year and has refused to participate in contact drills until his contract is renegotiated.

"I'm going to find out who was that person," Parcells said, "and when I do, that person is going to have a lot of trouble with Bill Parcells . . . I got it narrowed down to two guys. I have made no such statement of any such nature to anybody at any time. The guy is a bleeping liar."

Parcells Defends His Picks
May 6, 1986
By Bill Verigan

Bill Parcells knows what he likes.
"Defense is the key to any sport, baseball, football, basketball. Simple as that. If you wanta win. If you want to entertain people take 'em to Broadway to see Bingo Long's Traveling All-Stars and Motorcade."
So the Giants' first six picks in the draft were on defense.

Giants Rallied in Trenches

By Bill Verigan

A week ago, Bill Parcells was not pleased. His quarterback was being mauled and his running back couldn't find a hole.

It was time for a little chat with gentlemen of the offensive line.

"I spoke to them not too nicely," Parcells said. "I was disturbed by some things going on."

The coach probably was still disturbed by what was going on in the first quarter on Sunday in the Giants' 14-9 victory over the Raiders. It wasn't pretty.

"Anyone could tell things were not going real smoothly," said lineman Karl Nelson. "There were penalties and people were jumpy. We weren't into the flow of the game."

"I'd go offsides, then Brad (Benson) and Mark (Bavaro) would," said Bill Ard. "We kept facing third down and long yardage."

Parcells would have been worried, very, very worried if the same things had happened last season. Parcells was asked if the Giants could overcome such mistakes back then against an 0-2 Raider team a year ago in Los Angeles.

"I don't know," Parcells replied. "I doubt it."

But this time, they did.

"It's because they're more experienced," Parcells said. "More guys have been through such situations. They had to stay alert and take advantage of several situations on key plays in the second half."

In the second half, for the first time this season, the offensive line and running back Joe Morris looked as if they were working together. Morris said he could feel his timing returning. After gaining only 17 yards on seven carries in the first half, he broke loose for 93 yards on 11 carries (including a key 52-yard run) in the second half.

Parcell Vow: No Giant Letdown

By Rob Parker

The Giants are on a roll. They are like a downhill snowball, adding momentum and victories each step of they way. And according to coach Bill Parcells, the snowball won't stop until it reaches the bottom of the hill.

The Super Bowl.

"No, there is too much at stake," Parcells responded yesterday to the question of whether his team would let down in the final two weeks of the season. "I don't see it. The game (the Giants' 24-14 victory over the Redskins Sunday) is over. It's history. We now have to think about St. Louis."

Parcells said the Giants, by assuring themselves a spot in the playoffs, have reached one of their goals. Home-field advantage throughout the playoffs is next on the goal list.

"The idea is to get in," he said. "We did that. Then it's to get in the best possible position. And we're trying to do that."

Victories over the 3-10-1 Cardinals and the 3-11 Packers would assure the Giants of that second goal.

And the Giants have become tougher and tougher as the season goes on. Their victory against the Redskins not only was their first at RFK Stadium since 1981, it moved them one game closer to capturing their first championship, of any kind, since 1963.

The Giants have won seven in a row and are the league's only undefeated team at home (6-0). By winning in Washington, they have beaten three of the last four Super Bowl champs on the road, the Raiders and 49ers being the other two.

Parcells said his team's rough schedule has helped the Giants build confidence.

"If someone would have told you we would be 12-2 after the first 14 games, you'd probably bet the mortgage," he said to the press yesterday. "But the schedule has made us more competitive. Winning against the Raiders (Game 3) started it."

Then Game 11, the miracle in Minnesota, reinforced it.

"It certainly did," Parcells said. "When you hit one like that (the fourth-and-17 completion that set up the winning field goal), it helps.

"Demonstrated ability breeds confidence. You have to perform to pressure. If you yield to it, you'll end up on the short end of it."

John Madden and Bill Parcells look over Giants Stadium.

Parcells' Nuts-and-Bolts Style Builds a Winner

By Rob Parker

D on't call Bill Parcells a genius. You can call him lots of things: a player's coach, a coach's coach, blue-collar tough, diligent, obsessive, even superstitious.

But please don't tell him he's a genius. Parcells will be quick to point out that there are no longer dynasties or geniuses in football.

Some coaches want to be fathers to their players. Others want to be SOBs.

"I want to be remembered by my players as a guy who wanted to win," he said, "a guy who'll do anything to win."

You know what happens to geniuses? The Giants beat them.

Back on December 1, Bill Walsh's 49ers took a 17-0 lead into the locker room at halftime in San Francisco's Candlestick Park. That lead should have been enough, even if the 49ers aren't what they used to be.

But these are Bill Parcells' kids. They are the first graduating class of his system.

"If the defense stops 'em the next two times, we win," he told them.

Sure enough, the defense got on Joe Montana like bark on a tree, and the offense scored, with Mark Bavaro doing his famous impersonation of a cable car at rush hour, 49ers hanging from everywhere.

Then the defense did the job again. But this time, the offense sputtered, and it came down to fourth and 2 at the New York 49. Everything pointed to a punt. When the offense stayed on the field, it appeared to be a bluff to pull the 49ers offsides. Instead, hut, hut, Morris got the ball on a quick snap and gained 17 yards. One down later, Stacy Robinson caught a touchdown pass.

"It was no big deal," Parcells said. "It wasn't daring. We've had bigger plays and plays that were more daring. What else could we do? We were losing."

The next time the 49ers had the ball, it was one-two-three-punt for the third straight time. Robinson caught a 49-yarder, and the Giants won, 21-17.

That fourth-down call turned a very good season into a great season. It turned a wild card (which always smacks of jokers) into a champion.

It took that halftime speech and Bavaro's determination and Parcells' daring play and Morris' run and Robinson's catches and the defense's pressure.

But Parcells takes no chances. He believes in hard work and execution, but he also figures that maybe it worked out because he was too superstitious to practice at Candlestick the day before the game. You see, the Giants had lost both times on the road when they had practiced on the field where they were going to play.

"Sure, I'm superstitious," Parcells said. "I'd never touch a penny that's tails up. Two of 'em have been lying in the coach's room all season, and nobody will touch 'em. We work out on the same yard lines; the players and me, we arrive at the stadium in the same order and say the same things; I always stop at the same two places for coffee every day on my way to work."

When he accidentally hit a black cat a year ago on the parkway, he backed up to erase its spell. When he saw a trailer truck parked beside the practice field with the driver perched on top before a couple of victories, he made a note of it. The driver is always around now, even on road trips.

The driver also fits Parcells' blue-collar work ethic. Parcells views every Giant as just another worker on the assembly line. The one who bolts down the motor is equal to the one who sticks in the ash tray. It takes them all to make a car or a victory.

When the press started panting over Morris or Bavaro, Parcells would always bring them back down.

"Wasn't that a great play?" the press would ask.

"Not bad," Parcells would respond.

"Shouldn't he be in the Pro Bowl?" they'd ask.

"A lot of people should be," he'd reply.

But nobody puts in more hours than the head coach.

"I cannot allow myself to ever rest," said Parcells, who barely has time for his family during football season. "If you rest, you get beat."

He has competed since he was a kid at River Dell High in Bergen County. His mother and father died over the last two years, and Parcells now is probably closest to his high school coach.

He's still idealistic enough to believe the hardest worker usually wins. Indeed, he was disillusioned by what he saw college recruiters doing. When he was tempted to be part of that dirty game, he almost got out of coaching.

Like his team, he started at the bottom and worked his way up.

"I've done it all," he said. "I washed the uniforms in Cold Power at Hastings and got $1,000 a month during the season. I used a rope to get the dew off the field at Florida State. That was part of the job. But I loved it."

He has hinted several times that he won't coach forever. He has suggested he might not hang around as long as some of his players. But it's very difficult to imagine him doing anything else.

Since Parcells arrived, something has certainly worked for the Giants. They've gone from 3-12-1 to 9-7 to 10-6 to 13-2 and climbing.

In four years, Parcells has rebuilt this team with players in his image and taken it to the Eastern Division title, the Giants' first title of any kind in 23 seasons.

All he needed was enough time. George Young, the Giants' GM, got lucky when Ray Perkins hired Parcells as an assistant. And Young got lucky again when he botched Parcells' firing (and the hiring of Howard Schnellenberger) so completely after only one season that the Giants were obliged to keep him.

If Parcells had been fired after his first year, he would have gone down as just another head coach who tried and failed with the Giants. And Schnellenberger might have had about as much success as he has had at Louisville.

"Sometimes you don't get time," Parcells said. "That's the major question every coach faces: Will he have time to do it? A lot of coaches might be perceived as failures because they didn't get enough time. Take Kay Stephenson, who went to Buffalo at the same time I became head coach. Buffalo has had two coaches since him. But if Kay Stephenson was still around and had Jim Kelly, maybe the Bills would have a better record. It takes continuity, making a plan and staying with it."

Ironically, Parcells' ability to work with the man who had wanted to fire him is a basic key to the Giants' success. There are few similarities in Parcells and Young. It is no coincidence that the Giants' drafts have improved since Parcells has been head coach, and many of the players are obviously his draft choices. But Parcells and Young share the credit.

"A GM's job is to get the players for the coach," Parcells said. "The coach's job is to coach those players. But it's important to have a personnel philosophy that everybody understands."

In the end, no coach is better than his players, and every player on the Giants fits Parcells' specifications. A lot of them are gone because they were flawed in some way.

He started in 1981 as the defensive coordinator, and he still loves the defense best.

"If you don't play defense, you're gonna lose," he said. "I don't care what game you're playing."

He still recalls the first meeting in which he began to shape the Giants.

"We'd already moved Beasley Reece from strong to free safety, Brian Kelly inside in a move that might not have worked, and Harry Carson to the weakside from the middle.

"But we still didn't have a nose tackle. There was Myron Lapka, who fell off a truck. George Small and Jim Burt, who was still sleeping under the bed. Then we had Bill Neal, a defensive end from Pittsburgh we'd picked in the fifth round.

"So I said, 'Let's move him.' Almost everyone in the room had something negative to say, and I was getting madder. I finally said, 'If any of you bleeps have a better idea, let me know. Otherwise I'm gonna move him to nose in the morning.' Luckily it worked."

He has had failures, of course. He said he still gets mad because he couldn't turn Clint Harris into a player.

"If you make misjudgments, it costs you," he said.

There is a simple rule on trades: At the end of a season he wants draft picks; once the draft is over, he wants players. But he is always cautious about taking a player he doesn't know.

"The greatest mistake in making trades is overestimating current players on another team," he said.

What he looks for first is toughness.

"The scouts all know what I like," he said. "There are very good players who don't fit what I look for. Mark Bavaro wasn't rated high by some people, but our scout, Jerry Angelo, told me, 'You're gonna love this guy.'"

That's why there are few grumbles, even among the Giants playing limited roles.

"They listen to Phil McConkey, who knows what it's like in Green Bay," Parcells said. "Do they want to go somewhere and start and look up at the scoreboard and watch themselves getting hammered. Then a new coach comes in after three weeks and they're not starting and still losing.

"Earlier this year Pepper Johnson was moping around, and Gary Reasons said, 'Looks like a case of the no-down blues.' Reasons told him to forget it, no college player could come in and start on this defense.

"Our guys just want to win as much as I do."

He's the Coach of Work

But after 14-2, Parcells "rests"

By Phil Pepe

As of this morning, Bill Parcells is officially on vacation. Do not call him, do not write, do not ask him about the upcoming playoffs. For the first time since July 14, the coach of the Giants will not rise at 5 a.m., pick up a container of coffee and the newspapers at the local store and go to work.

As of today, Parcells is a man of leisure.

"I want to rest," he says. "Stay home. Talk to my wife. Reintroduce myself to her."

Tomorrow is another day. The vacation ends tomorrow. Bill Parcells goes back to work, back to his desk in Giants Stadium at the crack of dawn until late at night, back to his movie projector.

Parcells has earned his vacation. He has earned it with 14 victories in the regular season, the most ever for a Giants team, the last nine of them in succession. It is a long way from 1983 and 3-12-1, a gradual climb to the top that happened because the coach never eased up his workload.

As impressive as it is, 14-2 is nothing, Parcells knows, except an admission ticket to the real prize. "We still have a lot to do," he says. The improvement has been steady since Parcells replaced Ray Perkins—from three victories to nine, then 10, now 14. "I coach a lot better when I have good players," says Parcells. "That's one of my strongest points right now as a coach. I got good players."

Right now, there are no illusions about Parcells as a coach, or about his players. Everybody is saying the Giants are the team to beat for the Super Bowl. If they want to give him the Super Bowl ring, Parcells will take it, but he knows it doesn't work that way. That ring has to be earned. More hard work. It will not come if the coach takes too many days off.

"We're not that good," he says. "We have to play top-line emotional football. Fortunately, we have some good catalysts on this team."

Parcells says he will sit back and watch the wild-card game next week, Los Angeles vs. Washington, to see who the Giants' playoff opponent will be—the Rams or 49ers. He has no preference. He wouldn't tell you if he did. But he does like the idea that there will be no football for his team next weekend.

"It will help us with our bumps and bruises," he says. "You can't get hurt watching TV. I don't think you can."

The victory over the Packers yesterday means the Giants will have all their playoff games at home.

"I'm glad about that," says Parcells. "Our fans deserve it."

Some of those fans are the same ones who were calling for Parcells' scalp after 3-12-1. But Bill Parcells was in no mood for vindictiveness. He was feeling too good yesterday. And he was about to go on vacation.

1986 NFC East Final Standings

TEAM	WINS	LOSSES	TIES
Giants*	14	2	0
Redskins*	12	4	0
Cowboys	7	9	0
Eagles	5	10	1
Cardinals	4	11	1

*Qualified for playoffs

Carson Set for Big Splash

By Harvey Araton

I f the Giants win their next two games, Harry Carson is just about ready for Pasadena. He has a pair of slick, dark shades. He's going to write a column for New York's Hometown Paper. Better than that, he's got a Super Bowl schtick.

Carson dumps Gatorade on the coach, Bill Parcells, in the closing seconds of a victory, and that's at least two days work for the hungry media masses. Remember, Jim McMahon made a killing last year by merely covering his forehead and uncovering his behind. With that in mind, it may be time for Carson to think ahead. He may have to know the answer to such profound, probing questions as:

What percentage of water is in the Gatorade?

How much distance does he require for his running approach?

Does he prefer the horizontal flip or the vertical dump?

Carson promises to work on these and others. Yesterday, he couldn't even recall the exact details of his first celebratory attack. "Last year, two years ago, I don't remember," Carson said. "All I know is that it started with me and Jim Burt. And it wasn't Gatorade then. It was water."

It makes sense to Burt, the nose tackle, that Carson, the linebacker, is getting all the credit, now that the Giants are inside the Super Bowl territory, and driving. Linemen get knocked down. Linebackers step over them and make the tackle.

Burt claims he was the first to shower the coach, and that it was an act conceived, produced and directed by himself. It dates to the middle of the 1984 season. Mid-week. The Redskins coming in.

"He (Parcells) was on me all week," Burt said. "Why? I know why. Because I'm his damned dumping ground, that's why.

Parcells' sweetest Gatorade shower of them all, after winning Super Bowl XXI.

"Anyway, he's got me slamming five-pound weights against the wall for a half-hour, in front of the whole team. To fire them up, you know?

"So we go and blow them out, and he comes up to me on the sideline and says, 'Yeah, I got you ready, didn't I?' I said, 'Oh yeah, well, I got something for you, too.' I just went and got the nearest bucket. I didn't even think about what I was doing. Everyone around me just kind of backed off. They didn't know how he was going to respond. Then he smiled a little . . . then a little more."

Suddenly, the Giants were developing the habit of winning wet. In those early days, Carson remembers sponges and rags flying all over the place. The assistant coaches took a few baths, along with Parcells. At some point this season, when winning became almost a weekly occurrence, tradition gave way to superstition. This is all part of the program now. Toss of the coin. Game balls. Gatorade reverse, designed to sucker Parcells.

That's right, it's as organized as anything in the playbook. Or was, until Parcells caught on Sunday as the Giants were laying the Packers to rest.

The punter, Sean Landeta, was about to shake Parcells' hand, which all along has been the distraction planned by Carson. Parcells jumped back.

Landeta: "He said, 'Get outta here, Landeta, I know what you're up to.' I tried to act like I didn't know what he meant, but I couldn't hold back the smile. So then we decided that I'd get the jug, hide it for Harry, and get him from the other direction. Harry would've gotten him clean, but the fans started yelling."

Carson says Parcells once told him he'd "be fired" after the next bath. Carson told himself: "What the heck." Parcells gave up any such resistance. He's just promising "to get Carson one of these days."

There's a message here for many of these Giants, particularly the older ones who believe their time finally has come. Parcells, they believe, is a players' coach who has carefully nurtured a football family. They think the Giants, all of them, want to play for Parcells. To win one for the Gatorade.

"We've seen other situations here," said George Martin, the veteran pass rusher. "With John McVay, for instance, we had a relationship but not a good team. With Ray Perkins, we had a good team, but no relationship. Parcells encompasses the best of both worlds."

"It's just fun," Landeta said. "When you're winning, isn't that what it's supposed to be? Just fun, for everyone?"

Carson may not look at it that way. He knows the world will be watching in Pasadena. He is the man who does the honors, and he's just three victories away from a Super Bowl splash.

Parcells' Big Day Follows Knight's

By Mike Lupica

The friendship between the basketball guy and the football guy began at West Point in the 1960s.

Bob Knight was head basketball coach, Bill Parcells was assistant to head football coach Tom Cahill. Knight moved from West Point to Indiana. Parcells would move around a lot, from West Point to Florida State, from Florida State to Vanderbilt, then Texas Tech, then the Air Force Academy as head man, into private business for a while, to the Patriots, finally the Giants in 1981 as defensive coordinator.

"I been here longer than I been anyplace," Bill Parcells said yesterday at Giants Stadium. He likes to tell his players that everybody's in the same boat, players and coaches alike: "If you win, they let you stay."

Knight moved to the top of his field quicker, winning his first national championship at Indiana in 1976. Now here comes Parcells. He is two wins away. Twenty years from West Point, the football coach tries to catch up with the basketball coach.

The basketball coach says it figured all along, even if he couldn't watch Giants 49, 49ers 3 Sunday. In the Midwest Sunday, the first half of the CBS Sports doubleheader was the Giants game. The second half was Indiana vs. Ohio State. Knight got his team ready to beat Ohio state; his son Tim—who worked as a Giants ballboy the first year Parcells was head coach—watched the football game on a monitor with Billy Packer and Gary Bender and kept running back to the locker room with updates for his father.

"I explained to Parcells this morning," Knight said yesterday from Bloomington, "that I just couldn't coach two damn games the same day, not that he seemed to need me very much, as it turned out."

"The first thing he said on the phone," Parcells said at his meeting yesterday with the press, "was 'At least you didn't have to go to that damn prevent defense.' 'Course he wouldn't know a prevent from something a dogcatcher would use. He's just mad 'cause a couple of weeks ago I made fun of him for playing a bone. I watched him play on ESPN, and I called him up the next day and said, 'What do you call that defense when you got two guys up, three back, nobody on the ball, then they pass it underneath and score?'"

The West Point friendship, basketball and football in a nice collision, endures. Knight has been called the best basketball coach, by me and a lot of other people. Knight believes that one day Parcells will be called the best football coach. He says his friend is just getting started. He believes his friend is that good.

The coach of the Giants, you see, sneaks up on you, the way Harry Carson sneaks up on him with the Gatorade. And the coach of the Giants is a bit more than the Gatorade business. He is a man of toughness and intelligence, depth and humor. He like his players, and his job, at which he has become quite expert. The only things Parcells does not seem to have are a Super Bowl ring and an act. The ring is two wins away. An act is out of the question. Parcells, Jersey guy, isn't the type.

"You know, I'm a student of coaches, not just in basketball but in all sports," Knight said (he is; he likes generals, too). "And I've never been around one any better than Parcells. I'm not just saying it because he's my friend. He is able to recognize athletes as well as players. And believe me, there's a difference. There are some athletes who can't play, and there are guys who can play who aren't athletes. You've gotta know.

"Bill knows. He knows what he's doing, he knows what to look for, he knows how to get things to mix. He's really good with people. He's a lot more patient with people than I am, than a lot of coaches are. I've seen him. I've been in the locker room with him, on the sidelines. He knows when to raise hell and when not to. He understands that caustic is better than bombastic sometimes. I think he is extremely well-suited to coach those guys, because he seems to understand them so well. The only thing he isn't is famous."

He is the man for this team. Put it this way: This Giant team would be quite different without Parcells, diminished, lacking both personality and verve. The Giants might still be playing if Ray Perkins, old Mr. Zany, were still around. But they would not be as much fun. Parcells kept moving around after Army. He also kept learning about how to do it.

"There's always a way to do it," he said yesterday, "you've just got to figure it out." Then he talked about the old Yankees and said, "I think the key was that they had a lot better players than them other guys."

Then somebody wanted to know if he's a great coach yet and Parcells said. "Hey, what is this?" He lit another Marlboro and talked about coaching under Tom Cahill at West Point, things he learned.

"I'll tell you one thing I learned," Parcells said. "You can't tell 'em everything you know about everything."

Knight said, "We've got a swimming coach here at Indiana, very famous, named Doc Counsilman. I've always said that he could have been a great coach anywhere: the NBA, the NFL, the majors. Any sport he wanted to try. He's that type of personality. He would just go in and figure out the game, see what had to be done, what the right way was to do things and get people working together, and he'd win eventually. Parcells is the same type of man."

Parcells can be overprotective with his players. He has tried to bully the media at times. It is him and his players against the world. Giant writers have already written the words, "I'm proud of my guys" into their notebooks after the game before Parcells opens his mouth. But he is the indispensable member of the crazy Giant organization, and he has done more than anyone to build a machine that is two wins away.

"Mickey Corcoran (Parcells' old high school basketball coach at River Dell High in Oradell, N.J.) and I always thought he'd be a great coach," Knight said.

And Bob Knight said that when he was basketball coach at West Point, Parcells would look at a player without much physical talent and say to Knight, "That boy's in danger."

Twenty years from West Point, Bill Parcells is the one in danger. Danger of being famous. Two more wins and the football guy finally catches up with the basketball guy.

Parcells Takes the Offensive

Giants reminded of feeble showing in first game against Broncos

By Bill Verigan

Giants' coach Bill Parcells has a message for his offense: "Score."

"The offense didn't score a touchdown against Denver last time," he said. "Raul Allegre had four field goals and George Martin returned an interception for a touchdown. The offense has got to get some points this time."

The bettors have the Giants favored by 10 points in this town and the oddsmakers say the odds will go to 12 or 13 points. But the odds might be closer to reality out in Denver, where the Giants are only a six-point choice.

The Giants had one of their worst offensive shows in the regular-season meeting with the Broncos, running only 59 plays and generating only 14 first downs and 262 yards. Only against the Cardinals in Week Four did the Giants notch fewer first downs and run fewer offensive plays. Only against the Cardinals and the Cowboys did they amass less yardage.

Parcells tried to fire up the troops but, after 59 minutes of futility, the Giants gladly settled for a 19-16 victory on Allegre's final field goal with six seconds remaining.

The Giants were trailing, 3-0, when they got the ball midway through the first quarter and Parcells made what he later called one of his "gutsiest" calls of the season—a fake punt with Jeff Hostetler handing the ball to Lee Rouson on fourth-and-five at the Denver 44. The play went for eight yards.

"It was early in the game, and at midfield," Parcells said. "We had other choices. But I wanted to get something going."

Parcells Heats Up

Raging Giants' coach enflames fiery practice

By Bill Verigan

Bill Parcells turned the intensity to the max yesterday in the Giants' noisy, two-hour workout for the Super Bowl.

"The coaches had a bug in their ear," said Bill Ard. "Everybody was yelling."

"Parcells was at his best. On top of his game," Jim Burt said. "He went crazy. He was on everybody. He saw me giggling and started in on me."

When the hollering stopped, Burt walked back to the huddle chanting, "Show time. Show time."

About 75% of the workout was devoted to the passing game, both offensive and defensive. Although the players wore only shoulder pads and sweats, Chris Godfrey said there were almost a few "flareups."

"Everybody was very high," Godfrey said. "The tempo has really increased."

Even offensive coordinator Ron Erhardt noted the players were getting very antsy. "They were really getting after each other. It was strange seeing that when they weren't in full pads."

"Parcells is making sure everything is right," Burt said, "and I agree with him 100%."

Parcells was not pleased by the pressure being applied by the pass rush in one offensive drill and began yelling, "You guys can't go three days without hard work. Let's go harder. I want it harder than that."

When two New York television crews tried to position themselves for shots through a gate although practice was closed to the press, NFL security moved the team buses in front of them to block their view.

Parcells Molded Super Giants

By Mike Lupica

The football part comes tomorrow. The rest of it ended yesterday for the Giants, when coach Bill Parcells conducted his final press conference at the Anaheim Marriott.

Parcells and the Giants have done about as well as you can do at Super Bowl Week. In the five days when Parcells and his players were repeatedly asked to walk around with their pants down, the Giants comported themselves with dignity. It has a lot to do with the coach.

Lawrence Taylor snarled and complained, but it is his public nature. He stayed out too late and had to get up too early, but he did show up at all the places where he was supposed to show up. Maybe that has something to do with the coach, too.

This is not George Young's team. It is not the quarterback's team. It is not Lawrence Taylor's team, which is why Taylor's snarls were the only ones to be heard this week. It is Parcells' team. Parcells has stamped this team with his own toughness, his own modesty and his own ability to take a step back every so often and remember that football—and this vulgar pageant—is supposed to be fun.

"You gotta be able to laugh," Parcells said yesterday. "In this business if you don't laugh, you go crazy."

There have been very few Super Bowl coaches like him. In a lot of ways he is the new John Madden. Not the act. Madden didn't develop that until he got out of coaching and the red light went on. Parcells is human as a football coach. It is there to see. He was asked yesterday if he ever gets out of control on the sidelines. He said, "Out of control, no. Mad? Yes. To the point where I appear out of control? Yes." Just like Madden.

Somehow this week, Parcells carried everything off with an understated style. So did most of his players. If the Giants all do as well with the football part, they will win easy.

And if they do win easy, it goes back to Parcells. Young got the organization righted. Phil Simms had the season of his career. Taylor—whose star will begin to fall next season, I believe—kept himself under control and played like he was 23 again. Carl Banks emerged. Joe Morris did it again, like he did last autumn. But Parcells molded this particular team, gave it unity, imbued it with a confidence that this was its time and this Super Bowl was its destiny. He is leader and friend to this team. A lot of coaches and managers try it. Few succeed the way he has.

He tries to make it out to be simple. "If you win," he likes to say, "they let you stay." It his version of "Just win, baby." He talks about luck and the right personnel and being able to instruct the personnel the right way. But there is more to it with Parcells. Somehow, he has gotten it across to these Giants that their best support system is him. He is one of them when he has to be.

He quietly cleaned up what he perceived to be a drug problem on the Giants. He got rid of a player here, a player there—no fanfare, just goodbye. He was there last summer when Taylor needed him. I do not believe his relationship with Young is something from the Harlequin Romance series, but never in public has Parcells said a contrary word. Parcells is not an upstairs guy at Giants Stadium, anyway. He is downstairs all the way.

The endorsements are in place for so many Giants if they win tomorrow. Simms and Phil McConkey will do a book, Jim Burt will do a book. The Maras will be celebrated for staying with a goldmine like the Giants. And Young will get his due.

But if the Giants win, it is Parcells' triumph. If he stays around, he'll someday be known as the best coach the Giants ever had.

Lost Horizon: The Coach's Detour to Destiny

By Mike Lupica

In 1979, at the age of 38, 7 1/2 years before he would take the Giants to Super Bowl XXI, Bill Parcells stopped being a football coach.

It meant Parcells walked away from the only job he had known as an adult. It meant he gave up the one thing—aside from his family—that he loved most in the world. The year before, he had been head coach at the Air Force Academy. Then Ray Perkins, head coach of the Giants, offered him a job as assistant coach. Parcells accepted. He was New Jersey born, he was New Jersey raised; he was coming home. And he was in the National Football League. Everybody has dreams. Parcells' professional dreams were about Jersey, the Giants, the NFL.

Then Parcells changed his mind. He told Perkins he would take a pass on the dream and resigned from the Giants shortly after he had said yes. He went back to Colorado to his wife, Judy, and their three daughters. There was some difficulty at home. The difficulty: The home was in Colorado, the husband and the father was in New Jersey. Parcells loved his family and loved football. Torn between two loves and all that. His family won.

"I couldn't sell my house," said Parcells in his Giants Stadium office a few days before the Giants left for California and Super Bowl XXI. "But it was more than that. She (Judy) was there, my daughters were there. I was here, with no control over my life."

Parcells does not talk about specific problems at home. Really, there is no need to. You have a wife, you have growing daughters, you're away all the time, that is specific enough. He had only been in Colorado a year. The decision was the family could not stand another move, not then. He could not afford house payments in Colorado and New Jersey, not then. Parcells had been a football gypsy since graduating from Wichita State. He had averaged a new coaching job every other year and now it was causing his family to unravel.

There was a year at Hastings College, in Nebraska. Then back to Wichita State. Then three years at West Point. Three years at Florida State, two at Vanderbilt, three at Texas Tech, finally a year at the Air Force Academy as head coach. In Parcells' chosen profession, you move to upgrade, you move to build the reputation, you move to learn. He had moved. The Giants job was the big move. It was also his eighth job since college, even if it meant going home.

He stopped and looked at his life. He decided Judy Parcells and his three daughters needed him more than Ray Perkins. Parcells says there is nothing heroic at all about putting family first. It is done all the time, Parcells says, "I didn't feel like I had a choice. At that point, I couldn't do what I wanted to do and what I had to do."

Bob Knight is one of Parcells' best friends. It has been that way since Parcells was an assistant to Tom Cahill at West Point and Knight was head basketball coach. Knight, of course, was Knight as he talked about Parcells and 1979.

Knight: "I frankly think it took a helluva lot of guts to do what he did. What was he? Thirty-eight years old? A lot of guys talk about doing what he did, but they never do it. He stopped and reassessed what he wanted to do with his life. You know what I think? I think it's an indication of how smart this guy really is. He got out for a year and saw just where the hell he was. I've felt in my life like I was at that point, but I never took the step that Parcells did. Like I said, not many people have. And his career has gone full speed ahead ever since."

Knight can look back now and see the wake Parcells has left going full speed ahead. So can Parcells. But in 1979, out of football, he did not know that he would be back with the Giants in two years, head coach in four and coaching the Giants in Super Bowl XXI the day after tomorrow. He was 38 years old, he was unemployed and the one thing he knew how to do he couldn't do. His intentions were practiced and decent, but the situation is known as a mid-life crisis in non-football settings.

Parcells: "I didn't know what I was gonna do. I'd been a football coach all my life. I had confidence I could find something; I'm a confident person. But the fact was, it was May and I didn't have a job. I had some money, but not a lot of money. I had a house I couldn't sell and payments to make on it. I knew I'd survive. I figured we could get by for six months, maybe a year. But I really didn't know after that."

Parcells knew he had done the right thing by coming back to his family, but the reality of the decision did not hit him until he was back in Colorado, without prospects. The right decision had produced the wrong result. As

Parcells says now, "Leaving the job here (with the Giants) had created another sense of urgency in my family. The urgency went like this: 'Who was gonna pay the bills?'"

He knew people, because he had been head coach at Air Force. He made some calls. He still wasn't sure what he wanted to do, or could do: "I was thinking about some kind of sales deal, selling things to people, you know, that sort of thing."

He went to work for a company called Gates Land, a subsidiary of Gates Rubber, an important tire and rubber concern in Denver. Gates Land was developing 5,000 acres in an area called Cheyenne hills, adjacent to Broadmoor. The Country Club of Colorado was situated on the 5,000 acres and Gates Land was developing different areas for residential homes, track homes, custom homes, so forth. Parcells wasn't all that far from Colorado Springs and Air Force and still being a head coach—but that was only if you measured in miles.

In 1978, he was still a coach. At Air Force. In Colorado Springs. In the spring of 1979, Parcells was studying for his real-estate license. In Colorado Springs. He says the test wasn't so bad. Parcells: "Back to school. Fun, right?"

So it worked out this way: Parcells worked as an athletic director at the Country Club of Colorado Springs, organizing events and competitions and leagues. Like Julie on "Love Boat," only bigger. At the same time, he was talking to club members and local businessmen about buying something, building something, on the 5,000 acres in Cheyenne Hills belonging to Gates Land, subsidiary of Gates Rubber.

"I was miserable," Parcells says.

The Giants camp opened in July. All NFL camps opened in July. Parcells was making like Julie on "Love Boat" and peddling custom homes.

"I felt terrible," Parcells says. "By then, I was missing it pretty bad. I didn't know if I'd ever get back to football. Once you're out, you're out. As far as the NFL was concerned, I hadn't done anything. I hadn't been in the league. I had no reputation."

So he was dying as July turned into August and August turned into September and a football season was starting without him for the first time in his life. And so here was Parcells' link to the National Football League in the fall of 1979: The Denver Broncos. Same Broncos the Giants play today. Every home Sunday, Bill and Judy Parcells would sit in the end zone at Mile High Stadium, at the end of the stadium where the dressing rooms are, the opposite side from the press box, and watch the Broncos play.

"You could go ahead and fill every seat in the stadium and I could walk right to those seats today," Parcells says. Sometimes, he would know assistant coaches from the visiting team. They would have dinner the night before the game. Then, the assistant coach would coach on Sunday afternoon and Parcells would sit with his wife in the end zone, on the dressing room end, opposite from the press box.

Parcells says, "I was dying. I was dying to coach. And my wife thought I was having fun."

There was other football in Parcells' life. When Air Force was home, he drove up to Colorado Springs and watched Air Force play. On Friday nights, he was a color commentator on radio for high school football games. It was the city's radio Game of the Week. A prominent Denver broadcaster named Jeff Thomas did play by play. Parcells played John Madden. I asked him to describe his broadcasting style. He said, "Blabbering idiot. But, hey, it was high school football. It wasn't like I was describing art. Listen, I did it because I needed the money."

The high school season ended. The Air Force season ended. It was December. The home was a home again. The family had become a family. Parcells had survived. But he was still out of football, except for the three hours on Sunday when the Broncos played at Mile High.

Parcells: "I'm not gonna say it was the toughest year of my life. But it was still the toughest personal decision I'd ever had to make. When I took that job with the Giants, I was home. I was back home. And I was with the team I always wanted to be with." Parcells was born in Englewood, N.J. He had played his high school football at River Dell, in Oradell. From River Dell on, his life had been constructed around football; days were built around football practice, weekends were built around games. He became a coach and days and nights were built around practice and his life and his family's life were built around those games.

"Then I was in Colorado and I was leaving for work at 8:30 in the morning, like a normal person," Parcells says. "For my whole adult life, I had been gone for two and a half hours by 8:30 in the morning."

One December night, Bill and Judy Parcells were watching television at home. Judy Parcells said, "We've got to get back to football." Just like that. Parcells, who is built like a Toyota, did not jump up like the man in those Toyota commercials, but he had been waiting since the spring to hear those words, to be told it was time to get back to what he knew. Parcells says, "I heard what I needed to hear, but getting back to football was easier said than done."

He was on the phone again, just as he had been on the phone in the spring looking for work in Colorado. But these were football calls. He was looking for football work.

Steve Sloan, for whom Parcells had worked at Texas Tech, had gone to Mississippi. Sloan offered him a job. Parcells said that was music and accepted on a Tuesday. On Wednesday, Ray Perkins called. Perkins said there was a job as linebacker coach open with the New England Patriots and that Parcells should call Patriot head coach Ron Erhardt.

Parcells: "Here's Ray trying to get me back into the pros after I let him down. Well, I kind of let him down, let me put it that way, because I don't think Ray felt I had let him down, even if I did. Anyway, Ray hired me, then I had to give him the job back, and here he is being instrumental trying to get me another pro job. It's why I'm always going to have positive feelings toward Ray Perkins."

Parcells told Perkins, "I don't know Erhardt." Perkins said, "Call." He called and set up an appointment in Foxboro for Thursday. He called Steve Sloan and told him what he was doing, and Sloan said, no problem. Parcells flew east. He met with Erhardt. He asked how many men Erhardt planned to interview. Erhardt said a few, but Parcells was the first. Parcells told him about Ole Miss.

They went back and forth a little. Erhardt said he'd get back to Parcells by Tuesday. Parcells said, I'll be in Mississippi on Tuesday, working for Steve Sloan. It went like this for a couple of days. Parcells called Sloan again and Sloan said, "Don't worry about me, take your shot at the pros." By Friday afternoon, he was linebacker coach of the Patriots. Parcells was back in the game.

Judy Parcells flew to Boston that Sunday. On Monday, they agreed to buy a house in Norfolk, Mass. On Tuesday, they got a loan for the Norfolk house. They put the Colorado house on the market. This time, it got sold right away. Parcells was in New England for a year, then Perkins brought him back to the Giants as defensive coordinator the next season. Two years later, Bill Parcells was head coach of the Giants.

"And now, of course," Parcells says, "Ron Erhardt's here working for me as offensive coordinator. Funny how things work out, isn't it?"

Funny as a Gatorade shower. And a long way from 1979. He didn't know when he walked away from football for the right reasons he was really headed in the right direction.

Bill Parcells has his family, he has Jersey, he has the Giants, he's the boss, he is favored to beat the Broncos the day after tomorrow. It is a funny thing about dreams: Sometimes to really keep them you first must give them away.

Parcells Goes for the Ghosts

By Michael Katz

It was a game, Bill Parcells would say later, after two Gatorade baths, that "buried all the ghosts today." It was a game that played tricks with the memory, condensing history. The songs on the Giant hit parade went quickly from the haunting "Goodby, Allie" almost a quarter-century ago, to the taunting "El-way, El-way" of last night.

In New York or New Jersey or wherever the Giants call home, the 39-20 Super Bowl victory over the Broncos erases not only the bad ghosts, but the good ones. Have the Giants ever been better? Was Tittle-Gifford-Rote any better than Simms-Morris-Bavaro? Could the legendary Huff and Robustelli and Katcavage hold a Big Blue candle to the magnificent seven on the front line of this Giant defensive unit? Only the Jets-Mets-Knicks 1969-70 sports calendar had more red-letter dates than this one. World Series champions, NFL champions. Where is the Stanley Cup now?

The Giants have won one of those rare Super Bowl games that deserved prime-time TV. It was an entertainment spectacular—from controversial instant replay decisions to trick plays to the best catch in the Super Bowl maybe since Willie Mays robbed Vic Wertz in 1954 by Elvis Patterson on an interception of a John Elway pass.

That it ended in as much suspense as Sesame Street, well, blame Bill Parcells. He has a history of dampening fires.

In the ever-divided House of Mara where co-owner Tim Mara absented himself from the presentation ceremony of the Vince Lombardi Trophy to the winning Super Bowl team Parcells is the unifying, if somewhat untidy, figure.

He stood at the award ceremony where Tim Mara's uncle Wellington accepted the trophy, listening to commissioner Pete Rozelle accuse him of being "this year's NFL genius coach." He wanted to be with his guys.

Parcells can handle praise. It doesn't bother him, any more than the Gatorade baths. But his real thrill is not standing with the Maras and Rozelle, but on the sidelines, with his guys, making the big calls.

Like fourth-and-one on the Giants' 46, the play that turned what had been the best Super Bowl game into the expected Giant joy ride. John Elway, who does everything but kick field goals, had the upstart Broncos ahead, 10-9, at the half. The Giants took the second-half kick, and seemingly stalled when Phil Simms left the field and Sean Landeta, the punter, came in. But also entering the game for the Giants was Jeff Rutledge, the backup quarterback, first lining up as the up-man in punt formation, then switching to a normal T-formation QB, except how normal is a formation with Sean Landeta as the tailback?

The 30-second clock ticked off as the Broncos' defense jumped around nervously. Rutledge looked over the Broncos. His options were to take a delay penalty or gamble. The clock ticked off and Rutledge looked over at Parcells.

"I just nodded," said the coach.

Rutledge called for center Bart Oates to make the snap, took one step to his right and, behind RG Chris Godfrey, went two yards for the first down that kept the drive going. Moments later, Simms hit Mark Bavaro for the TD pass that put the Giants ahead to stay.

"It was what, two feet?" said Parcells.

"You know, you try to win the game. This is for the world championship. This is not for faint-hearted people."

His gray Giants sweater, obviously water-repellent, was dry now as he stood in the bright lights in the post-game interview room beneath the Rose Bowl stands. Bill Parcells, who grew up in Oradell, N.J., a couple of punts from the Meadowlands, a Giant fan who cried when the team lost, was smiling now.

"Bill Parcells," he said, "is one of the luckiest guys in the world. I don't know why God has blessed me this way."

Luck had nothing to do with it, but the man deserves it anyway. In a game that Parcells insisted was not over until the Giants scored their final TD, it was noteworthy that the player he chose to give that honor was Otis Anderson.

Earlier this season, Parcells had insisted the Giants trade for the former Cardinal as insurance for Joe Morris. Now this once-great running back, who unselfishly accepted his role with the Giants, was given a chance for a Super Bowl touchdown, which was more than Mike Ditka ever did for Walter Payton last year.

But the sentiment and the Gatorade can't overshadow the solid football mind. Last night, after Elway ran rings around the Giant defense in the first half, the Broncos were outgained in the third quarter—the Giants' quarter all season—163 yards to 2, outscored 17-0.

Parcells said there were no great adjustments, no mental manipulations, just his defense "settled down."

After winning Super Bowl XXI, Bill Parcells rode out of the Rose Bowl on his players' shoulders.

"Forget about adjustments," he said. "It was just execution. They were helter skelter out there, a little nervous for a while."

Lawrence Taylor would blame the first-half weather. The temperature was 76 degrees for the kickoff and California never looked better.

"It was so hot nobody could get their breath," said LT. "The second half, when it cooled off, we came out and played in our kind of weather. We started playing some ball."

"The third quarter turned it around," said Dan Reeves, the Bronco coach. "We came out at the start of the third and all of a sudden we're second-and-23."

The Giants were always second-and-23 when Reeves was Wellington Mara's choice to be head coach eight years ago. That's when Tim Mara stood up, when civil war almost broke out in the Divided House of Maras.

CHAPTER 5

THE AFTERMATH

DAILY NEWS   Pat Carroll

*Despite predictions of a Giants' dynasty, the Super Bowl celebration
didn't carry over to the 1987, '88, or '89 season.*

*I*t had been 30 years since the Giants last won a championship. And after Super Bowl XXI New Yorkers began to think that Parcells' championship showers would become an annual event. However, the next few years saw no more Super Bowl trips.

The strike-stricken 1987 season left the Giants in a hole. With his regulars intact for the full season in 1988, Parcells guided the Giants to a 10-6 record, but again missed the playoffs. It would be 1989 before the Giants would make the playoffs again. In those playoffs, the Giants lost a heartbreaker in overtime to the Rams.

But, just as the playoff loss a few years earlier to the Bears had laid the foundation for the Giants' first Super Bowl, this tough loss would lay the foundation for Parcells' second championship season.

Repeat? Why Not!

Want "more good players," warns Parcells

By Bill Verigan

There is no game, no more worlds for the Giants to conquer next week. But there is next season and another bit of history to confront them.

Only three teams have won back-to-back Super Bowls, the last being the Pittsburgh Steelers of 1979 and '80. Only eight teams have been in it twice in a row. Bill Parcells was already thinking about that yesterday.

"I don't think history means one thing in football," said the Giants coach. "Next year it's a new game."

And with some new players.

"To get more good players is the whole idea," said Parcells.

"We've got a good young team," Parcells said, "and if they don't get big heads they can be just as tough in the future. But I won't rest. Don't worry."

That the Giants know.

Falcons Covet Parcells

January 30, 1987
By Bill Verigan

Will success spoil the Giants? Bill Parcells tried to avert that possibility last night by terming reports of contractual problems "ridiculous."

But here's a situation that is sad and true. The Atlanta Falcons were denied permission this week to offer a $5-million, five-year contract as coach and GM to Parcells, the coach who dragged the Giants from the depths of the standings to a Super Bowl title.

Giants' management, which nearly made the tragic error of firing Parcells three seasons ago, shows every intention of holding him to the remaining two years of his contract at $300,000 annually—without giving him a raise.

And Giants' management asked commissioner Pete Rozelle to warn Atlanta to stay away from Parcells, according to sources close to the league office.

Parcells Still Supervising in Off-Season

By Bill Verigan

B ill Parcells, Super Bowl winner and coach of the year, wanted to make this point: "There's no difference in Bill Parcells."

Despite having a book in the works and being sought by the Falcons for $1 million annually to be their coach and pro football director, Parcells insisted, "I'm still hungry."

Indeed, he called the entire episode with Atlanta three days after the Super Bowl "embarrassing." "I feel like maybe our ownership didn't get to enjoy the Super Bowl win as much if something like that hadn't happened. They deserved to enjoy it, and I put George (Young, GM) in that group, too."

Parcells, who has two seasons left on his current contract, said he hasn't signed a new deal. But he said that he expects no fallout on his team.

"They know what they observe," he said, "I talked to the owners. I don't need to put out any olive branches."

This much is certain. The Atlanta episode is history. Since the Super Bowl Parcells has taken only two days off. He even skipped the team's visit to the White House and the owners' meetings in Hawaii. "What's the big deal?" he asked. "I also missed the meetings last year."

His players apparently are taking a similar business-as-usual approach to the off-season. Parcells encouraged them to enjoy the rewards that the Super Bowl can bring, but he also reminded them that the off-season is short.

He said there are "between 35 and 40 players" in the team's conditioning program at Giants Stadium. That's more than ever.

Calm before Giant Storm

Digging out of 0-5 'cyclone' will be rough

By Bill Verigan

Linebacker Carl Banks described coach Bill Parcells' brief message to the Giants returning players yesterday as a "calm-before-the-storm" speech. Twenty-seven days ago, players had trudged out of Giants Stadium with their possessions in garbage bags slung over their shoulders and an 0-2 record. After the replacements were banished with their jerseys and shoes, the loyal union players returned yesterday a minute after one o'clock with an 0-5 record. They might have to win the 10 remaining games to make the playoffs.

Parcells made it obvious yesterday that he will do "whatever it takes" to reverse that screeching skid from a Super Bowl title to the bottom of the NFL.

"We have to do things we did in the past, do them well and do them soon," he said. "When you're 0-5 and looking down this kind of barrel, things don't remain the same. We'll make every effort to get back on track. There's very little margin for error; we're starting over."

His staff was still putting together a game plan for Sunday against the Cardinals when Parcells addressed his players, then sent them out to work out on their own. Perhaps the message was that it's ultimately up to the players to salvage this sad situation.

Parcells will have the players on the field twice a day. During the first, he will walk the players through the plays and work on basics. In the afternoon, it gets tougher. The work day will be about two hours longer than usual.

And woe to any players who don't measure up. Parcells was not pleased by the regulars' performance in the first two games.

While the replacement players were limited in ability, Parcells said they "put out effort if they were in shape." But he said the regulars didn't perform well in the pre-season and that "10 of the 45 were probably playing well below their level of ability." He said they would be given a chance to "demonstrate through performances" whether they belong on the team.

"Nobody's pleased when you lose," said receiver Stacy Robinson. "It's not a pretty sight to be 0-5, and the garbage drops down on us."

Kicker Raul Allegre said that Parcells "wasn't down, but he wasn't jumping for joy that we were back, either."

Some teams might find players among their replacements, but Dan Morgan, a guard, and Mike Black, a center, were the only players retained by Parcells for the expanded roster and taxi squad. They will be handy on the scout team, especially with Chris Godfrey's sprained knee in questionable condition and Karl Nelson out for the year.

The two new additions and the four veterans who had crossed the picket line—Lawrence Taylor, Adrian White, Jeff Rutledge and Jeff Hostetler—were given yesterday off, so it was not possible to tell how they would be received.

At least one other offensive lineman, Bart Oates, welcomed them although he wasn't pleased by their participation during the strike.

Parcells compared his attitude to 1984 when the Giants went to the playoffs after a 3-12-1 record in 1983. He has not given up hope, even if the situation is grim.

"There's pressure, although some people might disagree," Parcells said, "and we've got to do something."

1987 NFC East Final Standings

TEAM	WINS	LOSSES
Redskins*	11	4
Cowboys	7	8
Cardinals	7	8
Eagles	7	8
Giants	6	9

*Qualified for playoffs

Parcells:
I'll Accept the Blame

By Bill Verigan

Joe Walton gets a break this week at Giants Stadium. The Jets aren't the home team.

The chants of "Joe Must Go" for Walton and the boos for the Jets' 6-8 record will be muted.

The irony is that the Giants' 5-9 record is worse, but Bill Parcells has escaped the wrath.

While Walton's critics wonder when he'll be fired, Parcells gets asked whether he has signed his contract extension.

The Giants have been spared abuse from their short-suffering season ticket holders. Injuries and the strike have been blamed.

But Parcells has pointed a finger at himself when it came to pinning this sad season on anyone in particular. He admitted he was frequently frustrated, and he said that might have spread the feeling.

There is no mystery why Parcells and the Giants have avoided beer baths and boos. They are the defending Super Bowl champions. But the Super Bowl is also where Parcells' troubles began. Walton probably would love to have such problems.

"Don't get me wrong, it was worth it; it was a great thrill, it's what we play for, and I'll never forget it," Parcells said. "I only hope we get back someday."

He promises he won't make the same mistakes again. But that triumph took a toll. The off-season was cut short, and Parcells now admits his preparation for this season was curtailed.

"I was dead," he said. "I just felt like I didn't have time to do anything in the off-season. Until the Super Bowl was over, I had to be concerned with Denver. And I had to be concerned with hotels and security and a lot more, too.

"Two days after the game I went to the combine meetings, and I looked at the players and wondered who in the world they were. I usually have a visual picture of 200 or 300 guys. I'm thinking about where they might fit in."

He won't have the same problem this year. That's for sure. He's got time on his hands.

Right now, he is plotting how to beat the Jets. But even that task figures into next season. Last week's victory over the Packers and another this week would be a positive starting point.

The Giants got off to an 0-2 start even before the strike, and by the time the strike ended they were 0-5. Parcells knows the importance of a fast start. Otherwise, he said, there is "no room for error."

"Once or twice I thought we were going to get it going. I thought so until the fourth quarter against Dallas. But we made those mistakes, and there was no room for error."

In the last week, Parcells has recovered a bit. He has rarely coached a team in decline before. His squads were always improving, and there was reason for optimism. Coach and players are closer when they win, and the Giants have developed some cracks.

"Losing is frustrating to everybody," he said. "You're supposed to win. You're paid to win. When you don't, it's frustrating to the players, coaches and organization."

He has to make some difficult decisions on players, but he said he'll take his time.

"I've got plenty of time," Parcells said. "When the season's over we'll discuss a lot of things. As of now I would rather not discuss any eventualities.

"I'll take a few days to myself, then really become analytical. I don't think the team needs wholesale changes. Transition is the word I like. There's probably not a coach in the league that doesn't feel that way."

Parcells will get the time, maybe Walton won't. The Super Bowl buys time, even if it creates some problems. Walton would gladly tackle the problems for a ring.

$3M Pact Extension for Parcells

By Paul Needell

The Giants put a year's worth of rumors and intrigue to rest yesterday when they announced that coach Bill Parcells has finally signed his long-awaited "multi-year" contract extension. Terms were being kept strictly hush-hush, but sources said the new deal will bring Parcells almost $3 million over the next four years.

Parcels was entering the final year of his contract at $325,000. The extension is believed to be for three more years through 1991 at about $750,000 per. In addition, a signing bonus of approximately $400,000 also is expected to be coming the coach's way.

Ever since Parcells had his much-publicized flirtation with the Atlanta Falcons following last year's Super Bowl championship, rumors have run rampant regarding his dissatisfaction with his overall role with the Giants. He and general manager George Young don't have the best of working relationships, and Parcells reportedly sought a situation that would bring him more power in personnel decisions.

"We've had a handshake agreement since last year," Young said yesterday. "I never worried about it."

Shortly after the aborted talks with the Falcons, the Giants and Parcells supposedly reached agreement on a lucrative contract extension. Mysteriously, that deal wasn't officially signed until yesterday.

The delay further fueled more recent speculation that Parcells might be headed to the Raiders to join his good buddy, Al Davis. Another report had Parcells possibly dickering with the Patriots, should coach Raymond Berry leave after the New England franchise is sold.

Asked why it took so long to finalize the extension, Young said: "Because that's what we decided to do. It's between Bill and I. Simple. It's our choice, nobody else's."

Pal: LT Relapsed at End of '87

By Bill Verigan

With a professional death penalty hanging in the balance, Lawrence Taylor began rehabilitation this week as an outpatient in a clinic in the metropolitan area.

Taylor, despite his own admissions and his failure of two NFL-administered drug tests, has a less severe problem than most outpatients, according to sources on the Giants. But his precise treatment is not known.

Drugs have been a part of Taylor's life for a long time. He has admitted that cocaine took hold of his life during the Giants' 1985 season, and his first attempt at rehabilitation was early in 1986 when he entered Methodist Hospital in Houston. It was a failure. Taylor was unwilling to admit he needed help to overcome the problem, and left after one week to barnstorm golf courses around the country.

Coach Bill Parcells always knew the problem wasn't solved. That's why he had Taylor tested every week during the 1986 season. Another Giant insider says Taylor was tested twice a week for two seasons, 1986 and 1987. A friend of Taylor's says he finds it hard to believe, but Taylor passed every test.

However, Parcells is fond of saying that no drug abuser is ever cured. Like an alcoholic, he is only off the stuff until his next whiff.

Parcells will not reveal the emotion he felt when Taylor was caught again in an NFL test this past August 15. Maybe it was anger, dismay and sadness, but it was probably not surprise. The coach has been involved in the battle against drugs for too long.

Parcells took over a dirty team in 1983. His methods might have offended some people, but he cleaned the Giants up before the NFL took over the drug program in July 1986. Even now, despite Taylor's highly publicized problems, the Giants are one of the most drug-free teams in the NFL.

One of Parcells' biggest challenges when he took over the Giants was to combat the drug use by many of his players, most notably Lawrence Taylor.

The cleanup began in Parcells' second season. Any suspicion was enough cause to subject players to random testing.

"More than a dozen guys were being tested regularly," said one former player.

Unfortunately, every time a Giant was waived or traded there were rumors, often false, that he was at least a suspect.

"A lot of those rumors weren't true," a player said. "There were players who asked to be traded. There were others who were simply replaced as starters and were expendable."

There were still probably a couple of guys on last year's team who had gone through rehab or failed their first drug test, but the Giants are cleaner than other teams.

Then in July 1986, the Giants were forced to relinquish control of their drug problem to the NFL. No one in the organization is happy with the way the NFL program is run. Some people hate the program, fearing it has too may loopholes.

Parcells Takes Dead Aim at the Absent and Lame

By Bill Verigan

It was open season on unproductive veterans yesterday at the Giants' minicamp.

Coach Bill Parcells accepted no excuses from the absentees and doled out no sympathy for the lame. They are often the easiest targets, and the coach was shooting at anything that didn't move.

Four unsigned players, Pepper Johnson, Terry Kinard, Zeke Mowatt and Lionel Manuel, and two with contracts—Lawrence Taylor and Phil Simms—were not present with the rest of the veterans.

"Don't let them tell you if they get hurt they won't get paid," Parcells advised the press. "They're guaranteed a certain amount of dollars if they get hurt. We've always done that on this team. The (10) players who are here without contracts know that."

The coach wasn't buying the pains and pulls that kept Jim Burt, Tom Flynn and Wayne Haddix from practicing, either. Burt showed up with a two-week-old pulled muscle in his backside. Flynn hurt his calf, and Haddix got a twinge in his hamstring.

"Those guys should be ready to practice," shot back Parcells. "We didn't hurt them. They hurt themselves."

Veterans beware. Parcells warned that "things are not going to be the same. There are some thing here I don't like. There are too many old guys (11 who will be 30 or older this year), and I want to get a younger, hungrier team."

Then, into this shooting gallery walked Kenny Hill. He also is unsigned, and he missed the morning practice because he was uncertain about his status. But after a conversation with Parcells and his agent, the prodigal player had returned. For the moment, Parcells put down his weapons.

Hill, you see, is one of those "old guys." The strong safety will be 31 the week training camp begins, and during the off-season he underwent surgery on both ankles. The young wolves are baying for his job, and Parcells already has said he likes the kids he has in the secondary.

But here was Hill, trying to fend off the wolves on his two recently healed ankles. Here was an example that Parcells could throw at the no-shows and sideline-huggers. Parcells was thankful for a player like Hill at this moment.

"The best trade I ever made," is what Parcells called Hill. "That kid's done a helluva job. He's someone I have tremendous respect for as a person and player."

The Giants rebounded from the disastrous strike-shortened 1987 season to post a 10-6 record in 1988. But, after missing the playoffs for the second straight year, Parcells got the Giants going in the right direction in 1989.

Just Call Him Thrill Parcells

By Gary Myers

Bill Parcels was making his usual post-game victory rounds. "Hey Old Red," he shouted at Ottis Anderson, hidden by reporters lined up five deep around him, "you want some Alpo?"

Parcells was in a good mood around 4 p.m. yesterday. The Giants had all but buried the Redskins for the season, beating them 20-17, the seventh time in the last eight non-strike meetings that Parcells had defeated Joe Gibbs, including a pair of three-pointers this season.

He was told that he was named star of the game by CBS, an award sponsored by a beer company. "I might have a few of those tonight," Parcells said.

Parcells had plenty of stars yesterday: Anderson, Parcells' old hunting dog, ran for 101 yards and picked up three key first downs—two on fourth down, setting up the Giants' two touchdowns, and the last on a third and five to ice the game; Phil Simms, bounced around by the Redskins defense, threw two fourth-quarter touchdown passes; and little Dave Meggett, who stuck his head in Wilber Marshall's chest on blitzes all day, including the key pickup on Simms' 25-yard TD pass to Odessa Turner to win the game.

But the difference in this game? The coach. Now, Parcells is not exactly Patrick Buchanan conservative—remember the fake punt in the Super Bowl?—but the Giants are hardly Pete Rose. Gamblers, they are not.

Parcells was standing outside the coaches' locker room now and was being asked about this apparent contradiction: The Giants are well known around the NFL as being a conservative organization. They rarely vote for change at the league meetings and make trades only in desperation. And yet here, in a game Parcells says is one of "the five or six that can make a difference in your season," he went for it. The Giants didn't have a wide open game plan, but at the key moments, Parcells took big chances.

"I coach just the way I want to. I wouldn't say I'm conservative, although I'm sure the fans would say I am," Parcells said. "I'm just trying to win the game and do the things to give my team a chance. It's hard to explain why I do things. It's almost instinctive because two weeks from now I might do something different."

Parcells went for a fourth and 7 from the Redskins' 24 on the first series of the game. "I raised my eyes for a second," Simms said. Then, he hit Mark Ingram for 13 yards, setting up Raul Allegre's 33-yard field goal. In the fourth quarter, Parcells gave the ball to Anderson twice, once at the Redskins' 42, then the Redskins' 40, each time needing a yard, each time getting a yard.

Parcells hates to punt in those situations and figured he had a much better chance of picking up a yard than Allegre did hitting a monster field goal. The Giants scored 17 of their 20 points following fourth-down conversions. Invariably, those things pump up a team."

"Bill will gamble as much as anybody," Simms said. "He's not scared to do anything."

More than anything, Parcells is conveying an attitude. He is a big believer in sending messages. By going for it, he's telling his offensive linemen that he believes they can push the defense. He's telling Anderson this is 1979, not 1989. And he's pumping up Jumbo Elliott, after he allowed two Dexter Manley sacks and was called for holding. Following the tough first half, Parcells cornered Elliott, who has been struggling with a bad back, and told him, "You're at the crossroads of your career. Dig out of the hole you've got yourself in or you will be in it for a long time."

The Giants were a down team after last week's loss in Philly. They blew a 16-7 fourth quarter lead, were damaged by a nonreversal on an instant replay nondecision and were in a foul mood after the game.

But Parcells did an excellent job of getting them ready for what so far is the biggest game of the season. Instead of the Redskins being tied for first in the NFC East, they are two games back, but really three since they are down the tiebreaker to the Giants.

"We put a stake in their heart," Meggett said.

The Giants are 5-1. They play in San Diego next week and then a Monday nighter at home against the Herschel Vikings. And their noninvolvement in the Walker Derby is another example of the Giants' attitude.

Nearly every team in the NFL was contacted last week by Walker's agents when it became apparent the Cowboys were going to deal him. The Giants said thanks, but we're not interested.

Conservative? Maybe not, considering the price. But they weren't interested regardless. And the decision looked good yesterday with Anderson picking up his first 100-yard game since 1985 and Meggett continuing to develop into one of the best situation backs in the league.

Bill Parcells said goodbye to two of "his guys" as Harry Carson and George Martin retired after the 1988 season.

Giants GM George Young says he doesn't want to take on "strangers," unless he's desperate. And the Giants obviously don't consider their rushing game to be a problem.

"We're realistic, not conservative," Young said. "I am the result of a lot of experience over a long period of time. My judgments are based on trial and error. That's what I'm supposed to be paid for. I'm not 25 years old.

"I look into every kind of deal when a good player is involved. I didn't overlook the Walker situation. But it would have been very difficult for me to make a deal like that unless we had an urgency."

Together, Young and Parcells were working on the ego of their team. By not making a move on Walker or the other running backs out there—Mike Rozier, Gary Anderson, Terrence Flagler—Young is saying that the Giants are happy with what they have. And by taking some gambles yesterday, Parcells is telling his team that he believes.

Maybe even as much as he did in 1986. The Super Bowl year. "Stop talking ancient history," Parcells said.

The Giants Return to the Grid Stone

By Bill Verigan

Vacation's over. The Giants' three-day layoff ended yesterday with a meeting and one-hour workout. It was back to basics, back to books, back to Parcells' dirty looks.

There will be no more rest for the weary warriors who clinched the NFC East championship on the final weekend of the regular season with a 12-4 record. Bill Parcells will see to that.

"I'm concerned because I've seen teams on TV that look like they can only play one half," said Parcells, adding that he doesn't expect that to happen to the Giants.

He has to avoid adding more players to the injury list, but Parcells promised he will "run 'em. We can do a whole lot in a week."

Last Sunday, the Giants clawed to get an extra week off, but the coach warned that it could backfire.

"Everybody says having a week off is an advantage," Parcells said. "That's not necessarily so. It's only an advantage if you make it an advantage. Otherwise, it's a detriment."

While the players were off for three days, Parcells and the coaching staff were looking at tapes and editing them for the players.

The Giants are facing the unknown in the NFC division playoffs on January 7. Their opponent will be either the Rams, who defeated the Giants 31-10 during the regular season, or the Vikings, who lost to the Giants 24-14.

Parcells said he has four objectives this week:

"First, we want to heal the bumps and bruises. We can't kill them off.

"Second, we want them to keep their timing.

"Third, we want to work on fundamentals and work on things the Vikings and Rams can hurt us with. We've hung in pretty well, but I see things we need to improve. Some of these young guys don't know what the playoffs are all about. That's obvious, and we have to make them aware. This is a different year and a different kind of team from 1986.

"Fourth is conditioning."

Parcells said, "I'm not saying I'm unhappy with the conditioning, I'm just going to reinforce it.

"There are problems in certain areas that every team has," Parcells said. "They come up during the season. They're sloughed off when a team is winning, and they become recurrent. Other teams look at the films. They say, 'Hey, let's try some of that, too.'"

Coach Parcells wasn't above reminding officials about how to do their jobs.

Parcells Lives, Can't Sleep, with It

By Phil Pepe

I n case you were wondering, Bill Parcells had no trouble sleeping Sunday night after losing to the Rams earlier in the day. He slept fine, Parcells said.

"Until 3:19 a.m.; then I was up and I couldn't get back to sleep."

What is there to do at 3:19 except think about an interference call against Sheldon White, think about Flipper Anderson taking a pass from Jim Everett and running all the way to the NFC title game, think about his season ending? What Bill Parcells did was what he does every day. He got dressed and headed for Giants Stadium. He was at his desk at 6:15.

A few hours later, Parcells was addressing his troops for the last time this season, going over the usual last items of business.

"Like what we're going to do with the fine money (it will be donated to charity), off-season addresses, plans for the off-season, rehab things and, don't laugh, reminding them to pay their taxes," Parcells said. "I told them they were a good team to coach, that I enjoyed coaching them very much—and I did. They gave me everything a coach could ask for. They're a good group of guys. We had very few discipline problems."

There was no talk about Sunday's game, what went wrong, what could have been done differently; no thought about what has to be done for 1990.

"This is a bad day to think about next year," Parcells said.

There was enough to think about with Sunday's heartbreaking 19-13 over-time loss to the Rams, idle thoughts creeping into his mind at unsuspecting times. It was going to be tough to get that game out of his mind; a game Parcells said, that gave him "one of the toughest losses I ever had."

He was asked if it was like losing to the Bears in the NFC championship game in 1985.

"Just about identical," Parcells said. "I didn't talk to anybody for about six hours after that game."

As much as the Bears game hurt, Parcells knew there was something to build on for 1986. He could sense the Giants were coming. He also has good feelings about this team that came so close, that was only minutes from San Francisco and the NFC title shot. A little help here, a few additions there; it could make a difference.

Only it's not that easy. The Giants don't start out next season as NFC East champions, needing only a few breaks, a few plays, to get to the conference championship.

"It starts all over," Parcells said. "The draft, the pre-season, the regular season, just to get to where you were standing yesterday, and you never know what's going to happen. It's going to take a lot of work to get in that same stupid position, but those are the games I want to coach in."

Regardless of an interference call and a sudden-death touchdown pass and the second-guessing of multitudes for refusing to sit on a lead and take 6-0 into the locker room at halftime.

"I have to live with the results," Parcells said. "I don't second guess myself at all, not one iota. Had we been getting the ball in the second half, I wouldn't have done it (try for another score)."

Instead, he wanted another score, even three points, to put the Rams down by at least nine. That would have meant they had to have two scores to win and it could have taken them out of their game plan and things might have been different.

All in all, it was not a bad year. A successful season, in fact. But Parcells knows success is relative.

"It's an ambiguous term," the coach said. "It means one thing to somebody, something to somebody else. To improve on what we did last year is a measure of success. But we're one of 24 teams not playing this week, and that's disappointing. It's mentally tough on me on a day like this."

It's going to take time for the wounds to heal. Soon, very soon, Bill Parcells will immerse himself in next year, what must be done to improve.

"What you want to do is try to improve it to give yourself a better chance," he said.

The healing process began yesterday with a meeting of his staff. Looking ahead to next season might make things a little easier. Parcells thought he might even sleep a little later this morning. Maybe until 4 a.m.

CHAPTER 6

HERE WE GO AGAIN

Giants' 1990-91 Season

*After the disappointment of the three seasons following Super Bowl XXI,
all Bill Parcells wanted was to return to the Super Bowl.*

*I*t was a simple question from Lawrence Taylor to Bill Parcells: "You think this team has the ability to go all the way, huh, coach?"

Parcells' one-word answer, "Yeah," said volumes to both men and served notice to the rest of the NFL. Parcells got his team off to a 10-0 start, but it wouldn't be that easy. The Giants lost three of their last six games and barely made it past the 49ers in the playoffs. Parcells even had to deal with a kidney stone. And in Super Bowl XXV, the Giants won by the narrowest margin possible when a Buffalo field goal was just wide at the end of the game.

Giants' Makeup Has Familiar Ring

By Gary Myers

I t was placed in each of the Giants' lockers last week. A flashy color brochure of jewelry available through a local distributor for the holiday season. Included were a nice variety of championship rings.

"Wouldn't mind having one of those," one Giant said. "But I don't want to have to buy it."

Maybe it won't be necessary.

The Giants were thinking Super Bowl as the 1990 season finally hit town last night. And the 27-20 victory over the Eagles only emphasized that. The nightmare of Flipper Anderson running up the tunnel with their 1989 season is gone. And unless you believe the 49ers have the divine right to make it three in a row, then the next thing you say is: Why not the Giants?

"The thing that hit me first when I got here was this team is hungry and it is loose," said safety Dave Duerson, signed last week after he was released by the Bears. "Those are two intangibles that you have to have. If you play tight like we did in Chicago the last few years, if you are afraid to make a mistake, it's hard to win."

The Giants sent a message to the Eagles, who figure to be elbow-to-elbow with them the entire season. It's real easy to overestimate the importance of the opener, especially when it's against the No. 1 rival. Remember, the Giants opened in 1986 by losing a Herschel Walker heartbreaker in Dallas. Then, they won 17 of their last 18, including the victory over Denver in Super Bowl XXI.

And the Giants opened with emotional Monday night victories against the Redskins the last two years. Still, in '88 the Giants didn't make the playoffs and last year the Rams didn't let them out of the divisional round. But last night's victory reinforced the idea that this definitely can be a Super Bowl season.

The 49ers appear out of sync. The Eagles' offense is a mess. The Rams have a ton of injuries. The Redskins have a shaky defense. And the Vikings have no heart. The Giants?

"I want my players to be smart, disciplined, confident, have strong will and come up with the kill shot when they can. If you don't have those things you can throw the talent out the window," coach Bill Parcells said. "The running, throwing, kicking and catching part is only 50%."

And it appears Parcells has constructed a team that meets his criteria. There's just enough firepower in the offense, as long as Parcells doesn't get rookie-itis and chicken out of playing Rodney Hampton. And although the front seven of the defense doesn't terrify teams like it did in '86, LT can still bring it at the key time. And picking up Duerson and cornerback Everson Walls gives Parcells two vets who have played in championship games.

Parcells may not be the best coach in the NFL—his offensive approach is frustrating—but it's hard to argue with his knack of reading the psyche of his team and preparing it to play. He knows when to take it easy, he knows when to turn up the juice. And he has a way of using his veterans to get his message across in the locker room.

"I got some guys I can talk to now and can get messages to the right people if we have to," Parcells said. "It's a vehicle a coach has at his disposal."

In the past, when something was going wrong, Parcells walked up to Harry Carson or George Martin and said, "Fix it." Walls and Duerson can be those players in the secondary. He also has Carl Banks to take care of the front seven and Simms has a grip on the entire offense.

So, can this be 1986 all over again? The Giants didn't find out they were on a magical mystery tour until Simms converted that fourth and 17 to Bobby Johnson in Week 11 in Minnesota. Then it became apparent something special was going on. The Giants didn't know it coming out of camp. And they don't know it this year, either. Too early.

Parcells' Team Super?

By Bill Madden

T his was late in the fourth quarter Sunday, and the Giants were in the process of running out the clock against the Redskins.

Lawrence Taylor strolled over to Bill Parcells on the sidelines and mumbled a question.

"You think this team has the ability to go all the way, huh, coach?"

"Yeah," Parcells said without elaborating.

"Um-hmm," Taylor, said, nodding affirmatively before walking away.

If you know Parcells, ever the one-game-at-a-time conservative thinker, then you know that "yeah" response he gave to Taylor said reams. Taylor must have thought so, too, because it obviously more than reinforced his own growing feeling about this team, which is 7-0.

Yesterday, Parcells was more characteristically cautious about the Giants' destiny this year, refusing to concede anything more than being assured of eating his Thanksgiving dinner as a playoff contender. Super Bowl? The San Francisco 49ers? NFC Eastern Division champions? Sunday, Taylor had caught him in an unguarded moment, but now this was Monday morning.

"There's not one guy on our team thinking about San Francisco," Parcells said. "I know these guys; that's why I've got so many veterans."

And that's why Parcells, however guarded about what December and January might bring, has a real good feeling about these Giants. What has given him that feeling is the infusion of veterans such as Dave Duerson and Everson Walls—and even the as-yet unused third-string quarterback Matt Cavanaugh and linebacker Lawrence McGrew.

"It's not just any veterans," Parcells said. "It's getting the right veterans. A lot of veterans you can put 'em all in rockers and let 'em sit on the front porch. Old players are not necessarily good players. The guys we've brought in here, though, have been the right players. They've fit in."

Which, of course, was important. The veterans Parcells has brought in this season especially did not come cheaply. Duerson, for instance, was signed for a $500,000 price tag. The same with Cavanaugh. Think about that: George Young paying a third-string quarterback a half-million dollars a year.

Parcells did.

"When (Adrian) White went down in the last preseason game, I went to George and told him I wanted Duerson," Parcells said. "He didn't hesitate. He said: 'Okay, go get him.' Then, right after that, Cavanaugh was available, and I told George I wanted him. There was never any discussion of cost."

And that is what first gave Parcells the good feeling that he expressed to Taylor on Sunday afternoon: The fact that the Giants' management, after completing some often bitter contract negotiations with Taylor and Leonard Marshall, now was showing its commitment to winning without any bottom-line restrictions.

"My players know I'll do anything to win this week," Parcells said. "I don't think about next year or even next month. If there's a veteran player out there who can help us now, then I want him. It turns out, though, that Duerson and Walls, I think, can help us beyond this year. I wan't sure of that when we first signed them, but that was before I got to see them and know them."

Again, though, this was not the time to be talking about next month or beyond—even if Parcells might be privately thinking about it. Tomorrow is Halloween, and that was far enough into the future.

"I have no illusions about what we've accomplished so far," Parcells said. "To have six division wins before Halloween is a very big plus."

That and an open checkbook from above.

Parcells: A Coach's Life No Life at All

By Vic Ziegel

What would Bill Parcells be doing if he weren't coaching his perfect football team? The coach played with the thought yesterday, and decided baseball was the answer.

The topic came up because Parcells was asked which of his players might move on to coaching careers. He wasn't sure, but he did have this piece of advice:

"I wouldn't advise any of them to pursue this particular profession. I really wouldn't," Parcells said seriously.

Was Parcells saying that if he had to do it all over again, he wouldn't have a parking spot all his own at Giants Stadium?

"If I had to do it all over, from the beginning, knowing what I know now . . ." Parcells said, pausing, then lowering his voice, "I probably wouldn't go into it."

He was giving too much away, so he decided to make with the jokes. "I'd be a bullpen coach," he said. A second later, he was saying, "No, it's too hot out there. I want to be the guy next to the phone. If he (the manager) says he wants a righty, then I tell the guy down there he wants a righty. And then I hang up. Then when it rings back, I tell the (manager), 'He's ready.'

"If he wants a righty or lefty, I think I could figure that out. And I could hit fungos. Maybe I could hit infield, but that's a little more dangerous because batting practice is going on."

If they needed him on the baselines, he would coach first, not third. What would he do about left-handed pull hitters?

"Never thought about that," he said. "I'd put a screen up."

When he was an assistant at Vanderbilt, Parcells said, he coached two innings of a game against Kentucky. "I got four runs: that's the truth. The manager came back, and I said, 'This is easy.'"

Where did the manager go? "To the bathroom," Parcells said.

When the laughs died down, a serious Parcells was back to explaining why a head coaching job in the NFL isn't his idea of heaven. "Based on what I've seen, the longevity isn't all that good," he said. "You know how many head coaches have been in this league since I've been a coach?" His guess, "and I'll be within five, is 60-something.

"I'm giving you a serious answer. I don't think it's all that advisable. And I think it's going to get worse. I enjoy the game, the competition, a lot of things I enjoy about it. But I see it's getting worse everywhere, on every level. It's not just professional football. It's the economics of the thing. And the pressure on people to win.

"You see the cycle. There aren't guys staying around forever. You see it happening."

Does this mean you're retiring after the season is over?

"Sheee . . ." Parcells said, ending the discussion.

Parcells had his team pointed in the right direction after a 10-0 start to the 1990 season.

Rejuvenated Giants Ease Parcells' Pain

By Gary Myers

Bill Parcells didn't try to hide a pained look as he moved gingerly down a hallway toward his office in the Giants' locker room. He had to go. Didn't want to. Had to. They were waiting for him at Morristown Memorial Hospital.

Parcells spent Saturday night at the hospital after he was stricken with a kidney stone, which on the pain meter, is the male equivalent of having a baby. It hurts like hell. Parcells showed up and coached the Giants to an ugly 23-15 victory over Minnesota, which ended their two-game losing streak and clinched their second straight NFC East title. And now he was heading right back to the hospital.

"I'm not exactly feeling great," Parcells said.

It was not going to be a fun night. The stone had moved from Parcells' kidney, but since it hadn't made its way to his bladder, he had not passed it on his own. And if it didn't, Parcells painfully explained a procedure where a tube will be inserted to push the stone back to his kidney and then ultrasound treatment will be used.

This is called coaching in pain. And the few players on the Giants who knew before the game about Parcells' condition expected nothing less than for him to stick it out on the sidelines. And he did, although he was a little less animated than usual. He didn't move around much and didn't look too happy.

"He's a trouper," Lawrence Taylor said. "We have to play. And he knows we need him to coach. It's as simple as that."

A few players wondered what was going on when Parcells wasn't on the field for the pre-game warmups. "Me and (Dave) Duerson were sitting in the locker room before the game saying that we hadn't seen Bill today," cornerback

Everson Walls said. "He usually talks to me on the field during the warm-ups and I didn't see him."

Then Walls looked up and Parcells was standing by the locker room door calling the players to get ready. Walls sensed something different during the game. "You mess up, he'll let you know. But I messed up once he just said, 'Everson, did you revolve on the play the way you're supposed to?'"

Last week, Parcells, who had an easier time with a kidney stone seven years ago, made a plea for his "bumps and bruises guys" to get back on the field pronto, not in three weeks. And that's why he escaped the hospital yesterday and was on the sidelines. He had challenged his players, "So you better show up yourself," he said.

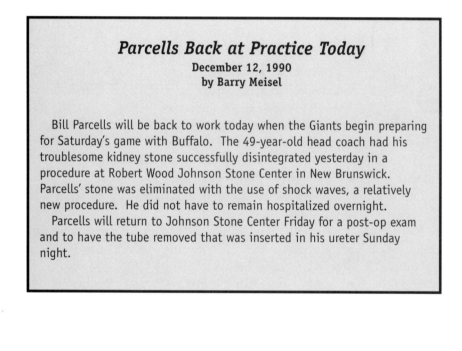

Parcells Back at Practice Today
December 12, 1990
by Barry Meisel

Bill Parcells will be back to work today when the Giants begin preparing for Saturday's game with Buffalo. The 49-year-old head coach had his troublesome kidney stone successfully disintegrated yesterday in a procedure at Robert Wood Johnson Stone Center in New Brunswick. Parcells' stone was eliminated with the use of shock waves, a relatively new procedure. He did not have to remain hospitalized overnight.

Parcells will return to Johnson Stone Center Friday for a post-op exam and to have the tube removed that was inserted in his ureter Sunday night.

Bill Parcells:
One in a Million

Turns press briefings into stand-up act

By Vic Ziegel

B
ill Parcells is sitting at the long table in the Giants Stadium press room, doing a wonderful imitation of a man enjoying himself. How can this be? His Giants are under a certain amount of pressure to paralyze the pathetic Patriots Sunday. Anything less—a vaguely vapid victory, say—and they will be found guilty of stumbling into the playoffs.

His team has won only two of its last five games. He doesn't have his No. 1 quarterback. His short-yardage game is yards away from where he wants it. The defense isn't as dependable as it was. And, look, he can still smile. Still carry on a conversation as if his shoes were off.

You don't have to win this Sunday, is how one question begins. "Sez who?" Parcells cuts in, but not irritably. Well, it's not going to affect where you go in the playoffs. "It affects my morale," he says.

The little game of ask-it-and-trash-it continues because Parcells gets off on this sort of stuff. Doesn't this Sunday give you a chance to learn about some of the guys you don't play much? "I hope to get some in the game," Parcells says, "but not at anybody's expense. That's all I got to do—tell my team, 'Oh, we're not gonna play you guys.'

"They'd look at me like I was nuts. I make them play in the preseason. Why wouldn't I make them play in the regular season?"

He wants to make sure we understand. "There's certain things we don't do. There's a certain policy in place. (The players) know what it is; they know we're not deviating. I think that's been very helpful to us over the years."

Hard not to like Parcells. If you're a fan, his team usually wins for you. If you're a player, especially an older player, he lets you know where you stand. If you're a rookie, you don't stand. You sit. If you block, learn fast, show good instincts, or if there's a large hole at your position, you get work. If you write about his team, you get tested. Because he reads you. Tells you he reads you.

He is asked about the Giants' skill at avoiding turnovers and his answer is, "If you're gonna write this column you're about three days late. About seven guys wrote it early in the week."

There's a question about his kickers. Would you use Raul Allegre—who was added to the practice squad this week—in the playoffs? "Sure, if I felt he gave us the best chance to win. But the other guy's (Matt Bahr) been kicking pretty well. There's no difference in their kickoffs. In fact, Bahr might be a better kickoff guy. In fact, he is. 'Cause he'll tackle. Unfortunately, for him. And he's kicking (field goals) 75% for us. I like the little son of a gun. What's not to like? He's been knocked lulu and he goes out and kicks. He hurts his back, and he goes out and kicks. All the professional football kickers that I've known were basically wimpy."

This is wonderful stuff. All the professional football coaches that I've ever known were basically dreadful. Weeb Ewbank, he was fine, but Weeb never had to play to this many cassette recorders.

"Anything else, gentlemen?" Parcells asks. This is supposed to tell us he's ready to leave. He has given us more than enough time, and we're back today, giving it again. There are no questions. Parcells can leave. Instead, incredibly, he lights a cigarette. So somebody asks who he likes in the Philadelphia-Washington wild card game. "Washington hurt themselves big-time (losing) Saturday night," he says. "I just think Philly's a different team in Philly than they are in Washington . . ."

There is more conversation. Small talk really. Hard to believe he'll be out on the practice field in a little while, making like Captain Ahab.

1990 NFC East Final Standings

TEAM	WINS	LOSSES
Giants*	13	3
Eagles*	10	6
Redskins*	10	6
Cowboys	7	9
Cardinals	5	11

*Qualified for playoffs

Parcells' Whip Works

Attitude change visible in team's prep for playoffs

By Barry Meisel

B
ill Parcells didn't want the Giants to "just cruise" through three days of practice, as Everson Walls said Wednesday.

He didn't want this to be a lazy playoff bye week after two uninspired performances over inferior competition, as his players admitted to displaying in three-point victories over Phoenix and New England.

So Parcells put psychology in motion: criticize the players, temporarily de-emphasize their regular-season achievements, bruise their egos.

That was accomplished by Parcells and his staff—some subtly, others more directly—in public comments Monday and in Wednesday's team meetings.

The purpose? Correct some legitimate mistakes while awakening those veterans who contemplated sleepwalking through the week, snap the rookies without playoff experience to attention, and tighten the 47-man bond vital to the Giants' Super Bowl chances.

The true results won't be known until the Giants line up for their NFC semifinal playoff game on January 13, but so far it appears the tactics are working. Carl Banks, Lawrence Taylor, Maurice Carthon and Mark Collins were among those who spoke during a 20-minute, players-only meeting before practice.

Then the team whooped and hollered through an unusually lively practice.

"Bill's a master of the psyche game," said Leonard Marshall, who has watched Parcells work since both joined the Giants in 1983. "You've got to give him credit because his timing was perfect. Guys could have very easily come here, just screwed around in practice for the next couple of days. But they've been intent. Guys have been working on fundamentals. Guys have been thinking and talking about what they're going to do to get this team ready for the playoffs."

Parcells spoke matter-of-factly Monday when he said of the playoffs that "if players can't get ready for this kind of game, then I need to get new players." He didn't say it in an ominous manner, but it's easy to understand how certain players unfamiliar with Parcells' tactics could have felt threatened.

"I've been here 10 years. I've heard all those statements," LT said. "I've heard every speech you can possibly make. I don't know how other guys received what he said. I don't think there was a threat in there intended for any particular people. We know we're all in it together.

"A lot of guys took what he said, if he said anything, the wrong way. And here we are, we won 13 games. You got people like New Orleans jumping up and down—they're 8-8 and in the playoffs and having a fit. They're partying, they're smiling, having a great time. And here we are, 13-3, and people are moping.

Marshall understood that Parcells might have been dying to startle the younger players who have little or no playoff experience into kicking it up a notch. But he wondered if they needed to be stroked this time of year.

"You can't sit back and continue to prod those guys, induce them with negative reinforcement," Marshall said. "You've got to tell them all the good things they did, what it took to win 13 games. What it's going to take now to win two more games and go to the dance (Super Bowl)."

So that's what the players did themselves yesterday.

"There's an altogether different attitude now," Collins agreed. "It's great. A lot better than (Wednesday)."

Parcells' Playoff Record with the Giants

	WINS	LOSSES	
1984	1	1	
1985	1	1	
1986	3	0	Won Super Bowl XXI
1989	0	1	
1990	3	0	Won Super Bowl XXV
	8	3	

Just a Jersey Guy

Parcells' pals stay close to coach's heart

By Bill Madden

Above the grill at Hagler's Diner in Oradell, New Jersey, a framed picture of the proprietor, George Hagler, standing arm-in-arm with a then-portly Bill Parcells, rests on a shelf. A thin film of grease from the tens of thousands of hamburgers, ham sandwiches and omelets that have cooked beneath it over the years now covers the glass and slightly clouds the visage of two longtime friends.

It is a small price to pay for resting in the place of honor at Oradell's pulse center, this 65-year-old landmark diner/restaurant where the "elite" who come to eat range from the Public Service and United Parcel truck drivers, to the local politicians to Gene Michael, who stops in on his way to Yankee Stadium, to Oradell's own, Duane (Bill) Parcells.

George Hagler is retired now from the rigors of standing on his feet all day, cutting roast beef. These days, he arrives at the old place around 12:30 p.m. and holds court at his reserved table in the rear of the restaurant area. On this day, two days before Parcells' Giants are to take on the Bills in Super Bowl XXV, Hagler is gazing fondly at the old picture, carefully wiping away the grease film on the glass.

"Back then, when he was a kid growing up in this town, he was Duane," Hagler says. "Course to the kids and guys like me, he was always Billy. He used to stop in here every day on his lunch break from school. Remember, this was before they had McDonald's and Burger King and you could get a hamburger for 15 cents here. Billy paid for them.

"But then, when he thought I wasn't looking, he'd go down to the soda bin at the end of the counter and pocket a couple of Nehis. Sometimes, he'd come back at the end of the week and confess that he took a soda and that he'd pay me for it."

Yet according to Hagler, payment is still due.

"Yeah," he laughs, "last year I sent him a bill for all those stolen sodas. I enclosed a note on it that said: 'Now you can afford to pay for them.'"

The stolen sodas story is, of course, a longstanding, running gag between Hagler and Parcells. Their bond goes far deeper than just those long ago 25-cent lunches. If you know Parcells as his friends and neighbors from Oradell still do, then you know that he is a guy who may have traveled the country—from Wichita to Florida to Texas to Colorado to New England before coming home to the Giants as head coach in 1983—but he never forgot his Jersey roots. And Jersey friends.

Today, when the camera scans Parcells roaming the Giants sidelines at Tampa, you will likely see a guy in a floppy hat and parka standing right behind him. That man is Mickey Corcoran. He is there, right behind Parcells, at every Giants' home game and every road game of any importance. And on the charter plane flights, the man always sitting next to Parcells is not Bill Belichick, Ron Erhardt or even George Young. It is Mickey Corcoran.

In 1958, Bill Parcells' senior year at River Dell High School in Oradell, his basketball coach was Mickey Corcoran. Even though everyone knew Parcells' future, in college and beyond, lay in football, it was Corcoran who influenced him most. And when Parcells' father, Chub, a Bergen County football legend at Hackensack High and later Georgetown, passed away a couple years ago, it was Corcoran who quite naturally emerged as a kind of surrogate father to the Giants head football coach.

"He was a gym rat," Corcoran recalled the other day. "Even back then, though, I knew Billy was born to coach. Why? Because of all the kids I had, he was the one who would always ask questions of me. He always wanted to know why we were doing certain things.

"I remember one time, his mom called me, sounding very worried, and said: 'I don't know what's wrong with Duane, Mickey. He's moping around the house.' Well, what had happened was that I really rode his butt that day and threw him out of the gym for wising off to me. I hated to do it because I loved the kid. But I also knew he'd be back to discuss it—on my terms."

Years later, after Parcells had gone on to an unhappy first year at Colgate, Corcoran helped him transfer to Wichita State, where he made some All-America teams as a linebacker and was selected in the eighth round of the draft by Detroit. Instead of following the pro dream, though, Parcells decided to get right into coaching, starting out as an assistant at tiny Hastings (Nebraska) College.

A couple of years later, Tom Cahill, Parcells' former high school coach at River Dell who had moved on to West Point, was looking for an assistant coach.

"When I heard that, I called Tom up at Army and said to him: 'I got the perfect guy for you.' He said: 'Billy Parcells.' Well, Tom starts to think about it and says: 'I don't know, why do you think I should hire him, Mickey?' And I said: 'Why? Do you have to ask, Tom? Billy's one of us! He's a Jersey guy!"

The rest, as they say, is history, although somewhat complicated. For upon reuniting with Cahill at West Point, Parcells became fast friends with the assistant basketball coach at Army, one Bobby Knight, who not coincidentally, also counts Mickey Corcoran as his guru. Parcells left The Point after three seasons and began his cross-country collegiate coaching odyssey, but, characteristically, remained close friends with Knight.

No matter where he went, Bill Parcells was never far away from his Jersey roots. One reason for that was Mickey Corcoran (left), Parcells' high school basketball coach and longtime mentor.

"They're both brilliant coaches, and brilliant motivators," Corcoran said unabashedly. "Bobby's a lot more complex than Billy, though. I've never seen anything like the love Billy's players have for him. I watch him in practices, the way he'll take them down a peg, then always leave 'em with something positive."

"The reason Willie has such a great rapport with his players is because he's so honest," said Parcells' youngest brother Doug, another Hagler's regular and Corcoran disciple who is now the recreation director in Oradell. "Maybe the best example I can give you of that is when Robbie McGovern got cut by the Chiefs a couple of months ago.

"Robbie's an Oradell guy, too, and I called Willie and asked him to give him a tryout. He did, and would have given him a job, too, but he just didn't have a place for him. Afterward, though, when he heard Robbie was considering going to law school, he told him: 'Don't fool around with football too much longer. You're a special teams guy and the big money just isn't gonna happen for you.' Robbie told me how much he appreciated his honesty and advice."

Talk to any of the people who know him best, from the blue-collar gang at Hagler's who'll be watching today's Super Bowl XXV over shots and beers, or guys like Bruce Battel, who went to high school with him and now handles his investments at Prudential-Bache, or Chuck May, who played Little League and Babe Ruth baseball with him in Oradell, and they all say the same things about Bill Parcells. He may walk with the Shulas, Walshes and Landrys now, but he's never forgotten his roots.

"All year long," Corcoran said, "Billy's been telling me: 'Mickey, I got to win it one more time and then I can walk away. But I keep reminding him that that's what he told me back in '86—that all he wanted was to win the Super Bowl. I told him: 'God put you on this earth to coach and now that you're here (at the Super Bowl) again, I couldn't be prouder.'"

Simply a Gigantic Effort

By Barry Meisel

They won by one point because Scott Norwood had never kicked a field goal from as far away as 47 yards on grass and couldn't in the biggest moment of his professional life. But it would be far too simplistic to say the Giants barely squeaked past the Buffalo Bills Sunday evening in the Super Bowl.

Bill Parcells' Big Blue won the silver anniversary classic, 20-19, by doing what worked all year. It was a complete game played on the Giants' terms. The offense hogged the ball for minutes at a time. The defense neutralized the most potent attackers with an aggressive style that was one part intelligence, one part intimidation. The special teams netted field position. And the coaching staff outmatched its opponents.

"This," veteran Dave Duerson said, "was a team effort."

Teams never had to worry about the Giants' offense racking up pinball points on the scoreboard, but by keeping the ball on the ground the Giants prevented the NFL's highest-scoring offense from getting on the field.

"Even our offense is on defense," Mark Collins said. "They took time off the clock."

The offense left little time for the Bills to rally in the final quarter, after Matt Bahr's 21-yard field goal gave the Giants a 20-19 lead with 7:20 left. The defense stopped the Bills once in two minutes, regained its breath while the offense ran another three minutes off the clock, and braced for the final 2:16.

The Bills were on their 19 with less than two minutes left when Thurman Thomas—the game's best player—broke off left tackle on third and 1. As he turned upfield, it appeared the Giants were doomed. There was only one defender left to beat, safety Everson Walls.

A cunning ballhawk he is. A pure tackler, he isn't.

"I just didn't want to take any chances," Walls said. "I wanted to play it smart."

Left: Giants pray before the field goal attempt of Buffalo's Scott Norwood in the closing seconds of Super Bowl XXV.

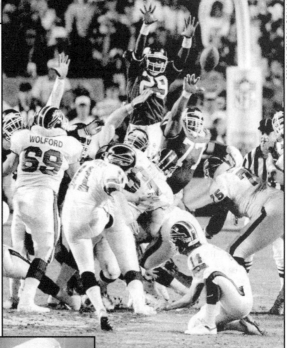

Right: Buffalo Bills kicker Scott Norwood (center) misses the field goal attempt in the last seconds of the game, clinching the victory for the New York Giants in Super Bowl XXV in Tampa.

Left: Giants head coach Bill Parcells gets doused with Gatorade in the wake of his second Super Bowl victory.

Walls brought Thomas down, one-on-one. It was the biggest tackle of the game. Buffalo reached the Giant 29 with 0:08 on the clock. Norwood trotted onto the field, just as Bahr had trotted onto the Candlestick Park grass with 0:04 left a week earlier in the NFC Championship Game. Bahr kicked the Giants into the Super Bowl with a 42-yard goal that nipped the 49ers, 15-13. Now the Giants were living a deja vu, only backwards.

"I watched this one," said Mark Ingram, who buried his head during Bahr's boot. "But I had to wait until the ball passed outside the uprights. And then I ran on the field and gave Walls a hug."

An entire season came down to one kick, but the entire game was the result of terrific preparation. Defensively, the Giants played the entire game with five or six defensive backs. They blitzed approximately a dozen times, far more than usual. They dealt with the no-huddle offense by trying to pressure Jim Kelly. They pressured Kelly by disguising where their pass rush would come from.

"We figured they'd be able to move the ball," defensive coordinator Bill Belichick said. "We wanted to play good in the red area (inside their 20-yard line)."

The Bills' most dangerous receiver, Andre Reed, caught seven passes in the first half. In the second quarter, however, after his sixth catch, Guyton threw a thunderous hit to jar a potential catch loose. Reed was no factor after that. He caught two passes for 10 yards, but dropped two and failed to make a first down.

"I think he was worried about us," Guyton said.

Throughout Super Bowl week, the Giant defenders were asked if they'd be able to keep up with the Bills' furious no-huddle pace. But by the time the fourth quarter arrived, Buffalo's defense was exhausted. The Giants' powerful offensive line hammered them early. In the first half, Jeff Hostetler rolled right often. When the Bills started overpursuing Hostetler on one of his many rollouts in the second half, the Giants fooled them by simply switching gears to the left. And on many straight handoffs, Buffalo's linebackers didn't stuff the point of attack aggressively because they were too concerned about Hostetler's mobility.

CHAPTER 7

BEHIND THE MIKE

DAILY NEWS

After this press conference, Bill Parcells would find himself in the broadcast booth, not on the sidelines.

*A*fter winning a second Super Bowl for his hometown Giants, Bill Parcells walked away, saying he wasn't sure he could still give all that the job required. Besides, what else was there to prove?

There were growing questions about his health, too. In 1991 Parcells had an angioplasty to open a blocked artery. In 1992 it would be open-heart surgery.

As a break from coaching, Parcells tried his hand at TV broadcasting for NBC. But the coaching speculation never stopped. Tampa Bay? Green Bay? Parcells never explained why he didn't pursue the job openings. Health concerns were the answers to the questions. With the health concerns finally behind him as the 1993 season got under way, Parcells could start looking for a franchise in need of a coach.

Parcells Mute on Mike

Won't discuss NBC tryout

By Bob Raissman & Barry Meisel

Although Bill Parcells auditioned for an NBC-TV football analyst job last month, it's common for the network to hold tryouts for former players and coaches, an industry source told the *Daily News* yesterday.

"Just because they auditioned him doesn't necessarily mean they're seriously interested," said the source after confirming that the Giants' head coach auditioned several weks ago for NBC by serving as Don Criqui's color man working off a tape of a 1990 AFC playoff game. NBC auditioned Steve Largent and Buddy Ryan and showed no interest after the audition.

And just because Parcells auditioned doesn't mean he has decided to quit coaching. He's entering the final year of his four-year contract with the Giants, a deal worth an estimated $3.2 million. A TV offer would substantially improve his bargaining position with GM George Young.

But Parcells has not said he definitely will be seeking an extension. He has not said he'd like to try another team, seek a TV job or retire.

Concretely, he has said nothing. And he remained quiet yesterday when reached at his Giants Stadium office.

"I have no comment," he said. "I have a contract to coach the Giants. It's been the same thing since February."

Not exactly. The TV audition raieses a question about Parcells' 1991 status since it is unlikely that NBC would, in the spring of '91, audition somebody for a job in the fall of '92.

Is Parcells definitely going to coach the Giants this year?

"He hasn't told me he wouldn't be," said Young, who insisted he still had no evidence yesterday that his coach had auditioned with NBC. "That's all I could go by."

Bill Folds 'em

Handley gets call as Giants' coach

By Barry Meisel

There was no frozen moment when Bill Parcells decided that 26 years as a football coach, the last 10 with the one team he always loved, was enough. In his eight years as head coach of the Giants, Parcells constantly told his players, "I go by what I see."

This time the 49-year-old Jersey guy from Engelwood, "Went by what I felt." For three months after his second Super Bowl championship he considered his football career, his professional future and his life. He came to a final decision last weekend and on Tuesday told GM George Young he was resigning with one year left on his contract.

Yesterday's press conference at Giants Stadium was Parcells' opportunity to explain, Young's to formally entrust the job to offensive coordinator Ray Handley and Handley's to begin mapping the smooth course of this well-oiled organization.

"I feel like it's time," Parcells said. "I'd given what I had for 10 years here. I just don't feel—and don't confuse this with burnout, I'm not burned out—I just don't feel I can give the same. I don't feel I could have given what I would have had to have given to get the job done."

Parcells called the decision emotional, but didn't once come close to breaking down as he spoke. He smiled and chatted easily, his blue eyes shining in the glare of the TV lights. Although he repeatedly insisted that his health had nothing to do with it, he privately confided to some that stress and cholesterol level tests taken as part of a medical exam May 6 had produced less than glowing results.

He turns 50 on August 22, but he said he doesn't know what he will do with his life. He said that although he has talked with NBC, MSG Network and WNEW radio, he has no concrete plans. Although he said he won't coach in '91, he wouldn't rule out coaching again. Although he'll have more time to spend at his Jupiter, Fla., vacation home, he said he'll still live in New Jersey.

"I hope to do some things with Judy (his wife) that I haven't done before," he said. "I'm not trying to be egotistical, but I don't have to base anything on financial decisions. I can make my own personal choices. I'm going to see what happens."

Parcells did not believe the timing of his decision—veterans' minicamp begins Tuesday—posed a problem for Handley. He said he believed the Giants' draft choices and assistant coaching hires—Jim Fassel for quarterbacks, Fred Bruney for the defensive backfield—would have been the same if he had resigned two months ago.

Handley agreed.

"He left the ship in good shape," he said.

The captain won a Super Bowl last year, a Super Bowl following the '86 season and another 83 games in eight years. Is Handley capable of surpassing Parcells?

"I'm not looking to improve," he said. "I'm looking to emulate."

Giant Memories

Parcells paid his dues, went out on top

By Barry Meisel

They were seated so close for the interview that if one of them was wearing a helmet they would have butted heads. An MSG Network microphone was all that separated Bill Parcells, ex-coach, from Harry Carson, ex-player.

This was at Parcells' farewell press conference Wednesday at Giants Stadium. Carson tried objectivity, but it didn't work. For every poignant question he asked, Parcells, always in control, jabbed back with a question or a good-natured needle for one of the special players in his life.

"You know me, Harry," Parcells said softly.

"Yes," Carson replied. "I do. It's difficult to do this interview because we are so close."

They had been through their wars together from 1981, when Parcells joined the Giants as defensive coordinator, to 1988, when Carson retired after 13 seasons.

Harry Carson was a Bill Parcells guy. Always will be. So will Lawrence Taylor and Phil Simms, Carl Banks and Maurice Carthon, Billy Ard and Joe Morris, and dozens of other dedicated players who Parcells molded into champions in his eight years as head coach of the New York Giants.

Parcells was born in New Jersey, grew up a Giants' fan, dreamed of one day running the club that in the '50s and '60s was one of the NFL's showcase franchises, but had slipped so far between 1963 and 1981 that it failed to qualify for the playoffs.

"A Bill Parcells guy, if called upon, would go play on the Brooklyn Bridge, at midnight, against anybody. It was a guy who would just show up and play," said Phil McConkey.

McConkey was a Parcells guy, too, a 5-10, 170-pound undrafted Navy lieutenant who played a fearless wide receiver and returned 277 punts and kicks from 1984-88. He—like Carson, Simms, Jim Burt and Kenny Hill—was one of Parcells' whipping boys, one of the mentally tough athletes who understood and accepted Parcells' iron-tongued approach. On one Saturday before a game a few years ago, McConkey absorbed one of Parcells' most brutal verbal poundings, a lashing so severe that he let his coach know how upset he was, something he rarely did.

McConkey paid a visit to Parcells the next morning.

"You were upset with me yesterday, weren't you?" Parcells said calmly, sipping from the cup of coffee he enjoyed five or six hours before every game.

"Yeah," McConkey said. "But I get upset with my father, too."

Parcells didn't only sculpt the Giants' game plan for eight years, he selected players who were as hungry as he was to win and shaped them so that they could. He loved challenges, and constantly challenged his players. He loved playing the sly villain, and demanded that his players relish invading enemy turf.

Interesting, isn't it, that Parcells' five biggest victories all took place away from Giants Stadium? That's one of the parts of the job he said he'd miss most.

"On the road in Washington. On the road at Philly, he said with a grin. "Those two places. They hate me so much there, they almost love me."

Love-hate aptly describes the way he kept his players close to his heart, but not so close they could afford to not meet his huge demands. Around the National Football League in the '80s it came to be known that when you played the Giants, you played a well-organized team that was mentally prepared, physically punishing, and highly motivated.

Parcells had an innate way of manipulating people so they'd respond in a manner that would help meet the challenge. Everything was done because he wanted to win.

And he knew his people better than they knew him.

"I hear all the rumors that run around the stadium," Simms said of the growing talk since February that Parcells would not return. "I heard 'em from time to time but I never believed them. When he told me, in all honesty, I was shocked. I didn't think it would ever happen."

It happened. Two Super Bowl rings to a large degree quenched his thirst for winning. Parcells, who'll turn 50 on August 22, had nothing more to achieve with the Giants. Even to win Super Bowl XXVI would mean nothing more than maintaining what he had already accomplished.

And so he leaves. He leaves with 85 victories, second-most in team history. He leaves with two world championships, three NFC East titles, five playoff berths. Is he headed for the Hall of Fame? Probably, but let's wait. He'll probably coach again one day. One hundred lifetime victories is a good bet.

He almost didn't get to 10. He was a deeply disappointed leader after his first season, 1983, a 3-12-1 year in which he chose Scott Brunner over Simms as his starting quarterback, lost a handful of key players to injuries, and went 1-10-1 after a 2-2 start.

After the season ended, general manager George Young asked Parcells to evaluate the team. Young wanted to hear what Parcells believed was wrong, and how he planned to improve it. The GM wasn't positive Parcells wanted to return. Parcells wasn't positive the GM wanted him back. They met on Thursday, December 21, 1983.

"He was pretty well organized," Young recalled. "He told me all the things I wanted to hear. The next day I told him he was all set for next year. I wanted him to know before Christmas."

The following season, Simms was the quarterback. Running back Rob Carpenter stayed healthy. Taylor and Carson had terrific years. The draft brought Banks, William Roberts, Jeff Hostetler, Gary Reasons and Lionel Manuel. The Giants began to resemble a band of aggressive, yet disciplined and mentally prepared, street-fighters. They punctuated a bounceback season when they marched into Anaheim Stadium, where they been walloped 33-12 three months earlier, and held the Rams to 214 yards in a 16-13 NFC Wild Card triumph. They lost their NFC semifinal the next week to the eventual Super Bowl champion 49ers, but could say they played well in a 21-10 defeat.

"And after the '84 season," Young said, "I stopped worrying about Bill Parcells."

Bill Parcells' Five Greatest Giant Victories

December 23, 1983 - Defeated the Los Angeles Rams, 16-13, in the NFC wild card game at Anaheim Stadium.

January 25, 1987 - Defeated the Denver Broncos, 39-20, in Super Bowl XXI at the Rose Bowl in Pasadena, California.

October 14, 1990 - Defeated the Washington Redskins, 24-20, in the regular season at RFK Stadium to start the 1990 season 5-0.

January 20, 1991 - Defeated the San Francisco 49ers, 15-13, in the NFC championship game at Candlestick Park.

January 27, 1991 - Defeated the Buffalo Bills, 20-19, in Super Bowl XXV at Tampa Stadium in Tampa, Florida.

Tube Time for Tuna; Parcells Is Netted by NBC

By Bob Raissman

B ill Parcells' short stint among the ranks of the unemployed is over. The Tuna closed a multi-year deal yesterday with NBC Sports. The ex-Giants coach will join the cast of "NFL Live" along with pulling limited duty on the network's Saturday "Prudential Update" show, the Notre Dame football post-game show, and possibly some work in the booth as an analyst.

Industry sources speculated the deal is worth $250,000 per year.

It is clear Parcells sees his TV work as a way to stay close to football. "I look at this as an opportunity to develop myself in a new field," he said. "I look forward to the challenge and the opportunity to stay close to the game."

But is sharing a studio with Will McDonough, Bob Costas and O.J. Simpson going to keep Parcells close enough? There has been much speculation that Parcells is looking at his TV work as a kind of sabbatical before returning to the coaching ranks.

He stopped short of saying there were any out clauses in his NBC contract. But in reality, if he wanted to leave to go back to coaching, NBC would not stand in his way. He indicated the subject already had been discussed with NBC Sports executive producer Terry O'Neil.

"I know there's always going to be speculation about that (a return to the coaching ranks)," Parcells said. He talked to Pat Riley about how he handled it. "But I'm in TV now and I'm going to make a go of it."

Parcells said he also talked to CBS about a gig there, but credited McDonough, his longtime friend who is also a columnist with the Boston Globe, and O'Neil as the main factors in his decision to go to NBC.

So, what will Parcells' on-air persona be? Will he be out looking for scoops to keep fans informed? "I've always tried to be straightforward with everyone," he said. "I'm not going into this to be a critic or to be controversial for the sake of stirring up things, but if someone fumbles five times..."

He said he would be hitting the phones, digging for info from his wide variety of NFL moles. Of course, his sources will include current NFL coaches. How will they react to Parcells now that he has joined the media fraternity? Will some of his ex-rivals still hold grudges?

"I think they have gotten over that," he said. "Well, maybe Joe Gibbs will take a little while to warm to me."

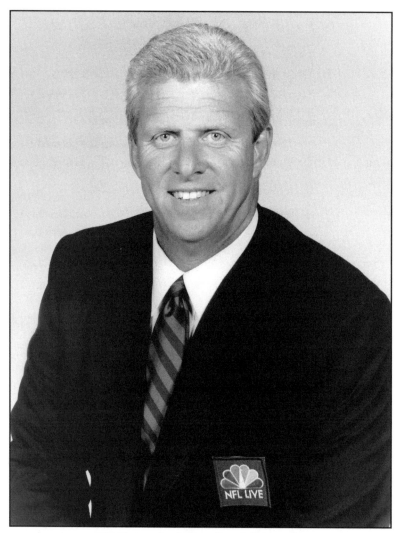

NBC's new football analyst, Bill Parcells.

Parcells Is Winning in Debut

By Bob Raissman

While the Rams were turning the Giants into sleepwalkers Sunday, Bill Parcells was definitely not stumbling in Miami. He would have been excused if he had; after all, this was his network debut on NBC as an analyst with only one dry run behind him.

The Tuna started slowly, working Colts-Dolphins, but he showed enough style and grasp of his new job to reason that if he wants a TV future, he could have a big one.

Working with Marv Albert at his side and NBC Sports executive producer Terry O'Neil in the truck (this is what's known as heavy preparation before B.P. hits the screen here), Parcells was glib and original despite what seemed to be some initial nervousness. During the opening on-camera shot, Parcells looked a bit like Rodney Dangerfield as he jerked his head around—maybe the tight collar bothered him—and wielded his microphone like a fisherman getting ready to cast.

But that's superficial stuff. One thing you look for is the way he described replays. Does the analyst add insight to the replayed action, or simply describe what viewers can see? Early in the Colts-Miami game, a totally boring game and a bad one to break in with, Parcells took the latter tack.

When Jeff George hit Bill Brooks with a pass early in the game, Parcells told us the obvious, that Brooks had run "a short out" pattern. But as he got into the action, Parcells became more detailed with his descriptions, telling us why things were happening.

When the Dolphin defense threw Eric Dickerson for a loss, after he caught a middle-screen pass from George, Parcells dissected the anatomy of a screen-gone-wrong immediately. "When you're defensing a screen one guy has to go into the middle of it, one guy has to turn it in and there has to be inside pursuit. That's exactly what Miami did." Parcells should have sued for lack of support on this play. His description begged for a replay—none came.

Parcells refused to come down directly on Colts coach Ron Meyer—earlier NBC's Will McDonough reported that Bob Irsay wanted to fire the coach after the first game—but clearly pointed out a couple of examples of poor coaching.

• With 13 seconds left in the first half and the Colts driving, Parcells said George would have to either throw the ball into the end zone or to the sidelines. George, however, delivered a pass over the middle that Dickerson dropped. "I don't know how they were planning to stop the clock with that play (if Dickerson had caught the ball)."

• With a second-and-long in the third quarter, Miami running back Mark Higgs picked up big yardage on a draw. "That's the fifth time on second-and-long that they've run the draw to the left side," Parcells said in a tone of voice indicating he was wondering why Meyer had not made any adjustments to stop the play.

The Parcells humor—very Maddenesque at times—was apparent. He coined a new term, "satellite player," for guys like Albert Bentley, Dave Meggett and Steve Sewell, who are running backs but who, more often than not, line up as wideouts.

The regular guy in Parcells came through, too. It wasn't forced or contrived. He seemed a bit harried at times. Chalk that up to excitement.

DAILY NEWS   Harry Hamburg

Since Parcells was not tied up with coaching, he had time to help his longtime friend, Cincinnati Reds manager Lou Piniella, win a couple of games.

PARCELLS

F Former Jets star **Joe Namath** joins Jets head coach **Bill Parcells** on the sidelines during *training camp*.

(Daily News/Dan Farrell)

(AP/Wide World Photos)

B **ill Parcells** and New York Jets owner **Leon Hess** pose for the media after Parcells was named *head coach* and chief of football operations for the *Jets*.

PARCELLS

Giants head coach **Bill Parcells** is carried off the field by his players after *winning Super Bowl XXI* in Pasadena, California.

(Daily News/Keith Torrie)

(Daily News/Keith Torrie)

Bill Parcells poses with the Vince Lombardi trophy before *Super Bowl XXV* in Tampa, Florida.

PARCELLS

Giants quarterback **Phil Simms** was on the receiving end of quite a few of **Bill Parcells'** tirades. In Super Bowl XXI, however, Simms played a *nearly perfect game*, completing 22 of 25 passes for 268 yards and three touchdowns.

Jeff Hostetler, who filled in for the injured Phil Simms late in the 1990 season, helped **Parcells** get his *second Super Bowl win*.

WHAT IF NEW YORK HAD A BRIDGE
THAT WENT ALL AROUND THE WORLD?

New York is home to hundreds of bridges. Including one called American Airlines®.
And over 220* times every business day it stretches from the New York area to
Los Angeles, London and hundreds of other cities around the world. Call your
Travel Agent or American at 1-800-433-7300. Or book online at www.aa.com
Getting where you want to go is easy.   **AmericanAirlines**
As long as you take the right bridge.   *New York's Bridge To The World*™

member of oneworld

PARCELLS

Bill Parcells and **Drew Bledsoe** took the Patriots from a 2-14 record in 1992 to Super Bowl XXXI in 1997.

In 1998, **Bill Parcells** brought Long Island native **Vinny Testaverde** back home to the New York Jets. Testaverde responded with one of the *finest seasons* in New York Jets history.

Tom Seaver
Hall of Fame Pitcher and
Chase Middle Market
Spokesperson

No matter how good you are... you need to know the team is behind you.

IN BASEBALL, BUSINESS AND BANKING, IT TAKES A TEAM TO REACH THE TOP.

More growing companies rely on Chase, the leading bank for business

Your Chase Relationship Manager heads a team of professionals dedicated exclusively to growing companies

As your guide and advocate, your Relationship Manager gives you access to credit, cash management, investments, leasing, merger and acquisition advice and financing, derivatives, international – a full range of products and services

We're the leading bank for business because, like you, we play hard. We play to win. And we love the game. Get the best team in banking for your business.

CHASE

THE RIGHT RELATIONSHIP IS EVERYTHING.®

www.chase.com

PARCELLS

Unheralded quarterback **Ray Lucas** helped **Bill Parcells** end his coaching career on a positive note after the disappointing start of the 1999 season.

Named in honor of the great American hero, Mickey Mantle's features museum quality baseball memorabilia, a sports art gallery and TVs tuned to today's big games, sports and blooper videos!

Step up to the plate for Mickey's favorites– Southern Fried Chicken Fingers, Blue Corn Nachos, Roast Duck Quesadillas, Juicy Burgers, Grilled Sirloin Chili and Chicken Fried Steak.

Visit our retail store for a wide array of Mickey Mantle's Restaurant souvenirs, including Mickey Mantle autographed baseballs, and a selection of balls, bats, pucks, helmets, jerseys and books autographed by your favorite sports stars!

"The Best Ribs in New York"
–Arthur Schwartz, *N.Y. Daily News*

Mickey Mantle's Restaurant
42 Central Park South NYC
(59th St. Bet. 5th & 6th Aves.)
(212) 688-7777
www.mickeymantles.com
Open 11:30 AM to Midnight, 7 Days a Week

Parcells Faces Toughest Fight

Heart surgery likely tomorrow

By Bill Madden

A little more than a week after having the time of his life playing manager with Lou Piniella, Bill Parcells is back in Philadelphia today confronting the fear of his life—open-heart surgery.

He had hoped it would not come to this—that the "scraping out" procedure doctors in Cleveland performed on the blocked artery to his heart a few weeks ago would take. But then last Tuesday, during his daily running routine, Parcells once again felt familiar pain in his chest that has caused him so much anguish over the past year. The doctors had told him there was a 50-50 possibility that the artery blockage would re-occur in time. Worse, though, they said that if it did, the only recourse left to correct the problem was bypass surgery.

"I feel fine," Parcells said yesterday. "I'm just unlucky. At least that's what the doctors tell me. The problem is that the scar tissue from the scraping they did has caused the blockage. That happens with certain people no matter how well they follow their diet."

After consultation with his doctors, Parcells, who will be 51 in August, elected to check into Temple University Hospital in Philly and will undergo an angiogram today. Based on the results of that, he likely will undergo the bypass surgery tomorrow.

Throughout these past few months, Parcells has not wanted to make a big deal of his heart problems. He probably could have saved himself a lot of bashing from the media over the winter had he detailed the real reason he went back and forth on whether to take the Tampa Bay coaching job. He chose not to, and only his closest friends knew the personal torment he put himself through.

"Billy wanted to coach . . . he wanted to build that Tampa Bay program," said Mickey Corcoran, Parcells' mentor from high school. "At the same time, he was having these problems. That's why he asked them for more time. When they squeezed him, he went with his first—and right—instinct. He backed off and decided he was going to look after his health first."

At the same time, however, the pull to get back into coaching after a year's layoff would not subside. A week went by, Parcells was feeling good and he decided to throw caution to the wind. He called Tampa Bay owner High Culverhouse back and said he had reconsidered. If worse came to worst, he thought, he could have an angioplasty done that would correct the problem and enable him to be ready in plenty of time for training camp.

He had lunch with Piniella, a Tampa native, in Moonachie on January 7 and the two talked about the Tampa Bay job. Piniella was excited for his friend and gave him a list of the best areas to live in Tampa. The next day, Parcells met with Culverhouse in Washington, only to be told to forget it.

In Culverhouse's mind, it was sweet revenge after having had his initial advances rejected. In retrospect, he probably did Parcells the favor of his life. Instead of having to plunge head-first into a massive building job on an organization that has known nothing but losing, Parcells comes out of likely surgery tomorrow with a summer of leisure ahead of him. They say it takes about three months to fully recuperate from bypass surgery. Now he will have that.

He brought this town two Super Bowl championships. Let him rest on his laurels another year before getting back into coaching. He doesn't have to ever coach another game as far as New Yorkers are concerned, but he probably will.

"I miss it," he said the other day. "I miss the challenge . . . the workouts . . . the rush on Sundays."

That was obvious when he got together with Piniella in Philadelphia last week. As Corcoran is fond of saying, Parcells was born to coach, and there he was, sitting up in the press box at Veterans Stadium, managing and thinking along with Piniella, putting on plays, changing pitchers. The Reds won both those games and kept on winning, reaching a season-high six in a row before losing yesterday.

"Tell Lou, he's on his own for a while now," Parcells joked yesterday. "I've got this other thing I've got to take of. But I'll be ready to give him a hand for the stretch run."

June 6, 1992

Parcells Recovering Like a Champ

By Bill Madden

Bill Parcells had just completed a slow but steady stroll around his bed and was gazing out his hospital window at the hard spring rain yesterday afternoon when Mickey Corcoran, his high school mentor and closest confidant, came into the room.

Other than his wife and daughter, Parcells had not received visitors since undergoing heart bypass surgery on Tuesday and at the sight of Corcoran, his face brightened.

"This was a real buttkicker, Mick," Parcells said as he gave his old basketball coach a gentle hug. "I won't be doin' any rebounding for you today."

He was in pain—as one might expect from someone who had just had his breast-bone cut in half with a buzz saw and half his chest cavity pulled out so a new "left anterior descending artery" could be installed in his heart. But he did his best to conceal it, and he looked remarkably well so soon after the ordeal.

"I can't believe how good you look Billy," Corcoran said. "I mean, it was just three days ago!"

"It was something," Parcells said. "I mean this place, the people here, they're unbelievable. Before I went in the operating room there was this 25-year-old girl before me who was getting a heart transplant. I'm looking out the door and I see all these doctors, about 10 of 'em, and they're pacing back and forth talking.

"I can tell it's like a big game, you know what I mean? They're all getting their game faces on!"

When it was his turn to be wheeled into the operating room, however, Parcells found he could not escape his fame. He may be just a blue-collar Jersey guy to Corcoran and his friends from Oradell who grew up with him, but to football fans—even those in Philadelphia—he is a member of the coaching elite, one who has won two Super Bowl championships.

"Would you believe it?" Parcells said. "They're rolling me in and these guys are asking me to sign autographs for them. One of the interns says, 'Hey coach, you mind signing this for my brother Joey?'"

As he talked, Parcells continued to slowly pace back and forth across the room.

"Larry Ennis (one of his football coaching friends who also underwent by-pass surgery) told me you gotta keep moving," he said. "When you wake up in the morning, you don't want to move, but you've got to fight it to get up. Now, it feels so good to sweat."

Finally, he sat down and began sifting through a stack of cards and telegrams.

"Everybody's been great," Parcells said. "I got a telegram from Lou (Piniella) that said, 'Never mind getting well soon, just get me some damn runs!' Then there's this one from (former Giants' defensive back) Kenny Hill. I used to always get on him. I'd tell him, 'You can't play unless something hurts.' So look what he says in this card: 'Some people can't function unless they create illusionary obstacles to overcome for themselves.'"

He laughed, and if there was one thing that was clear, it was that for all he had been through, Parcells had lost neither his iron will to succeed nor his often-biting sense of humor.

Bill Won't Fan Flames

By Gary Myers

Bill Parcells found the place, no problem. He followed his old route, said good morning to the same security guard when he arrived at 9 a.m., even teased with Phil Simms when he bumped into him in the stadium tunnel.

"I'm not into nostalgia," Parcells said. "But I'm not without memories."

Parcells worked in the NBC booth yesterday while many Giants fans wished they could zap him back onto the field to switch places with Ray Handley. Parcells is the link to the two Super Bowl championships. Handley is the link to the turmoil and misery of '92.

Parcells, who says he feels 100% better than he did a year ago after heart bypass surgery in June, could be back on somebody's sideline in 1993. "I'm not counting anything out," he said. "I'm not saying I'm going to do it. I'm not ready to say it. I'm not saying I will or I won't. There are no vacancies. I want to give broadcasting 100% this fall. I wasn't able to do that last year."

He said he had nice visits yesterday with Giants co-owners Wellington Mara and Bob Tisch, GM George Young, assistant GM Harry Hulmes, secretaries, office staff. But Giants fans want to know: Will Parcells ever coach their team again? It seems like such a longshot, even if Handley gets fired. Could Parcells ever see himself coaching the Giants again?

"It's a hard question," Parcells said. "There aren't any vacancies here. The job is not open. I don't anticipate anything in the future."

Parcells said he feels sorry for Handley "to a degree," and that with a football team "you must let a ship run its course and make a judgment at the end of the season."

It was clear as the Giants were beating the pitiful Seattle Seahawks, 23-10, that the fans have made their judgment. No banners are allowed in the stadium, but pro-Parcells banners popped up. Sections of fans under the broadcast booth turned around at halftime, saw Parcells, and chanted, "We Want Bill."

Minutes later, after the Giants had allowed Seattle its very first touchdown since September, a creative "Ray Must Go," chant to the tune of the Atlanta Braves tomahawk chop enveloped the stadium. And when the Seahawks, the NFL's worst team, encouraged the fans to get louder, well, it was a low point in Giants history.

"It bothers me," Parcells said. "But I'm not saying the fans are being unfair. Fans are fans. I know. I've been down there. I know what it's like. I'm not saying I wasn't in tune with what's going on. It's unfair to the guy coaching. I'm flattered by the fans and all the great people I've come into contact with."

Will he be back? "I'm not trying to create openings," he said.

Bill Parcells in the broadcast booth with Marv Albert at Giants Stadium.

Torn Taylor

And with LT goes a piece of Parcells

By Mike Lupica

The stat man, Elliott Kalb, pushed the note in front of Bill Parcells. This was at Rich Stadium yesterday, early in the game the Buffalo Bills were playing against the Pittsburgh Steelers.

Parcells was working the game as a broadcaster for NBC. Now he looked down at the note and saw, "Lawrence Taylor. Ruptured Achilles tendon . . . Unconfirmed." And now it wasn't Buffalo, wasn't anywhere near there. It was Giants Stadium, and it was personal for Bill Parcells. It was him and Lawrence Taylor and it was all the Sundays.

"It was like a knife to my heart," Parcells was saying now.

It was Sunday night, Parcells was in a Buffalo hotel room. He had seen the play where Taylor got hurt against the Packers, seen Taylor go out of Giants Stadium, maybe for the last time, on that golf cart. Parcells had talked about Taylor at half-time of the Bills-Steelers game. Parcells knew what everybody knew. If this was it for Lawrence Taylor, it figures he went out on a day the Giants won, and it figures he went out chasing a quarterback. There was a time when he would chase them all the way to Monday morning, but not yesterday. Yesterday was the ruptured Achilles on a play that looked like nothing, and most likely the end.

Parcells, who saw the very best of it from Taylor, which means the best there has ever been from a Giants player, got it in two notes from Elliott Kalb in the Buffalo Bills press box. The second one just had one word on it, and the word was "Confirmed."

"I remember a lot of days," Parcells said in a quiet voice. "He was very special to me. Now I'm not too nostalgic. People who know me know that. I'm not too nostalgic and neither is Lawrence. We never had to do too much talking. You know what our relationship was? He knew and I knew."

"There is a lot of guys still playing for the Giants who played for me," Parcells said. "And a lot of them are special to me. You have to put Carl

Banks in there, and Leonard Marshall. Doug Riesenberg. But the only two who went the whole way with me are Taylor and Simms. Now neither of them may be playing. Maybe that's another reason why this got to me the way it did."

Then he talked about that night in New Orleans a few years ago, when the Giants were fighting for their playoff lives and Simms was hurt and Taylor had a ruined shoulder. The Giants won, 13-12. Taylor did it with one arm. He forced plays and fumbles and made tackles with one arm. The Giants stayed alive. "The greatest game I ever saw," Parcells said. "I went up to him afterward and got him alone in the trainer's room. I put my forehead on his forehead and said, 'You were great tonight.' And he said, 'I don't know how I did it.' But I did. He was Lawrence Taylor."

Tuna Sandwiched between Two Jobs
December 6, 1992

Heading down the stretch of the NFL season, expect the doses of Bill Parcells speculation to get even bigger. The situation will take on soap opera-like proportions.

Call it "As The Tuna Melts." Will he coach again? Will the Giants come calling? Will he stay in TV?

The guessing game will continue. But as far as Parcells' TV career is concerned, there are some new facts.

The first tidbit concerns Parcells' feeling about being in the booth to analyze a Giants game on NBC. Well-embedded NBC moles say Parcells, who is in Buffalo today to work Jets-Bills, has asked NBC Sports executive producer Terry O'Neil to pull him off the December 19 Giants-Chiefs game. Tuna and Marv Albert where scheduled to work it.

Same spies say O'Neil has agreed to use other announcers on the telecast. Parcells was not happy about being put on the grill—answering Albert's questions about Ray Handley and the Giants—during the October 25 Seahawks-Giants game. He likely didn't want to be on the spot again, especially if he aspires to return to coaching.

Second chunk of Tuna concerns NBC's Super Bowl XXVII coverage. Parcells was slated to work on the pre-game show with Bob Costas and Co. Now, our moles say, Parcells has asked O'Neil if he can do without him on the Super pregame. O'Neil apparently told Parcells he does not have to work the show.

Why does Parcells want out of the Super? Well, maybe he figures he will again be the center of stories concerning his future and doesn't want to be hassled. Or maybe he thinks he will have a coaching job by January 31.

CHAPTER 8

BACK TO THE SIDELINES

AP/Wide World Photos

*After a two-year hiatus, Bill Parcells got back to coaching.
He took over the 2-14 New England Patriots.*

*A*fter a 2-14 season, the New England Patriots needed to do something. What they did was land Bill Parcells as their new head coach.

Parcells wanted to mold the woeful Patriots in his own image: tough, focused and disciplined. To do that, he filled his coaching staff and player roster with familiar Giant faces. But, like his first Giants team, it was going to take time before the Patriots would become a Parcells team. Even when the Patriots started winning, they didn't look like a typical Parcells team. While the Giants slugged it out on the ground and played punishing defense, Parcells' Patriots were shooting it out in the high-scoring AFC. And a No. 1 draft choice, Drew Bledsoe, was leading a prolific air attack.

Patriot Gains

Parcells returns to New England

By Paul Needell

The news conference in this downtown hotel ballroom was over yesterday, and so was the live interview on the Boston sports radio station, and the one on ESPN, and the stand-up with the local cameras. Bill Parcells found his wife, Judy, and walked to the bank of elevators down the hall as four reporters from New York tossed a few last questions.

The former Giants coach fresh from agreeing to be the new coach of the New England Patriots for a cool $5.5 million over five years, according to an NFL source—finally had to stop by the elevators. Parcells was asked if he knew why George Young never called him about the still-vacant Giants' job.

"You'll have to ask him," said Parcells. "Don't ask me."

Someone wondered if Parcells ever considered contacting Young himself. "No," he replied. "Never thought about it."

Why not? "I don't really want to get into that," Parcells said. A few seconds later, he stepped on the elevator with his wife and a few Patriots people. "Good luck," someone offered. As the elevator doors closed, Parcells said, "Thanks," and then the new coach of the 2-14 Pats was gone.

During his news conference, when Parcells was asked if he had thought about a return to the Giants, he said, "That was a long time ago, in my mind. I have to say that the Maras, Wellington and Tim, are probably the two men responsible for what Bill Parcells has. So I have, and always will have, a very loyal place in my heart for them, and the New York Giants.

"But I think that it was time for me to go in a different direction, and I think it was time for them to go in a different direction, and we both decided to do that. So what my thoughts were, what may have been in my mind, I'm just going to keep to myself."

All Parcells wanted to share yesterday were his thoughts about the Patriots. While owner James Orthwein also announced executive VP/football operations

Patrick Forte and executive VP/business operations James Hausmann would form a triumvirate with Parcells, make no mistake: Bill is in charge. Even if he denies being all-powerful.

In their first meeting, Orthwein asked Parcells how he would turn the Pats into a "competitive team."

"I told him I wasn't interested in a competitive team, but if he was interested in attempting to bring a championship team to New England, then I was his man," said Parcells, who was an assistant coach with the Pats in 1980.

Why New England, this year, after backing out of a deal with the Buccaneers last January? "Because I felt good, and I look forward to returning to the profession that I love," said Parcells, who underwent heart bypass surgery last spring.

"It's something I missed very much. It's like the school-yard when you're a kid. You have to grow up sometime, but fortunately, I haven't had to. But this is my last coaching job, without question . . . this is my last deal. I'm John Wayne after this one."

He sounded like a man eager to ride off into the sunset with six-guns blazing.

Bill's Giant Raid

Perkins, five assistants to Patriots

By Barry Meisel

Bill Parcells has landed a staff of familiar expatriates to become Patriots. Five Giant assistant coaches in limbo since Ray Handley was fired on December 30 have agreed to join Parcells in New England. The Patriots yesterday announced that Romeo Crennel will coach the defensive line; Fred Hoaglin, the offensive line; Johnny Parker will be strength and conditioning coach; Mike Sweatman will handle special teams; and Charlie Weis will work with tight ends.

All five coached with Parcells during the former Giant head coach's eight-year tenure. Parcells hired all except Crennel, who started with the Giants in 1981 and was the team's most senior assistant. Parcells and Crennel both were hired by Ray Perkins.

Speaking of Perkins, he is going to be the Patriots' offensive coordinator. He will leave after coaching one year at Arkansas State, where he finished 2-9 in the school's first year in a Division I-A program.

Perkins was New England's wide receivers coach from 1973-77 under Chuck Fairbanks. In 1978, he was San Diego's offensive coordinator, where Giants' GM George Young found him and hired him to coach the Giants from 1979-82. When Perkins left to take his dream job at the University of Alabama, Parcells took over the Giants.

"Working with Bill again is something I think I'll enjoy," Perkins said yesterday from his Jonesboro, Ark., office, confirming his new job. "Coaching is what I want to do right now. Just coach and not worry about anything else."

Parcells' defensive coordinator will be Al Groh, who coached the Giants from 1989-91. He was Handley's defensive coordinator in '91, but left for Cleveland last year before Handley could fire him. Groh, a defensive assistant under Bill Belichick in '92, was being considered as the Browns' offensive coordinator.

"This is an advancement in (Groh's) career," said Browns' owner Art Modell, who has strongly advised Belichick to hire an offensive coordinator instead of doing it himself. "He's rejoining Parcells. I don't know how long Parcells is going to coach. He'll coach fewer years than Bill Belichick and Al could very well be the next head coach up there."

Parcells' eighth assistant will be running back coach Dave Atkins, formerly of the Eagles. Parcells is expected to hire three more assistants to fill out his staff.

With a bunch of "his guys," Parcells got down to the job of turning around the Patriots.

Man at Work

Bill Parcells brings a familiar fervor to New England

By Bill Madden

B ill Parcells has chosen to begin his resurrection of pro football's worst franchise in a small motel room just off I-95 on the outskirts of this small town 25 miles south of Boston. Eventually, the new $1.1 million-a-year coach of the New England Patriots is expected to move into more spacious digs, but for now the only urgency is a place just to sleep.

Besides, you can't beat the commute.

Every morning, for the last three weeks, Parcells rises at 6 a.m., is in his black Cadillac by 6:15, and makes the short trek through town, around the traffic circle to his office at Foxboro Stadium on old Route 1. There is one stop to be made along the way—Donut World—where Parcells grabs a coffee to go (make that a decaf, please) and he's at his office by 6:30.

On this morning a few of Parcells' coaches—who are staying at the same low-budget motel as their boss—have beaten him to the stadium. They are already studying films and perusing Patriot personnel reports when he arrives. The sun will not rise for another half hour or so, and by the time Parcells and his coaches return "home" to the motel for dinner in the coffee shop—served as usual by the ever-obliging Gretchen—it will have set again.

"This job," Parcells says, "is like being a full-time resident of the Lincoln Tunnel. I haven't been off these little roads and the Foxboro circle since I got here. There's a couple of nice restaurants in town, but I've never been to them. Just Donut World. This isn't what you would call a cultural experience."

Overhearing this, Ray Perkins, Parcells' offensive coordinator, adds: "I've been eating twice a day at the hotel, early in the morning and then at night but no matter when I'm there, Gretchen's on duty. She must put in longer hours than us."

Truth is, this spartan existence is no different from the 14-hour regimen Parcells put himself through in his eight years as head coach of the Giants—with just two exceptions. Back then, Parcells routinely smoked a couple of packs of cigarettes a day and his ever-present cup of coffee was full of caffeine.

It took his heart bypass surgery last summer to break those habits. It was thought that 18 months away from the rigors of coaching had broken him of that, too. By his own admission, seeing the sunshine at the Jersey Shore, at the racetrack of Shea or Yankee Stadium was an afternoon delight he had all but forgotten. But old habits die hard. Question: How long will it take before the daily stress of rebuilding an organization and the pressure to succeed bring the cigarettes and coffee back into his life?

"One of the first people to call me when I accepted this job was (Rams head coach) Chuck Knox," Parcells says. "He said to me: 'I know how you are. You're going to plunge into this thing full throttle and kill yourself. You can't do it like you used to.' He's right. I almost killed myself with the Giants . . . but it was worth it.

"These 18 months away from it have helped me to put more discipline in my personal life. Smoking is one of the things that I've eliminated and I would leave the job before I did that again. Believe me, I thought a lot about the stress and my health before I took this job."

Parcells' new job is not so much a job; it's a mission. A mission impossible perhaps. Certainly, it was that to all his predecessors with the worst franchise in football. But Parcells' arrival has sparked a groundswell of football hysteria here. Two weeks after his hiring, nearly 5,000 season tickets were sold.

From Parcells' office window, he can see the brown, chewed-up terrain of the playing field of Foxboro Stadium, where many of the best seats in the house don't even have backs. Giants Stadium this isn't. The office view only hints of the depressed state of the Patriots. Even the offices look temporary.

"Ah, it's not that bad," says Parcells as he grabs the huge stack of mail in a bin on his desk. "It'll look a lot better in the spring when the new sod is put in. It's not like this is some high school stadium. It holds 60,000 and there are plans to expand it by another 15,000 or 20,000."

Since the Patriots settled here in 1971—after spending 10 nomadic years bouncing around as tenants at Boston University's Nickerson Field, Fenway Park, Harvard Stadium and Boston College's Alumni Stadium—they have been hard-pressed to average 40,000 per game, dreadful by NFL standards. There has recently been scuttlebutt about constructing an 80,000-seat domed stadium in downtown Boston for the Patriots, but as Parcells says: "That won't happen in my tenure here."

With a five-year contract and a personal commitment to be coaching a Super Bowl team before the pact expires, the stadium is the least of Parcells' concerns. Build a winner and they will come, even if their seats don't have any backs.

Parcells needs players. By virtue of the NFL-worst 2-14 record last year, the Patriots will get the No. 1 pick in the April 25 college draft. But in the weeks leading up to that, Parcells and his staff will be scouring the free agents lists, too.

"There are more vehicles available now to improve your team," Parcells says. "This year especially is a window of opportunity with free agency coming in. Nobody knows what's gonna happen, but next year the salary cap kicks in. This team was 2-14 for a reason. In football you are what you are. So I'm figuring out how to get players."

One way, however, is not apparently by mail order. As he continues to sift through his mail, Parcells pauses to read one letter and then chuckles.

"This is a good one," he says. "Guy here says he was a world-class Frisbee player. Describes himself as being 'sneaky fast' but says he hasn't played football since Pop Warner League. Just wants a tryout."

He tosses the letter in the trash can and gets up from his desk.

"C'mon," he says, "let's go up to the war room and see what Charlie's got for me today."

Charlie Armey is the Patriots' college personnel director, but his duties also include the procurement of free agents. His office, one floor up from Parcells', serves as the Patriots' pulse center of operations—three huge grids rating college players and NFL free agents hang on the walls. The list of present free agents is largely comprised of released players so the pickings are rather slim.

But every day, Parcells and Armey go over the list, discussing players, deciding which are worth bringing in for a tryout. In Parcells' first three weeks, though, only one free agent—center Dean Caliguire, who was cut by both the Steelers and 49ers last year—was deemed worthy of signing.

"Got a couple of guys here you might want to consider looking at, Bill." says Armey.

"I hope so, Charlie," replies Parcells. "You know, there's an old saying that you judge a trapper by the number of pelts he has hanging on his door. So far, Charlie, you got only one pelt."

Armey laughs nervously as he gives Parcells the "skinny" on the three players whose name cards he's pulled out on the board. After a brief discussion of each, it is decided to bring in one of them, a linebacker, for a tryout. It is almost noon now and Parcells, glancing at his watch, heads back downstairs.

"Time for my workout," he announces and heads off to the weight room where he'll spend the next hour on the treadmill—another new wrinkle to his coaching workday. When he returns to his office he finds a tuna fish sandwich and a giant iced tea—his regular lunch fare—waiting on his desk.

The rest of the afternoon is spent in meetings with his coaches in their various offices down the hall from his—from which Parcells periodically emerges just long enough to call Armey to discuss negotiating strategy with the free agents. It is nearly 7 p.m.—and dark outside again—when he gets into his car and heads back to the hotel.

At dinner, his mind is still on football, even though Gretchen's recommendation of the vegetarian pizza has proven to be an excellent call. The subject gets around to the Cowboys and how, in just four years, Jimmy Johnson has taken them from 1-15 doormats to Super Bowl champions with dynasty potential.

"I watched Jimmy Johnson as close as any coach who's come into this league and I saw him early on as a dangerous adversary, a guy who is aggressive, not afraid to take chances and who doesn't care what anybody else thinks," Parcells says.

"A lot of people snickered at him after that first year, but the first thing he did was to solidify the quarterback situation. One of his good fortunes, though, was to have Troy Aikman sitting out there waiting to be taken No. 1 in the draft. Without him, this meteoric rise probably would not have been so quick."

It is easy to see how one could compare the Cowboys' situation four years ago to the Patriot challenge facing Parcells. This year there are two blue-chip college quarterbacks—Washington State's Drew Bledsoe and Notre Dame's Rick Mirer—who may be drafted No. 1. Parcells offers no hint who he will take; his only objective is for an equally meteoric rise.

And what if resurrecting the Patriots really is a mission impossible and returning to this down-to-dusk grind is all in vain?

"There's another old saying," Parcells says, "that the best way not to fail is not to take the chance."

Parcells Picks Bledsoe in Effort to Arm Patriots

By Gary Myers

B ill Parcells wanted to keep Drew Bledsoe a secret. But it's no secret that to win the Super Bowl—a concept foreign to the Patriots—it's not a bad idea to have a quarterback. So, Parcells did the wise thing, resisted temptations to deal away the first pick in yesterday's draft and took Bledsoe, who has a pretty good chance to be the next Troy Aikman.

Typical of Parcells, he is already playing mind games. He announced that he "detests" the term franchise quarterback, saying, "I think it's a term that has to be earned on the field by performance." But it's pretty clear Parcells took Bledsoe, the guy with the cannon from Washington State, to be his franchise quarterback.

"When he is ready, I will use him and not before," Parcells said.

Parcells said he never came close to making a trade and he knew weeks ago his pick would be Bledsoe. There had been some talk that he liked Notre Dame's Rick Mirer, but Bledsoe became the very clear choice Saturday morning when New England sent two representatives to the Marriott Marquis and they negotiated for 12 hours with Bledsoe's attorney, Leigh Steinberg.

Bledsoe mentioned that he heard Phil Simms was asked what the one thing Bledsoe will need playing for Parcells and Ray Perkins. Simms' answer: "Thick skin." Bledsoe smiled and said, "His players all love him. He's very vocal and very intense."

There wasn't much draft drama after the first 60 minutes. By that time, Parcells had taken Bledsoe, breaking the hearts of the Seahawks, who saw the local kid as the cure for an offense that scored 140 points last year. The Seahawks took Mirer, who some, but not many, think in the end could be better than Bledsoe.

Familiar Fire Fuels Parcells the Patriot

By Gary Myers

He's five hours to the north of his last training camp in New Jersey, 2 1/2 half years removed from his last game with the Giants and who knows how many seasons from his first Super Bowl with the Patriots.

There's been an extraordinary number of changes since Bill Parcells last coached in the NFL. But not much has changed in the Parcells package. He has surrounded himself with the core of his old Giants coaching staff and still loves to tease his players, send little messages to get his points across, tactics and tricks that resulted in two Super Bowl rings.

The only difference: He has a bad team. No need to reserve any fingers for Patriots jewelry.

In a season in which Mike Ditka and Joe Gibbs flip-flop with Parcells—he goes to the field, they go to TV—the bounce is back in his walk, the toothy grin back on his face and the competitiveness back in his soul.

For those who wonder if Parcells' heart is still in coaching after being out for two years and undergoing coronary bypass surgery, he simply says, "Go by what you see. I'll be into it."

"Go by what I see" has always been one of Parcells' favorite expressions. It's how he judges players, how he says he will decide on his starting quarterback, although rookie Drew Bledsoe just signed a six-year, $14.5-million deal with a $4.5-million bonus and is competing with journeyman Scott Secules, Tommy Hodson and Scott Zolak.

Parcells quit the Giants on May 15, 1991, because he knew something was wrong physically, although doctors didn't know at the time he had major heart problems.

"I never wanted to be out of football," he said.

But the first year out, he didn't miss it simply because he was too concerned about his health. That's why he turned down opportunities to get back on the sidelines in '92 in Tampa Bay or Green Bay. But last August, a couple of months after the bypass, he started feeling frisky again. "I missed the competition," he said. "During the broadcasting season last year, I kind of missed it quite a bit."

He will miss some of the things he did the last two summers that, frankly, being stuck in Smithfield preclude him from doing. Like spending time at Saratoga, which he loved. But you can tell by the look on his face that he's back in his element, calling Andre Tippett "fatso" for being three pounds overweight, kibbitzing with players about the conditioning run Friday, and having his staff back together.

"I think he's still the same guy he was two years ago," said Romeo Crennel, the ex-Giants defensive-line coach who followed Parcells. "He might have a slightly different outlook on things because he was able to sit back and look from the outside. But he's the same guy as far as football. He knows what it takes to win football games. I don't think his philosophy or attitude has changed at all."

Parcells took along a bunch of his former Giants assistants: defensive coordinator Al Groh, who worked for Bill Belichick in Cleveland last season, special-teams coach Mike Sweatman, offensive-line coach Fred Hoaglin, tight-end coach Charlie Weis, conditioning coach Johnny Parker and secondary coach Bobby Trott, who worked two years for Ray Handley but had been with Parcells at the Air Force. And he hired Ray Perkins, who hired him with the Giants in 1981, named him offensive coordinator and entrusted him with developing Bledsoe. Strangely, Perkins and Parcells, the two coaches who quit the Giants, are reunited.

The last time this staff was together in camp was at FDU in the summer of 1990. "We knew we were on the brink of really doing something with the team if everybody in the organization had a great year," Groh said. "Now, I think he's equally excited, as we all are, over a very different prospect. I think this is a perfect situation for him. He understands where we are and what needs to be done."

It will take Parcells time, but he will find his go-to guys in the locker room. He won't find Phil Simms or Lawrence Taylor, but Parcells will find out which players he can trust to take care of things. He has some familiar faces on the roster, signing former Giants Reyna Thompson and John Washington as free agents, trading for Adrian White and inheriting safety Roger Brown. Certainly, he doesn't have anybody with the stature or influence of Simms, LT, Harry Carson or George Martin.

Parcells will drive the players like always, but nobody will complain. "We're so happy to be around someone who can lead us," linebacker David Howard said. "We're not afraid of him, but we respect him so much. He demands that by his presence. And I'd like to have on my resume that I was coached by one of the greatest coaches."

No Place Like Parcells'

By Gary Myers

Bill Parcells won't be stopping at Elmer's in Upper Saddle River, New Jersey, for coffee and doughnuts. And he won't be following his pre-Giants Stadium game rituals just for luck or even old times' sake.

Parcells has not been on the sidelines at Giants Stadium since January 13, 1991. But when he returns Sunday night as his winless Patriots play the Jets, there will be no goosebumps or hint of sentiment and certainly no tears.

Parcells is the master of sending messages. And this week's message: don't make a big deal out of this.

"A stadium is a stadium," he said. "I have no feelings. I'm just going. That's just the way I am. I've never been too nostalgic."

Parcells had just finished a 30-minute news conference dissecting Sunday's 17-14 loss to Seattle and was sitting off to the side, sounding awfully sincere when he claimed that a return to his home state, a return to the stadium where he coached two Super Bowls teams, was just a business trip. He doesn't have a home in New Jersey anymore and will be staying at the team hotel Saturday night.

He will be on the opposite sideline. His Patriots will be in the visitors' lockers room. And it will be a Jets' crowd, not a Giants' crowd, and that means a different clientele. But some of his former players might show up since the Giants have a bye this weekend.

"Most of the reactions that I term important come from the people that are involved," Parcells said. "It's from people. That's the only thing that ever made Giants Stadium personal to me was the people.

"The players playing in it and the people supporting us when I was there. That's what made it special. That's no longer the case. So that's why it has no meaning to me anymore."

Pats, Past Haunt Parcells

By Curtis Bunn

A ll week long, Bill Parcells downplayed the significance of what it meant for him to coach another game at Giants Stadium. And after his Patriots' pathetic performance last night against the Jets, it's no wonder he wanted to deflect the attention.

But Parcells could not have expected New England to be so inept. Who would have expected him to suffer the indignation of a 45-7 defeat at the stadium where he celebrated so many triumphs in eight years as coach of the Giants? There were times that the agony and embarrassment were written on his face. Most of the time, Parcells stood on the sideline expressionless.

Afterward, Parcells was not in a mood for nostalgia. Asked about "special feelings" returning to the facility where he led the Giants to so many conquests, he said, "There was no strange feeling, not at all. . . . You want a history lesson? What's that got to do with this game? Let's talk about this game."

OK. From the outset, the Jets functioned against Parcells' Patsies with unbelievable ease. Enough said.

"There's not much to comment on when you perform like that. I'll take the responsibility for it and tell you that we weren't prepared." Parcells. said. "We did very little to stop them and we helped them along the way."

Even though his Giant team never suffered such defeat, Parcells said he is not frustrated at the obvious growing pains. "I know what the process is," he said, "and it's going to be a long one.

"We've played four games and haven't won any."

Parcells' prized rookie quarterback, Drew Bledsoe of Washington State, had similar sentiments after a performance about which Parcells said, "I didn't think he played well at all, did you?"

No, Bledsoe did not, either.

"I didn't play a particularly smart game. I didn't throw the ball well," said Bledsoe, who was 19-for-42, 195 yards, no touchdowns, and two interceptions.

Tuna Learns to Take Bad with the Bad

By Steve Serby

He sat in the NBC booth and the television studio for two seasons and found out once and for all that coaching football was his addiction. The pull of the game lured Bill Parcells back to the sidelines. So even though his Patriots are 1-9 as they brace again for the Jets on Sunday, even though he is as far removed from Pasadena and Tampa as he can possibly be, Bill Parcells has no regrets about coming back.

"There are days when you say, 'What am I doing this for?' quite honestly," Parcells said yesterday, "but no, I don't have any second thoughts."

Someone asked Parcells, 85-52-1 with two Super Bowl championships as Giants coach, what answer he comes up with in those moments when he starts asking himself why he left Bob Costas to duel Don Shula.

"My answer to that is because you like doing it," he said. "Even though things aren't going the way you hoped they would, you have to take some measure of satisfaction in what you're trying to accomplish with the players. My team is hanging in there. We're not playing sloppy football and we're pretty determined and we don't have anything to show for it, and as long as it stays that way, I think eventually things'll work out. I do everything I can to make sure that we do stay that way."

The Patriots have lost two overtime games. They have lost six games by four points or less. Parcells, who taught them how to be competitive after the Jets humiliated his team, 45-7, September 26, didn't expect to be a contender with a rookie quarterback. He had no inkling he would be 1-9 either. So even for Parcells, there are days and nights filled with insecurities.

"I'm not into prognostication," Parcells said, "but certainly, when you're in as many close games as we've been in, you would like to think you can do one thing that would help your team get over, and they haven't been able to do that.

"I think it does create a little bit of anxiety on the part of the coach. Certainly we're competitive, but you're on the threshold of winning but you don't win. You have a tendency to look at yourself and say, 'What's the one or two things I could have done that allows us to win instead of lose?' That can be exasperating."

After all the heart problems, you worry about Parcells' health at age 52. "I'm doin' all right," he said, conceding he'd be doing better with a few more wins. "But that's the way it is," Parcells said. "You get in a few games like we've been in and you realize you're just gonna have to wait awhile."

He was 3-12-1 as a rookie head coach in 1983 and is certain better days are ahead with Drew Bledsoe, quarterback of the future. "I think he's finally figured out that he didn't get it," Parcells said, "and that he's starting to make some progress toward getting it."

Parcells was asked if Bledsoe could take him to The Promised Land five years or so down the road. "Certainly I hope it's not five years," Parcells said.

Steve DeOssie recalled how Parcells always instilled in the Giants that winning was a habit. When asked how he keeps his team playing hard in the absence of positive results, Parcells said. "Like I tell 'em, I'm not worried about their morale. They better worry about mine."

1993 AFC East Final Standings

TEAM	WINS	LOSSES
Bills*	12	4
Dolphins	9	7
Jets	8	8
PATRIOTS	5	11
Colts	4	12

*Qualified for playoffs

Team Tuna Star Kissed

By Gary Myers

B ill Parcells has created tremendous expectations in New England after a red-hot finish in his first year with the Patriots. And Parcells' history with the Giants indicates a drastic improvement in the second year.

Parcells was 3-12-1 in 1983, his rookie year with the Giants, and nearly lost his job. He held on and did an amazing turnaround in 1984, behind Phil Simms, who threw for 4,044 yards. The Giants finished 9-7, won a playoff game, and two years later won the first of two Super Bowls.

New England was just 5-11 in '93, but was actually much better than that. The Pats suffered through a seven-game losing streak before beating the Bengals, Browns, Colts and Dolphins in their last four games. But in the last six games of that seven-game losing streak, New England was outscored by only 20 points, with the most lopsided loss a 6-0 defeat to the Jets in a monsoon in Foxboro.

New England has become the trendy pick in the pre-season. The Pats have a shot at their first playoff spot since 1986. It's called expectations. The tough part is fulfilling them.

"My expectations are higher, too," Parcells said. "I frankly don't pay much attention to prognostications. But I told the players at the end of minicamp that the expectation would be greater this year as individuals and as a team. All I know is we will be better than last year. Whether that translates into more wins remains to be seen."

Parcells said he has more offensive players in place with the Pats than he did with the Giants at a comparative stage, but that the Giants' defense was stronger. It's likely the Pats' improvement this year will be totally dependent on the development of second-year quarterback Drew Bledsoe, who got bounced around last year but kept improving.

After eight years with the Giants, two years in television and now his second year with the Pats, Parcells is having a great time building this team. He related how much he likes being around young people and how the exchanges between his offensive linemen and quarterback before Friday morning's practice "was like a comedy club. It was hilarious."

His two years away, he said, "gave me a perspective substantially different than I had."

He's said he's not nearly as "narrow-minded" as he was before or "as singularly focused as I was. My whole life was just that one thing. Getting out and seeing how other people live and did their jobs, I had never really done that.

"The physical problems I had during those years also gave me a perspective. I think I do this job now in a much better consistent frame of mind. I don't mean I'm a better or worse coach, it means my frame of mind is better dealing with the everyday things that I know I can't control. I have a better outlook on that."

A few wins out of a tough opening schedule will probably improve that outlook even more.

The expectations created by the Patriots' strong finish in 1993 were realized in 1994. Parcells' team finished with a 10-6 record and the Pats' first playoff game since 1986.

Hungry Pats Will Fill Bill–Tuna or Later

By Gary Myers

Bill Parcells, overnight bag slung over his right shoulder, walked out of Cleveland Stadium yesterday toward the Patriots bus, the disappointment of a wild-card loss very evident.

The New England Patriots came from nowhere to make it to the postseason, but Parcells now will deal with the emptiness of his first playoff defeat since Flipper Anderson of the Rams caught an overtime touchdown pass and kept going right up the Giants Stadium tunnel five years ago.

The Pats, an embarrassment before Parcells arrived, started 3-6 and then ran off seven straight victories to make the playoffs for the first time since 1986, but were bounced by the Cleveland Browns, 20-13, in a game they could have won.

"I think our team made progress," Parcells said moments after the game. "I think we're a better team than we were last year at this time. We don't get to go on. We don't play this to progress, we play this to try and be champions."

Parcells, the teacher, lost to Bill Belichick, the former student. The Browns are a year ahead of the Patriots and it showed in a defense that limited Drew Bledsoe to 21-of-50 and picked him off three times. Meanwhile, Parcells' defense allowed Vinny Testaverde to play lights-out, completing 20-of-30 for 268 yards and no interceptions.

The Pats had two big chances that in another year they might be capable of converting. They were down 17-10 with a first down at the Browns' 48 midway through the fourth quarter. "You got a real chance to do something and we didn't do it," Parcells said.

Bledsoe's pass for fullback Kevin Turner was too high, bounced off his hands right to Cleveland defensive back Eric Turner, whose 28-yard return set up Matt Stover's 21-yard field goal. And then after Matt Bahr kicked a 33-yarder and the Patriots recovered the onsides kick with 1:30 left, they moved to their 48 before Bledsoe, with the season on the line, threw four straight incompletions. Overtime would be for another season.

After the game, there was a Giants reunion at midfield, with Parcells hugging Pepper Johnson and then Carl Banks, two of his former linebackers now with the Browns, before giving a hug to Belichick. Banks said he and Parcells said, "We love you," to each other.

Parcells goes home while Belichick, 1-0 as a playoff head coach, goes to Pittsburgh on Saturday. The most emotional game is behind him. "I didn't want to play Bill and he didn't want to play me," Belichick said.

Why?

"One of us had to lose," Belichick said. "I wouldn't be here if it wasn't for Bill. I have a real debt of gratitude to him. I think he's done a heckuva job with that football team. They left here 3-6 (on November 6). When they came back, they were 10-6."

"I think Bill has done a terrific job here. My relationship with him: He's just another coach when the game is going on, just like I am," Parcells said. "Tomorrow it will be a different story."

Parcells, who does his best work in the playoffs, nearly squeezed a playoff victory out of this team. He is not known as a gimmicky coach, but for at least the third time in his playoff coaching career, he used a gimmick on a punt to set up a key score.

In Super Bowl XXI, he shifted Jeff Rutledge under center and split Sean Landeta wide. Rutledge ran a successful sneak to keep a third-quarter drive alive that resulted in a momentum-changing touchdown the put the Giants ahead of Denver for good.

In the NFC Championship Game in San Francisco four years ago, he had the snap go to upback Gary Reasons, who ran for a first down, setting up a crucial field goal in a 15-13 victory. The next week, the Giants won their second Super Bowl.

And yesterday, Parcells set up a field goal that tied the score 10-10 at the half when Pat O'Neill threw to a wide-open Corwin Brown, a backup safety, for a 21-yard gain. Banks said it was typical Parcells.

"I bet the first thing out of his mouth in his meeting on Monday was, 'Guys, if you do what I tell you to do, I'm going to give you a chance to win the football game. We'll be in it at the end and we'll have a chance to win it,'" Banks said. "That's how he coaches in these situations. It makes it extremely tough to prepare for a guy like that because you know he's going to put as much into it as you are.

Steve DeOssie, who played for Parcells with the Giants and joined him in New England, said Parcells turned up the intensity this week.

"He took it on himself," DeOssie said. "We don't have a tremendous amount of veteran leadership. We've got some veterans who are excellent leaders, but we don't have a lot of them. Bill took it upon himself to set the example, set the tone."

Tuna Cans 'Super' Talk

By Gary Myers

Bill Parcells is the best coach in the NFL. Drew Bledsoe, $42-million man, is ready to jump into the Troy Aikman-Steve Young-Dan Marino elite quarterback level.

And the Patriots, a 10-6 wild-card playoff team in '94, including a regular-season-ending seven straight wins, have an awful lot to build on.

Even though the AFC lacks a Dallas-San Francisco superpower, the Patriots still have a long way to go before they can start thinking about Phoenix in January. They are an incomplete team.

But there's no question Tuna has things cooking in New England. For so long, the Patsies were No. 4 in Beantown popularity, the only NFL team that ranked behind the baseball, basketball and hockey teams in its town. But a recent newspaper poll put the Patriots in first place in Boston. They are totally sold out, preseason and regular season, for the first time in their 36-year history.

That has everything to do with Parcells, who has turned around a sorry franchise, and Bledsoe, who has the money, if not the rings, of Aikman and Young and the explosiveness of Marino. And with last season's first playoff appearance since 1986, the Patriots are a team ready to take the next step deeper into the playoffs.

"I don't care about prognostications," Parcells said yesterday between practices. "I don't care about expectations. The criteria I use are my own, if I can get my team to play to its potential, whatever I perceive it to be, then I feel like I did a good job. If I can't, then I feel I've failed.

"That's what I've always said. I said it when I was in New York and I still say it. I don't care what anybody else thinks."

It became quite clear last season that Parcells was a coach who knew how to adapt. In 1986, he won a Super Bowl with the Giants with a great deal of the offense coming from Joe Morris. He won another in 1990 by choreographing classic smashmouth football.

But last year was culture shock for a Parcells team. It was a team totally dependent on Bledsoe. He threw 691 passes. New England ran the ball 478 times. So long, smashmouth.

"It's going to be a different image," he said. "The '86 team was different than the '90 team, which is different than the '95 team."

Parcells has seven Giants in New England who played for him on the '90 Super Bowl team: David Meggett, Bob Kratch, William Roberts, Myron Guyton, Matt Bahr, Steve DeOssie and Bobby Abrams. Amazingly, Dan Reeves has only five left from that team: Rodney Hampton, Jumbo Elliott, Doug Riesenberg, Howard Cross and Brian Williams. Parcells also has almost his entire Giants coaching staff with him. Parcells takes no thrill in signing Meggett away from the Giants. "You know better than that," he said. "I'm trying to get players. They are trying to get players. It's a competitive industry, like Coca-Cola and 7-Up."

But these '95 Pats don't play defense like either of Parcells' two Super Bowl teams. And certainly they can't run the ball like them. Parcells doesn't have the big bruising back after letting Marion Butts go in the offseason. And he lost a lot when he didn't match fullback Kevin Turner's offer from Philadelphia.

New England will have a running game of Corey Croom and rookie Curtis Martin, fullback Sam Gash and, of course, Meggett, who will get his hands on the ball about 15 times a game.

"Are we better? I don't know," Parcells said. "As I've said, it's all players, all money."

The loss of Turner, wide receiver Michael Timpson, safety Harlon Barnett, nose tackle Tim Goad, defensive lineman Ray Agnew and running back Leroy Thompson brought New England into uncharted territory in free agency: getting nicked.

"We made normal progress by virtue of not being depleted by free agency for two years," Parcells said, "but now we're in the mix with teams that suffer along with prospering by free agency. We were a team that was just prospering."

Parcells said he hasn't had to resort to any psychological games to keep Bledsoe from getting full of himself after getting that seven-year, $42-million deal with the record $11.5-million signing bonus.

"I told him when I got here I didn't want a celebrity quarterback," Parcells said.

Bledsoe hears the talk of great expectations. "I'd rather be an optimist and be wrong than be a pessimist and be right," he said.

Parcells? Check with him in January.

Martin Paints
a Blue Streak

By Hank Gola

Giants football returned to Giants Stadium yesterday, but it wasn't the Giants who played it.

Rookie running back Curtis Martin wore down the Jets for 170 yards on 34 carries as the Patriots ground out a 20-7 victory. Martin turned in the eighth-best rushing performance in club history and the best in 12 seasons, with two former Giants on the offensive line and Bill Parcells calling the plays.

"Just like old times," said left guard William Roberts, who was used to these kind of days from Joe Morris, Ottis Anderson and Rodney Hampton. "It felt good, just running, running, running."

For the Patriots, it more often has been throwing, throwing, throwing. Drew Bledsoe was averaging 42 passes a game before yesterday. His 27 attempts against the Jets was his lowest since 1993.

According to Roberts, the offensive line "lobbied" the coaching staff to run the ball more and the Jets, who held Marshall Faulk to 30 yards on 15 carries last week, couldn't make them stop. It was mostly straight-ahead stuff with fullback Sam Gash leading Martin through the hole, not unlike how Maurice Carthon used to escort Morris and Anderson.

"If we ask for it, we'd better make it successful," said Roberts, who has sparked the running game since entering the starting lineup four weeks ago. "You could see the frustration the Jets had when we had success with it. So you just keep going. It was nothing special. They kept sending in the play. We kept executing it."

Martin's 170 yards were the most gained by a Patriots running back since Troy Collins had a club record 212 on September 18, 1983. That happened against the Jets, too. By scoring both of the Pats' TDs yesterday (from 2 and 9 yards out), he also set a club rookie record with seven for the season.

Martin prepared for the workhorse role by watching the tape of the Jets' stuffing of Faulk about "12 or 14 times.

"I said to myself, 'That's not going to happen to me.' It became a personal thing to rush for more yards."

Martin, who carried the ball 36 times in a Monday night win over the Bills two weeks ago, said he didn't feel that sore after the game. That's probably because he wasn't hit that hard. It was almost too easy. He had 116 yards by half-time, including 29 and 49-yard runs.

"They were being aggressive, trying to blitz," he said. "The linebackers were creasing and once I got through the line, there was no one there."

Roberts feels that Martin has been improving.

"He's starting to get a good feeling how we block and he's using us better," Roberts said. Or as Parcells said, "the kid's learning."

"That's true, " Martin said. "The more I'm out there, the more I get to know my offensive line and fullback. Like today, just knowing what shoulder my fullback was going to block with was how I got a couple of big runs. The experience has really helped me out. The more you play, the more comfortable you feel."

Bill Parcells watches as his Patriots beat the Jets, 20-7, with a brutal running attack. Despite that win, they finished 6-10 in 1995 and missed the playoffs.

CHAPTER 9

A THIRD TRIP
TO THE TOP

Patriots' 1996-97 Season

Bill Parcells demonstrates the flight of a field goal attempt in a news conference. In his fourth year as Patriots coach, Parcells flew his team back to the Super Bowl.

*T*he pairing of Bledsoe with Parcells wasn't supposed to work. There was evidence to prove that it didn't work. Two losing records in three seasons with the Patriots didn't sit well with Parcells. He asked to void a fifth year off his contract, and thought he was done after the 1996 season.

The Patriots dropped their first two games and it looked like Parcells was on his way out of New England. The season turned around in a hurry as the Pats finished with an 11-5 record, winning the AFC East. Parcells capped off his regular season with a dramatic 23-22 win over his old team in Giants Stadium. And after a pair of wins in the playoffs, Parcells was back in the Super Bowl.

However, his owner, Robert Kraft, was in an uncomfortable spotlight. Tensions between the two led to media speculation about where Parcells would be working the next season. All the questions soured what should have been a festive week for both men.

Parcells Walking Away after '96?

By Gary Myers

Former Giants coach Bill Parcells, who says he makes his decision to coach on a year-to-year basis, could be coaching his final year in New England. ESPN reported last night that Parcells had renegotiated his five-year contract, which was to run through the '97 season, down to a four-year deal, with the contract expiring after this coming season. That lends credence to speculation that Parcells intends to step away from coaching after this season.

Neither Parcells nor Patriots owner Robert Kraft could be reached for comment, but it's widely known around the league that Parcells' personnel power has been reduced by Kraft. And the perception is his relationship with Kraft is not what it once was.

Personnel director Bobby Grier ran the recent draft, which included taking wide receiver Terry Glenn with the seventh pick in the first round when Parcells wanted a defensive player.

Parcells also was not involved in the controversial drafting of Nebraska DT Christian Peter, who was let go three days later. In fact, Parcells did not even attend the scouting combine in Indianapolis in February.

Parcells joined the Pats in 1993 after taking two years off following his second Super Bowl championship with the Giants in 1990. He led the Pats to the playoffs in 1994, but last year they slipped to 6-10.

If this indeed turns out to be Parcells' final year in New England, it would be fitting that his final regular-season game will be at the Meadowlands against the Giants on December 21 in the 10-year anniversary season of the Giants' first Super Bowl.

Pats Cite Tuna for Calling He a She

By Associated Press

N ew England Patriots coach Bill Parcells has been admonished by owner Robert Kraft for referring to rookie wide receiver Terry Glenn as "she." Kraft told The Associated Press he was offended by the remark and let his feelings be known to Parcells.

"That's not the standard we want to set. That's not the way we do things," Kraft said. "It's just like there was a player last year that gave the finger to the crowd: He's not here anymore."

Patriots observers say Parcells, who did not return calls, has similarly addressed other players in the past. But it attracted more attention this time because of the draft-day power struggle over whether to select the Ohio State wideout in the first place.

Then, Glenn injured his hamstring and missed the entire exhibition season with what Parcells insisted was a mild strain. Asked about Glenn one day at training camp, Parcells said, "She's making progress."

The problem also was magnified because of the Christian Peter problem. The team drafted the Nebraska defensive lineman and then renounced the rights to him after an outcry over his history of violence against women.

At last week's Patriots kickoff luncheon, Kraft's wife, Myra, called Parcells' comment about Glenn "disgraceful."

"I hope he's chastised for that," she said. "It was the wrong thing for anyone to say."

Robert Kraft said he contacted Parcells about the comment. Asked about the content of that conversation, Kraft repeated the story about the player who made the gesture to the fans and its moral: "He's not here anymore."

Parcells Sells
Bill of Goods

By Ian O'Connor

Seeing green, pacing the visitors' sideline, presiding over a run-and-gun game, Bill Parcells was entirely out of his element. With one exception. Somewhere in the basement of Giants Stadium, somewhere between a lost cause and a dramatic comeback, the coach was asking his players if they wanted to be champions.

When Parcells was young and the walls were blue, this was standard Sunday afternoon conversation. But at half-time yesterday, the thought of the New England Patriots winning the Super Bowl was about as credible as the thought of Evander Holyfield pummeling Mike Tyson.

So with the Jets up 14, with 30 minutes to go, Parcells reminded his Patriots of the events in Vegas, gambling they could handle the stakes.

"If you carve out a championship," he told them, " it will be with you the rest of your life. A prime example was the guy last night."

Parcells was raising the bar in the Meadowlands. An old exercise for the coach, a fresh one for his team.

"There's still time to win the game," continued the half-time speech. "You need to decide if you want to be champions."

There is danger in such challenges, but Parcells is no dummy. When you ask for the improbable, it is a good idea to make the request in the company of the Jets.

Yesterday, the Jets held a 21-0 lead. In the stands, in the press box, folks were only trying to guess how they would lose it.

As it turned out, the Jets would quit scoring touchdowns. Drew Bledsoe would honor his immense talent. An official would make a terrible call.

It added up to a 31-27 score, New England's seventh victory in eight games. Forever in search of silver linings, the Jets offered a tired spin, finding gain in the collapse. The Patriots were less predictable. After defeating the most miserable lot in sports, they were talking title.

"This team," Bledsoe said, "has shown characteristics of teams that go on and win games in the playoffs and win championships."

Parcells' two championship teams aren't among them. The Giants might not have been as deliberate and heavy-footed as we remember them, but they never tried their hand at Arena football.

In their run of good fortune, the Patriots are averaging 32 points. They throw short. They throw long. They run reverses. They run flea-flickers. They go for it on fourth down.

With 6:45 left and the Jets holding a 27-24 lead, Parcells faced fourth-and-2 at his own 49. Bledsoe threw to Ben Coates, who was tackled by Marvin Jones and Bobby Houston a full yard short of the first down. Charles Stewart, line judge, made a ridiculous spot.

Granted an undeserved extension, Bledsoe would complete a 28-yard pass to Terry Glenn off a pitch from Curtis Martin, then a 2-yard pass to Keith Byars for the winning score.

The way Parcells saw it, he had to make that fourth-down call. After asking his players to act as champions, how could he kick the ball to the Jets?

"I'm trying to win the game," Parcells said. "I just had a feeling we could do it. We made it. Just by inches, but we made it."

Bledsoe was white-hot in the second half, 17 for 22, two touchdowns.

His streak of 11 straight completions across the second and third quarters started on a third-and-11 pass from his own 19, the Patriots down 21. Shawn Jefferson, Aaron Glenn and Lonnie Young all bobbled it. Jefferson finally caught it.

"That catch," Bledsoe said, "was the turning point."

The quarterback was talking about the game. The coach was talking about the season.

"We've been showing some maturity," Parcells said. "That (comeback) wasn't about maturity. That's about getting your butt kicked and having enough guts to get back up.

"We've been talking about (being a champion). I've been trying to point out to them what it takes to be one of those."

William Roberts, left guard, doesn't need the lesson. He won twice with Parcells, won when the offensive line was supposed to drive defenders, not just get in their way.

Asked if New England has shown the capability of winning a title, Roberts said, "That's yet to be determined." The Giants, Roberts said, used to walk like champions. These Patriots need work on their strut.

"What I need to see," Roberts said, "is guys walking off the field with their chests so expanded, knowing it's just a matter of time before we take this game away from them."

Tuna Makes Splash with Players

By Rich Cimini

L et the speculation begin: Who will be Rich Kotite's successor?
The Jets' locker room was buzzing yesterday with players who were wondering about the future. Several players told the *Daily News* they would like to see the club pursue Patriots coach Bill Parcells, whose contract expires after the season.

Because of tampering rules, the players spoke on the condition of anonymity.

"I'd love it," one player said of Parcells coming to the Jets. "He's a proven winner, and that's what we need."

"It would change everybody's expectations of this team," another player said. "We need a strong leader like him, someone who will make sure we don't cut corners anymore."

A third player said, "You've got to respect Parcells. He's won everywhere he has been. There's no reason why he couldn't make a difference here. (Parcells) is a no-nonsense guy, and he could get rid of a lot of the nonsense around here." Said a fourth player: "He's a proven winner, and he knows how to get it done. We need a guy of that stature to bring some stability." No one knows Parcells better than offensive coordinator Ron Erhardt, who served as Parcells' coordinator on the Giants' two Super Bowl teams. Erhardt declined to speculate on what might happen, but he expressed an interest in returning.

"You always like to stay where you start something and haven't finished it," he said. "I think we have a pretty good foundation (on offense), and I'd like to build on it. But that's up to the powers that be."

For Parcells, a Pat Answer

By Gary Myers

B ill Parcells didn't get much sleep Friday night. He got up when the hotel clock said it was only 2:08 a.m. and that was it. He waited around, drove to Giants Stadium, and was walking the field in an empty stadium long before kickoff. He was back home, against the Giants for the first time, and it was going to be an emotional day.

It didn't hit him right away, not until he was standing on the visitor's sideline and saw the Giants across the field. "Looking over there at the uniforms—I've never looked over there at those," he said.

Parcells had no idea about the down-and-up ride the Patriots were ready to take him on. They fell behind, 22-0, and came back to win, 23-22, on Drew Bledsoe's fourth-down 13-yard TD pass to Ben Coates with 1:23 left. It's a dangerous pattern the Pats established here November 10 when they came from 21-0 down against the Jets to win, 31-27.

When it was over yesterday, Parcells turned to the crowd behind the Pats bench and raised his fist where he thought his two daughters were sitting. He ran on the field and jumped into Bledsoe's arms. He was emotional with his team and hugged and clenched hands with owner Robert Kraft. The Pats had already clinched the AFC East, but this clinched the first-round bye and a home game in two weeks in Foxboro.

Parcells didn't look forward to coaching against the Giants and was glad when it was over. "Everybody knows how I feel," he said. "I grew up just up the street. This is not my home away from home. This will always be my home. Right now, I'm just not living here."

No doubt Jets fans are hoping Parcells will return home. Don't count on him showing up as an employee at Weeb Ewbank Hall anytime soon. Parcells' contract is up after the season and by mutual agreement, he and Kraft are

Parcells embraces then-Giants coach Dan Reeves after the Patriots earned a first-round bye in the playoffs by defeating the Giants, 23-22, at the Meadowlands.

waiting until the Pats are done playing before discussing a new deal.

There is every reason to believe that unless the Kraft-Parcells summit blows up, then Parcells will be coaching New England in '97. And if not, he might not be coaching at all. Why would he give up this team for the Jets? Parcells would be the perfect antidote to two seasons of Rich Kotite. Even better, a team of Parcells and Packers GM Ron Wolf, a former Jets executive and close friend of Parcells, would be the equivalent of the Jets hitting the daily double.

But call this the curse of the Jets: Parcells is pretty attached to his team, and Wolf, already under contract in Green Bay past this season, has been offered an extension by the Packers. And officially cross former Redskins coach Joe Gibbs off the list. He reiterated yesterday he has no desire to coach again.

"I am saying nothing about New York," Parcells said. "All I'm talking about is getting ready for the playoffs."

At Parcells' request, Kraft eliminated the fifth and final year of his contract at the end of last season, along with a penalty clause of about $1.5 million if Parcells didn't finish his deal.

"Last year, the day we were 6-10 and finished the season, Bill was tired. It was a long season. He had a bit of a medical problem in Kansas City," Kraft said. "He asked me to release him from the last year of his contract. There was the penalty that had been set up by the previous owners. I tried to accommodate him and be a good guy and let him out without asking for anything."

The draft day disagreement, when Parcells wanted a defensive lineman, the scouting department wanted wide receiver Terry Glenn and Kraft sided with the scouts, led to speculation Parcells was gone after '96. Glenn yesterday set a rookie record for most catches. And Parcells sure seems like he's coming back.

After the Pats were down 22-0 at the half, Parcells showed he would be worth every million it would cost Leon Hess to get him. The Patriots didn't quit on him. "The '27 Yankees can't win playing like we did the first half," he said.

After Glenn caught one TD pass, ex-Giant David Meggett ran a punt back 60 yards for a score. It was 22-17 when the Pats got the ball on their 25 with 7:08 left. Troy Brown made an acrobatic third-down catch to keep the drive alive and Bledsoe's game-winner came on a fourth-and-7 from the Giant 13.

"We were lucky to win. Lucky to get out of here alive," Parcells said. "I'll tell you, these kids here, they got champions' hearts. We may not be the best team, but mentally they are pretty tough."

The Jersey guy came home for a day and beat his old team. He was off with his daughters after the game to visit one of his favorite restaurants. But it doesn't look like he will be coming back home to work again any time soon.

Parcells Shows Who's Boss

By Mike Lupica

The public address at Foxboro Stadium had counted the last seconds all the way down now to the AFC Championship Game, to be held on this same field next Sunday afternoon. Now the game between the Patriots and Steelers was finally over. Bill Parcells walked off the field and out of the fog and the rousing college noise and into the music that played above the noise, rousing Jersey music from Bruce Springsteen, the song called "Glory Days." You give Parcells enough time, enough team, he still brings those days with him. Now he had brought one here.

The score was 28-3 for the Patriots, against a Steelers defense that was supposed to scare Parcells all the way into his next job. But Parcells attacked it from the start, from the Patriots' first play from scrimmage. Rod Woodson of the Steelers came up on Terry Glenn and Glenn gave him a fake and left him and Drew Bledsoe threw it to Glenn for 53 yards.

Parcells had called the whole thing the day before.

"Woodson will come up on first down and try to intimidate my quarterback," he said. "We'll see if we can get him to bite on an up-and-go."

Once in the Super Bowl, he went right after the Buffalo Bills with passes down the field to Lionel Manuel when no one expected those. Six years later, another January, he went after the Steelers.

"They press you," he would say in the locker room later, "you press them."

Soon it was 7-0 for the Patriots and then Bledsoe threw a touchdown pass to Keith Byars and it was 14-0. Early in the second quarter Curtis Martin ran right up the middle and was gone for 78 yards and another touchdown. It was 21-0. The Steelers should have been chasing the team bus there, not Martin. The Patriots, for the first time in their history, would play the AFC Championship Game at home, against Jacksonville. If they win that, Bill Parcells goes back to the Super Bowl.

"When I came here my goal was to compete for the championship," Parcells said after the game. "Now we're trying to do that." He paused and said softly, "It's why I coach."

It is why he coaches. It is why, if he can beat Jacksonville, he has a chance to be the second NFL coach—Weeb Ewbank was the other—to win the championship with two different organizations. He may leave the Patriots, win or lose. He left the Giants after the Super Bowl, so you know he can do it again if he cannot resolve his differences with Patriots owner Robert Kraft. Only Parcells himself knows if he is moving towards the door already. But if he does not coach the Patriots next season, he will coach somewhere. The shot at the glory days keeps him at this. The teams change, the stadiums. Not that.

He did not talk about his coaching future when it was over, and only people who know absolutely nothing about him expected him to. The owner, Kraft, said he wanted him back. He said he wanted to keep his organization intact, and his coach in place. That means Parcells does not have control over everything, the drafting of the players, the spending of the money.

At halftime, in his private suite high above the stadium, Kraft had said this: "I want to keep him. But I'm not going to give him final say." Then Kraft was talking about how the Patriots might not have gotten to this Sunday without Terry Glenn, a No. 1 draft choice Parcells did not want.

No one except Parcells knows what he wants now. Maybe he himself does not know. Maybe, because of his troubled relationship with Kraft after an equally troubled relationship with Giants general manager George Young, what he has found with the Patriots is this: There are no perfect situations. Maybe the only perfect situation for Bill Parcells is on the field, in the game, in a big game, coaching his team. He does this as well as anybody of his time. He is one of the great coaches, now one game away from his third Super Bowl.

"I love Bill," one of his former stars with the Giants was saying the other day, "but if God put him in charge of the world on Sunday, Bill'd find something to be upset about by Tuesday afternoon."

This is a good world for him right now. All these young athletes have the same dream: A career year in the last year of a contract. Now Parcells is having that kind of year, last year of his contract. He knows what Pat Riley got in Miami. He knows what the players get. If Neil O'Donnell is worth $25 million to the Jets, what is Bill Parcells worth? Think about that one.

Somebody asked him about the fog.

"I could see just fine," he said.

Then he looked at his watch and told his wife Judy he wanted to go home and watch Carolina vs. Dallas. He took her hand and they walked into the rain and the people outside waiting for him cheered. Glory days. If not at Giants Stadium then here. If not here next season, somewhere else. You hire Parcells, he brings them with him.

From Vince to Bill

Ex-coach sees Lombardi in Parcells

By Ian O'Connor

Mickey Corcoran remembers his ballplayer forever asking questions, settling only for the most thorough explanations. Bill Parcells wanted to know all about coaching, and Corcoran would tell him what and why. This was a sharing of Super Bowl secrets, though the participants hadn't a clue. Vince Lombardi had taught Corcoran how to win. Corcoran would teach Parcells how to coach. They worked on a rough draft of football history in the gymnasiums of small-town New Jersey. At St. Cecilia's High in Englewood, where Lombardi moonlighted with the basketball team, the coach inspired his favorite player to follow his lead. At River Dell High in Oradell, Corcoran had the same effect on his hot-blooded shooter.

Now 75 and a full-time fan of the Patriots, Corcoran remains the link between the best coach then and the best coach now. He says Lombardi and Parcells have more in common than a pair of Super Bowl trophies and a probable association with the one awarded in 19 days. Corcoran sees the same man, same style, same result.

"Bill is like Vince in so many ways: very emotional, organized, a tremendous disciplinarian," Corcoran said yesterday. "They both had great player-coach relationships. They always knew there was a fine line between player and coach, that the line couldn't be crossed. Like Bill, Vince was a master of handling that line.

"They both could really get on a guy. But at the end of the day Vince and Bill would find a way to pat a guy on the butt and tell him that tomorrow would be better. That's a great talent they shared."

"Vince would always hang around other basketball coaches to research the game," Corcoran said. "He learned so quickly. We once had this historic game with Bogota High, which was playing in the state (tournament) the next night. Bogota got the opening tip, just held the ball, and Vince ordered us to stay in the zone. It was 0-0 after three quarters, then we won, 6-1.

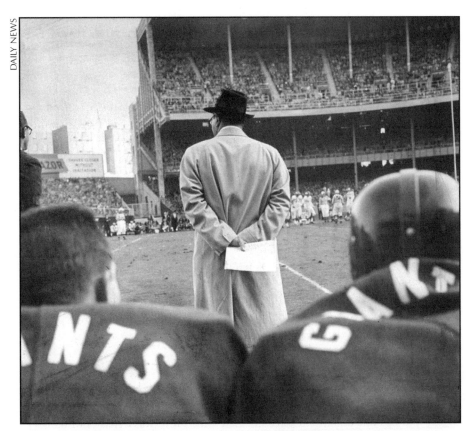

Vince Lombardi had more in common with Bill Parcells than just serving as a Giants assistant coach. Although he didn't know it, Lombardi passed his Super Bowl-winning secrets to Parcells through Mickey Corcoran, one of Lombardi's players and Parcells' former high school basketball coach.

"We had the discipline to pull that off because of Vince. I was one of his pets, but he inspired everyone who ever met him."

Corcoran was moved to run his own team, to become the basketball coach at River Dell and then Horace Mann in the Bronx. He came across some pretty good players in his day, but none that made the impression Parcells did.

A three-sport star, Parcells drew the attention of Division I recruiters and major-league baseball scouts. But above the talent, Corcoran was impressed by the kid's curiosity. The coach took the player to games at Columbia and Fordham, and the rides home—much like they were 20 years earlier—amounted to question-and-answer sessions.

"Bill had such an inquisitive mind," Corcoran said.

And such a quick temper.

"It wasn't all roses when I coached him," Corcoran said. "He was so competitive that I had to throw him out of the gym three or four times. But he was always back at 7:30 the next morning, his tail between his legs, hoping to get the air cleared.

"He never challenged my authority, but would kick a ball to the ceiling. I remember once we were winning by 17 and he picked up a technical. I took him out and then our lead goes down to three. But if I put him back in, he sees the transgression didn't matter when I needed him. So he stayed out and we lost. Hopefully, it was a lesson worth teaching."

Parcells talks of the lessons learned in Corcoran's locker room, of his mentor being the reason he got in the game. They still speak and visit regularly, Parcells asking his old coach to Foxboro for games and practices.

Corcoran attended a workout in the days preceding Sunday's victory over the Steelers, and saw Parcells set a Lombardi tone.

"No fooling around allowed," Corcoran said. "There was a little snow up there and a player came out with a snowball. Bill said, 'What do you think this is, a schoolyard? Get rid of it.' But the players love him there, just like they did with the Giants. He commands that respect."

Corcoran has an idea how his friend feels about the Jets, but won't speculate for public consumption. Parcells has muzzled his inner circle.

For now, Corcoran is content to make the four-hour drive to Foxboro. He was there for the Steelers, will be there for the Jaguars. Parcells has a chance Lombardi never had, to win a Super Bowl with a second team. Lombardi only had one year to rebuild the Redskins before doctors found the cancer in his colon.

"Vince was one of the greatest men you could ever meet," Corcoran said. "With Bill, you could always tell he'd be special. I remember his first year at West Point, going up there to watch practice when Bill was coaching the line, seeing how he stood out among all the coaches. That hasn't changed."

Nor has the link. In small-town Jersey, Lombardi talked to Parcells. Mickey Corcoran was the messenger, passing Super Bowl secrets across the generations.

New England coach Bill Parcells yells from the sidelines while his Patriots beat the Jacksonville Jaguars, 20-6, in the AFC championship game.

Big Blue Know if Supe's On

By Gary Myers

P hil McConkey was sitting by his locker 10 years ago, a few days after the Giants defeated the Redskins to make it to their first Super Bowl, when Bill Parcells approached him with a seating chart of the Rose Bowl on a posterboard set up on a tripod.

McConkey developed a routine for games at Giants Stadium: He sprinted onto the field before kickoff, waving a towel to get the fans all pumped up. Parcells, a master at controlling situations, had a pre-game job for McConkey at the Super Bowl.

"He showed me where our fans would be sitting," McConkey said. "He told me to get out that damn towel and get them revved up and make it seem like home. The fans were behind our bench. I was thinking, 'I'm a Naval Academy graduate, Bill, you don't have to bring out a seating chart.' Then again, he leaves nothing to chance."

Parcells and the Giants won that Super Bowl against Denver, 39-20, and another four years later against Buffalo, 20-19. And now The Tuna is going for the third ring Sunday when the Patriots play the Packers in Super Bowl XXXI at the Superdome.

Parcells is the one thing the Patriots have going for them. He loves being in The Show and knows how to push the right buttons with his players—psychologically and with the Xs and Os. Give him two weeks to work on the Patriots' minds and he will build their confidence. Give him two weeks to prepare a game plan and he will come up with something special. He will leave nothing to chance again, but it's doubtful his Patriots will be good enough to pull it off.

This is the greatest one-game challenge in Parcells' 12-year NFL head coaching career. New England is a double-digit underdog and the Packers are this year's NFC superpower. Parcells has seven days left to convince his players they can win and break the AFC's 12-year losing streak.

Tuna and Kraft Like Best Fins

By Gary Myers

Bill Parcells and Robert Kraft walked together across the Superdome field yesterday. They didn't even need a security guard between them. In fact, they looked pretty chummy as Parcells related Super Bowl stories to his boss, who was smiling despite food poisoning from some Caesar salad the night before.

And this morning, when Parcells conducts his fourth news conference of Super Bowl week, he will be accompanied to the podium by Kraft. That's something Jimmy and Jerry never did. "No announcements," Parcells said. "No scoops."

Maybe a little damage control is going on as Parcells' future with the Patriots has totally overshadowed the presence of his team in the Super Bowl. Parcells and Kraft may be attempting to quell speculation for the rest of the week by providing a unified front.

Parcells refused to say where he will be coaching next year. But so many signs point to him packing up his belongings and staff, getting on Route 1 South to 95 South, and coming home to coach the Jets and collect Leon Hess' money for a few years.

Talk about his deteriorating relationship with Kraft has become spicier than the Cajun food down here. Parcells and Kraft met yesterday and claim everything between them is just fine.

"Fellas, whenever we see each other, we talk," Parcells said. "It's not like we're from some foreign countries or something and we don't talk. It's funny. I get a kick out of this. It's so ludicrous."

Parcells and Kraft are expected to meet Tuesday. A quick resolution is anticipated. "I've made it clear to him I want him back," Kraft said. "I'd be silly not to."

Parcells was asked to rate his relationship with Kraft on a scale of 1 to 10. "It's fine," he said.

"A five?" someone joked.

"It's fine," Parcells said.

And Kraft said: "I'm saying right on the record—I do not dislike him. I like him. He's fun to be with most of the time. I understand how he operates and I adapt to it. The bottom line is we are in this game. If everyone wasn't pulling together, we wouldn't be here. And I'm going to enjoy it."

Kraft offered no prediction if the Tuna will be back. "I would say he's mercurial," he said. "What he feels at this moment, he might feel something different in a day or two.

"I've learned a lot from this man. When we sit quietly in his bunker or my office, we have wonderful discussions. We've been out to eat. We've done different things."

Next week a divorce is apparently on the agenda. This morning, they will be at the podium together. What's in store? A vaudeville act, perhaps?

"I'll be a saltwater tuna," Kraft said. "Bill will be a freshwater tuna."

Parcells Explains the Origin of 'Tuna'
January 22, 1997
By Hank Gola, Rich Cimini & Thomas Hill

Bill Parcells was born in Englewood, N.J., in 1941. The Tuna was born in Foxboro, Mass., in 1980.

Parcells was the Patriots' linebackers coach under Ron Erhardt when he was tagged with the "Tuna" nickname. Parcells explained the genesis of the fish story at yesterday's photo session at the Louisiana Superdome.

He said it stemmed from an old StarKist commercial, featuring Charlie the Tuna.

"My players were trying to con me on something one time, and I said, 'Well, you must think I'm Charlie the Tuna, you know, a sucker,'" Parcells said.

"We started with it that year, and they used to wear these little tuna helmets, little tuna pictures on their helmets. So that's where it started."

Worst of Times for Tuna

By Gary Myers

Bill Parcells went over to Bill Belichick in the Patriots locker room, they said a few things to each other, then Parcells embraced his longtime assistant and friend.

He walked through the New England locker room and down a hallway. A Super Bowl loser for the first time. And almost certainly, a Patriot for the last time.

This losing the big one was a new experience for Parcells. Somebody else got carried off the field. There was no Gatorade bath. No LT to run off with in triumph to the locker room.

Parcells contributed two victories during the NFC's 12-game streak coming into last night's game. And now, after New England's 35-21 loss to the Packers in Super Bowl XXXI, he put lucky No. 13 onto the AFC's losing streak. Parcells found out how the other half lives in this game. And it stinks.

"I know how hard it is to get here and it is very disappointing," Parcells said. "Anytime you get to this game, there is a measure of satisfaction. When you lose it, you're disappointed."

Fifteen minutes earlier, Parcells addressed his players. He said nothing to them of his plans for the future.

"I told them I appreciated what they had done for me this year and the effort they have given," Parcells said.

But Parcells, who oddly is not flying home with the team today, but instead is taking a private plane, is expected to meet with Pats owner Robert Kraft tomorrow in addition to meeting with his players.

And NFL commissioner Paul Tagliabue will likely have to rule on Parcells' contract. The worst-case scenario for the Jets is that Tagliabue will rule Parcells has a valid contract with New England in 1997 and Kraft will not allow Parcells to buy his way out or accept draft-choice compensation from the Jets. The best-case scenario is the Jets introduce Parcells as their new coach Wednesday.

"Right now, we are coming down from a situation (the loss)," Kraft said. "Bill and I will talk sometime early this week. Then we'll have something to say. It's been a great season. I just hoped we had brought the trophy back for our fans."

This Patriots team was hardly built in Parcells' smashmouth mold. The only way New England was going to win was if Drew Bledsoe was able to match Brett Favre in a shootout. No way Parcells was going to be able to shorten the game like he did six years ago in the Giants' 20-19 victory over Buffalo.

Even though the Patriots had given up just three field goals in playoff victories over the Steelers and Jaguars, it meant little against Green Bay, which led the NFL in scoring.

On the Pack's second play, Favre audibled, found Andre Rison behind Otis Smith, and hit him with a 54-yard TD pass. Parcells' defense later allowed a Super Bowl record 81-yard TD from Favre to Antonio Freeman, who was being covered by safety Lawyer Malloy.

In the first 14 playoff games in Parcells' career, 21 was the most points one of his teams gave up. The Packers had 27 at the half. The Giants gave up 39 points in two Super Bowls.

This was not the typical Parcells team. Further evidence: After New England had closed to within 27-21 in the third quarter, Super Bowl MVP Desmond Howard, who set up the first TD with a 34-yard punt return, took the kickoff and set an NFL playoff and Super Bowl record by running it back 99 yards for a touchdown.

"I thought we had one real good window of opportunity when we closed the gap to 27-21. But that put it back to a fairly comfortable lead," Parcells said. "I think the game turned on that kickoff return. That was the biggest play of the game. The difference was on special teams. It's the first time this year we've been outplayed on special teams. We were worried about (Howard). But you can't cancel the game. You have to play and I credit him."

As Mike Holmgren was being carried off the field, Parcells reached up to shake his hand. In the interview area, he worked his way through a crowd of reporters to congratulate Favre. And then Frank Winters and Dorsey Levens. He was gracious in defeat.

But winning a shootout is not the way for a Parcells team to win a Super Bowl. In the Giants' two Super Bowl victories, Phil Simms and Jeff Hostetler combined to throw 57 passes. Bledsoe threw 48. Curtis Martin managed only 42 yards rushing with 18 coming on a touchdown run. Bledsoe was sacked five times and threw four INTs.

Defensive coordinator Al Groh said Parcells told the team "some of the things we need to do to get to San Diego next year."

Bledsoe said Parcells told them about the Giants using a divisional playoff loss as motivation to get to the Super Bowl. That was the '85 Giants, who lost in Chicago and won the Super Bowl the next year.

"That's what we are going to try and do—use this loss to motivate us," Bledsoe said.

He said he "had no idea," if Parcells would be back. "I would say Bill is my coach and it's been a privilege to play for him," he said.

The theory was to give Parcells two weeks to prepare and he would find a way for the Patriots to win. But the same could be said for Holmgren. Nobody was going to get outcoached in this game. It was a wild game, a shootout, a game in which the Patriots could not keep up.

So, the 1996 season is over. Tuna season begins today. Parcells won the Super Bowl in his fourth season with the Giants. He reached the Super Bowl in his fourth season with the Patriots. That makes the Jets the early favorite to be in Tampa in January of 2001.

Bill Parcells congratulates Green Bay Packers coach Mike Holmgren after the Packers defeated the Patriots, 35-21, in Super Bowl XXXI.

CHAPTER 10

JOINING
THE
JETS

It wasn't easy, but the Jets were finally able to announce that Bill Parcells was their new head coach.

*F*or the second time in his career, Bill Parcells walked away from a team after taking it to the Super Bowl. But this time, instead of leaving coaching, Parcells intended to head south to New York and turn the Jets around. However, the Patriots had no intentions of making it easy for Parcells to take over the floundering Jets.

It finally took a ruling from NFL commissioner Paul Tagliabue, four draft choices, and $300,000 of Jets owner Leon Hess' money to make Bill Parcells the head coach of the New York Jets—ending the six-day reign of temporary head coach Bill Belichick.

Tuna Will Land with Jets

Alimony is the only question that remains

By Gary Myers

The Bill Parcells-Robert Kraft divorce proceedings start today. And the end result, no matter how Paul Tagliabue rules after his conference call, should still make Parcells the next coach of the Jets.

If Tagliabue agrees with Kraft that Parcells has a valid contract to coach the Pats in 1997, then it comes down to what Kraft wants from Parcells or the Jets to let him go. No matter what happens, Parcells is done in New England.

Kraft, who made his millions by being an outstanding businessman, will be in position, if he wins, to demand compensation, either financially from Parcells and/or the Jets or draft picks from the Jets. If Kraft is not satisfied, there's the possibility he can prevent Parcells from coaching in '97.

He won't be thrilled with the idea of letting his Super Bowl coach set up shop down the road in the AFC East, and conceivably could make him sit. But that's a longshot.

If Tagliabue rules for Parcells, the most the coach might have to do is buy out his contract for $1.2 million, probably with Leon Hess' money. It's a question of what was put in Parcells' contract when it was amended last December and what remained from his original deal.

It seems that when Parcells renegotiated the deal, he must have figured at the end of this season he would retire or stay with the Pats. But things changed: His relationship with Kraft deteriorated and the Jets job opened up back home. Kraft thought he was doing Parcells a favor last December. It has come back to haunt him. The whole issue put a damper on what should have been the owner's fun week in New Orleans.

In any case, Parcells will certainly be in Hempstead very soon. And that's the best thing to happen to the Jets since Super Bowl III.

Jets Weighing Price of Tuna

By Rich Cimini

As it turns out, the Jets can have their Tuna and eat it, too. Translation: they can get Bill Parcells without surrendering the No. 1 overall pick in the upcoming draft, but they still will have to pay a handsome price for the three-time Super Bowl coach.

How does this grab you? A second-round pick this year, a first-round pick in 1998, plus a $1 million payment.

Patriots owner Robert Kraft, who owns the rights to Parcells for the 1997 season, will accept that package as compensation for his floating-in-limbo coach, an NFL source said last night.

The Jets, who initiated discussions yesterday with the Patriots, are adamant about keeping the No. 1 pick, several sources said. They offered the Patriots their second-rounder this year, their second-rounder in '97, plus $1 million in up-front money, as reported in yesterday's *Daily News*.

If the Jets bump next year's second-rounder up to a first-rounder, they could have one of the top coaches in NFL history. The Jets-Patriots negotiations have evolved into a high-stakes poker game.

Kraft, declared the winner Wednesday in a league-mediated contract dispute with Parcells, sent out signals that he would demand the Jets' No. 1 pick as compensation.

It's believed that Kraft informed the Jets of his demand, but that was his jumping-off point in the negotiations, a source said. As of last night, the two sides still were talking. Kraft is playing hardball.

"I've been through hell because of this," he told CNN/SI. "I'm just supposed to hand Bill Parcells to a team in my division? I don't think so."

Parcells has had his eye on the Jets' vacancy for weeks, according to NFL sources. If the teams can agree on the compensation, the Jets-Parcells contract negotiations would be a rubber-stamp.

Perhaps the most shocking development was that the Jets, tight-lipped throughout the five-week coaching search, acknowledged for the first time they're interested in Parcells.

The Jets released a statement last night that said, "Discussions were held between the New York Jets and the New England Patriots regarding Bill Parcells, and there is nothing substantive to report at this time."

The Jets, who have not interviewed any other candidates, contacted the Patriots in the afternoon. It was a "brief conversation," according to a Patriots statement, which also said there were "no substantive matters to report as a result of this conversation."

In his ruling Wednesday, NFL commissioner Paul Tagliabue advised Parcells and the Patriots to resolve his coaching status as soon as possible.

The Patriots can't hire another coach until Parcells makes his decision. He can quit or return to the Patriots, which is highly unlikely.

Publicly, Kraft has said repeatedly that he wants Parcells to coach in 1997, but he doesn't want that to happen, according to sources. Kraft still is fuming about the events of Super Bowl week, which turned into a sideshow because of the contract dispute. Kraft blames Parcells for that.

If the Jets-Patriots negotiations reach a stalemate, they could request Tagliabue to settle the matter. As of yesterday, the league wasn't anticipating that scenario.

Parcells met with his assistant coaches at Foxboro Stadium. Their contracts expire today, and they're wondering what will happen. More than likely, they will accompany him to the Jets.

According to one assistant coach, Parcells told them, "Give me your phone numbers and I'll be in touch."

Jets Hire Belichick

Call Pats' bluff, pass on Parcells for 1997

By Rich Cimini & Gary Myers

The Jets have a new head coach, and it's not Bill Parcells. It's Bill Belichick, the *Daily News* has learned.

In a sudden conclusion to a bizarre, seven-week coaching search, the Jets hired the former Patriots assistant head coach, sources close to the situation said last night.

Belichick, who met with the Jets' hierarchy yesterday in Manhattan, will be introduced early this afternoon at a news conference at Weeb Ewbank Hall at Hofstra.

The Jets wanted to hire Parcells, who resigned from the Patriots on Friday after leading them to Super Bowl XXXI, but they turned to Belichick after failing to acquire the rights to Parcells in negotiations with the Patriots.

The Patriots own the rights to Parcells until January 31, 1998, and they demanded the Jets' first-round pick (No. 1 overall) as compensation. The Jets refused. They never made a formal offer, but they apparently realized the Patriots weren't going to budge on their demand.

The Jets weren't bluffing. They had Belichick in mind as their No. 2 choice since the offseason began.

The Jets didn't interview any candidates other than Belichick. They never received permission to speak with Parcells. The Jets requested permission Sunday, according to Patriots owner Robert Kraft, but they were told they couldn't talk to Parcells until an agreement was reached on compensation.

It's believed that Belichick, 44, will serve as a one-year interim coach with the understanding that Parcells will step in for the 1998 season. It's an unconventional situation that raises serious questions, but the Jets believe they can have their Tuna and eat it, too. By waiting for Parcells, the Jets won't have to pay compensation to the Patriots.

Belichick replaces Rich Kotite, who resigned two days before the final regular-season game. He compiled a 4-28 record in two seasons.

Belichick is no stranger to New York. He served as the Giants' defensive coordinator on their two Super Bowl teams, both under Parcells.

He was the Browns' head coach from 1991 to 1995, compiling a 36-44 record with one playoff appearance. His teams went 6-10, 7-9, 7-9, 11-5 and 5-11. His last season in Cleveland, 1995, was undermined by the tumultuous news that the Browns were planning to move to Baltimore.

Belichick is widely regarded as a bright coach and a strong disciplinarian, but he lacks media savvy. He isn't particularly glib. In fact, Parcells affectionately refers to Belichick as "Doctor Doom."

Patriots owner Robert Kraft was left wondering yesterday why the Jets hadn't made an offer. It had been five days since they initially contacted the Patriots about negotiating a deal for the rights to Parcells.

Kraft said he talked yesterday afternoon with Jets president Steve Gutman, who, curiously, didn't work out of his office at Weeb Ewbank Hall.

According to Kraft, Gutman asked if the Patriots were going to back off their demand for the No. 1 pick.

"I thought that should be part of the solution, but they haven't made a formal offer," Kraft told the *Daily News*. "I said, 'Make me an offer with players or picks,' but he has made no offer. I don't know what they're doing."

The owner also said the Jets called Sunday to request permission to speak with Parcells. Kraft denied the request, claiming he wanted to complete the trade before he allowed Parcells to talk with the Jets.

"Gutman suggested to me that perhaps they'll talk to Bill without talking to us," Kraft said. "I told them make me an offer we can agree to, and then they can talk to (Parcells and his agent.)"

Jets' Tuna Surprise

Bill is a 'consultant' and Belichick is coach

By Rich Cimini

O nly the Jets could turn the hiring of a coach into a circus. Only the Jets could replace one coach, who didn't quit and wasn't fired, with a coach who may not last the season—or the rest of the week, for that matter. Only the Jets could hire two coaches in one day.

The Jets, desperate to rebuild their tattered image, called it good business. The Patriots, burning with anger, called it a "transparent farce," and plan to fight it with the NFL.

In perhaps the strangest chapter in their star-crossed history, the Jets yesterday announced a Twin Bill hiring—Bill Parcells and Bill Belichick, who will serve in the roles of paid "consultant" and head coach, respectively.

On February 1, 1998, Parcells, who agreed to a multi-year contract, will assume the head-coaching duties and become the chief of football operations. But "it's conceivable he could assume that role earlier," said Jets president Steve Gutman, raising the possibility that negotiations could continue with the Patriots to free Parcells to coach the Jets in 1997.

The Jets, taking a page off the Al Davis playbook of deception, circumvented last week's ruling by commissioner Paul Tagliabue, who affirmed the Patriots' belief that they own Parcells' rights for 1997. Not surprisingly, Patriots owner Robert Kraft was livid upon learning of Parcells' arrangement with the Jets.

"It's like rules don't matter for the Jets and Bill Parcells," Kraft told the *Daily News* last night.

The Patriots called Parcells' consultant role "a de facto coaching position."

Claiming the Jets violated the NFL's tampering policy, he filed a formal protest with the league office. It could take a week before Tagliabue renders a decision. A hearing could be held.

The Jets, who have been trying to negotiate a compensation package for Parcells since last Thursday, refused to yield to the Patriots' demand for a No. 1 overall pick in April's draft. So the Jets never received permission from the Patriots to speak with Parcells. They claimed no such permission was needed to make him a consultant.

On Monday night, the Jets contacted the NFL's legal department. They were neither denied nor given permission to make a consulting agreement with Parcells. Any ruling on the consulting agreement would depend on the specifics of the arrangement, the league said. It's a vague role, to be sure.

The 55-year-old Parcells won't have the final say on personnel matters — that belongs to Belichick, who will become the assistant head coach when Parcells is elevated—but he can be consulted on the day-to-day football operations.

Parcells, claiming he is "re-energized" and committed to finishing his career with the Jets, will have an office at Weeb Ewbank Hall. He will attend games (not on the sideline) and he's permitted to sit in the war room on draft day.

Skeptics might say the situation could be akin to an ejected baseball manager making decisions from the clubhouse.

"Consultants consult," Gutman said. "He does not make decisions. He does not run the football team. He does not coach the football team."

According to Parcells' contract with the Jets, he will coach a minimum of two seasons. When Parcells decides he doesn't want to coach anymore, Belichick will return to the head-coaching job, said Gutman. At that time, Parcells could move into a front-office job.

Belichick was interviewed at 5 p.m. Monday at owner Leon Hess' office in Manhattan. Two hours earlier, the Jets broached the "consultant" role to Parcells. By 7 p.m., the three-way deal had been consummated.

"This is designed to create an element of stability and create an opportunity to put a football program together, and have it last for a very, very, very long time," Gutman said.

The idea of an interim coach raises serious questions: Will the players respect a lame-duck coach? How will the specter of Parcells affect Belichick? What if Belichick does a terrific job? Would he still be replaced? The answer is yes.

That could be controversial, but Gutman, in a rare moment of candor, said, "A piece of me wishes we almost had it."

Tags Orders Tuna Today

Parcells comes home & this time it's for real

By Rich Cimini

After 28 years of unprecedented failure and ridicule, the Jets discovered heaven on the 47th floor yesterday.

A penthouse conference room at a midtown law firm became the scene of the Jets' greatest triumph since Super Bowl III in 1969. It took 6 1/2 hours of emotionally charged negotiations with Patriots owner Robert Kraft and NFL commissioner Paul Tagliabue, but Jets owner Leon Hess and president Steve Gutman pulled off the coup of a lifetime.

Bill Parcells is the Jets' coach. Effective immediately. The Jets landed their Tuna, and they get to eat it, too, because they didn't surrender the No. 1 overall pick to the Patriots.

"We're very happy, and the commissioner did a hell of a job," the 82-year-old Hess, in a rare public appearance, said at an impromptu news conference in the lobby of the office building. "This ought to be the turnaround of the Jets."

Finally, there's hope for one of the most star-crossed franchises in professional sports.

The most bizarre chapter in Jets history ended at 5:40 p.m., when Tagliabue announced that he had resolved the bitter two-week dispute between the Jets and Patriots via binding arbitration.

Tagliabue, authorized by both sides at 4:30 to serve as the arbitrator, needed only 20 minutes to rule that the Jets must pay the Patriots a compensation package that includes four draft picks—third and fourth-round picks in the 1997 draft, a second-round pick in 1998 and a first-round pick in 1999. The Jets also are required to make a $300,000 charitable contribution to the Patriots football foundation.

Hardly a steep price for a three-time Super Bowl coach. Of course, if Parcells transforms the Jets into winners, the first-rounder in '99 would be a bottom-of-the-round choice.

There was no doubt how Jets fans felt about Bill Parcells becoming the new head coach.

Parcells, his short-lived consulting career over, reports to work today. He will be coronated at a 1 p.m. news conference at Weeb Ewbank Hall.

"The club has shown tremendous faith and confidence in me and my staff," Parcells, who didn't attend the hearing, said last night in a statement. "I can't wait to get to work (today) to start rewarding the tremendous confidence Leon Hess has placed in me."

Kraft, who also appeared with Tagliabue and Hess at the news conference, didn't appear ecstatic.

"We were looking for a much higher settlement this year," said the Patriots owner, who had publicly demanded the No. 1 overall pick.

Later, Kraft tried to put a positive spin on the result, claiming it was "a good settlement for Patriots fans." He added that he would not pursue tampering charges.

Tagliabue, working behind the scenes the last few days with the hope of reaching a settlement, said "both sides gave more than they wanted to give, and neither side got as much as it wanted to get."

Parcells, who signed a six-year contract Friday (with a minimum four-year commitment to coach), will replace his longtime aide Bill Belichick, whose head-coaching reign lasted just six days. Belichick will become the assistant head coach and will run the defense.

"This is the arrangement we came here hoping for," Belichick said. "I'm glad Bill's here. He's the best."

The hearing began at 11:15 a.m. The Jets were represented by Hess and Gutman. The Patriots' contingent consisted of owner Robert Kraft; Andy Wasynczuk, the vice president of business operations, and Richard Karelitz, general counsel. Team Parcells was not invited to participate, according to a league spokesman.

The first hour was spent discussing Parcells' controversial consultant agreement with the Jets. As it turned out, the consultant arrangement—a circumvention of Parcells' contract with the Patriots—became a masterful move by the Jets, because it forced Tagliabue to intercede.

After an hour on that subject, Tagliabue instructed the two sides to begin negotiations.

The Jets' initial offer was two third-round picks, according to a source close to the situation.

At 4:30, hopelessly deadlocked, the clubs each presented a proposal to Tagliabue. Twenty minutes later, he made his ruling.

"We think Jets fans have something really extraordinary to look forward to, and we hope we're able to produce it for them," Gutman said.

Hess was asked if he ever experienced a day this enjoyable as the Jets' sole owner.

"Not in the last five or six years with this football team, you know that," he said.

This was the first face-to-face between the two teams since the controversy began two weeks ago, in the aftermath of Super Bowl XXXI.

Under his contract with the Patriots, Parcells couldn't coach another team or hold a "comparable position" without the Patriots' consent. The Jets ran an end-around play by naming Parcells a consultant. In a meeting last Friday with Hess, Tagliabue admitted he was "concerned" over that arrangement.

Not surprisingly, Kraft fumed, claiming the Jets' move was a "transparent farce." Tagliabue, drawn into the fray once again, put Parcells' consulting job on hold. According to the commissioner's directive, Parcells was not to perform any services for the Jets until the matter was reviewed in the hearing.

Parcells' consulting days are over. Now he's the coach.

Now there's hope. Finally.

Players Applaud Parcells

By Rich Cimini

In eight seasons with the Jets, Marvin Washington never has experienced a winning season. Now that Bill Parcells is the coach, he expects that to change—fast.

"They finally got it right," the veteran defensive end said last night after learning the Jets had landed Parcells to coach in 1997.

"We went from laughingstocks the last two years to a legitimate football organization. I'm happy for the Jets. They finally got someone who can turn it around."

Parcells is a law-and-order coach who will bring much-needed discipline to a complacent team that was known for committing stupid mistakes.

Parcells, a three-time Super Bowl coach, also brings instant credibility. That's what the Jets needed after 3-13 and 1-15 seasons under Rich Kotite.

"It got to a point where we couldn't back up anymore," safety Lonnie Young said. "We had to go for the big fish. Thank God luck was on our side. We were finally able to land the big one."

Running back Adrian Murrell, one of the team's cornerstone players, said he was thrilled with the outcome of the bizarre two-week Parcells odyssey.

"I'm definitely excited about getting coach Parcells in 1997, not 1998," Murrell said.

Murrell also was happy that the Jets didn't have to give up one of their veteran players in the compensation package to the Patriots.

"I'm glad we didn't have to lose someone like Aaron Glenn or the other guys (Keyshawn Johnson and Hugh Douglas) that Bob Kraft mentioned in the newspaper," Murrell said.

Young said it's "one of the best things to happen to the Jets in years." The 33-year-old safety had only one lament.

"I just wish I could turn the clock back three or four years, so I can be around to enjoy the whole thing," he said.

CHAPTER 11

BIG COACH, BIG TOWN

Jets' 1997 Season

AP/Wide World Photos

Bill Parcells was back on the sidelines of a New York team and as fiery as ever. Side judge Mike Pereira found this out after Parcells thought Pereira's call cost him a game against the Dolphins.

*A*fter only the third undefeated preseason in franchise history, it looked like Bill Parcells was worth every penny the Jets had paid for him. This was essentially the same team that had gone 1-15 the year before.

Even a quarterback controversy couldn't stop Parcells from leading the Jets to their first visit atop the AFC East in 10 years. This from a team that had gone 38 consecutive weeks in last place. Eventually, the Jets' limitations caught up with them and they finished the season with a 9-7 record. While the improved record may have been a tie for the biggest turnaround in NFL history, that was small consolation to Parcells. Winning another Super Bowl was his only goal. That goal was closer than anyone imagined.

Tuna Meets the Press

By Rich Cimini

B ill Parcells' first day on the new job started before sunrise—6:27 a.m., when he pulled into the Jets' parking lot yesterday at Weeb Ewbank Hall. That the Parcells Era began in darkness seemed only fitting, considering the recent plight of the franchise. But now, with the future Hall of Fame coach running the organization, the Jets can almost see the light.

The newly discovered hope was reflected in the voice of owner Leon Hess, who, in introducing Parcells at a packed news conference/coronation at Hofstra, praised the new coach as the ideal choice to revitalize the star-crossed Jets.

"His record speaks for itself," the 82-year-old owner said in his second public appearance in as many days, "and I just pray some of it rubs off on us in the next few years."

The hope was expressed in the mood of wide receiver Keyshawn Johnson, who had a morning meeting with Parcells and came away feeling as if he had won the Rose Bowl again.

"One of the things I said to him was, 'I want to win,'" Johnson said. "He stopped me short. He's said he's not into winning football games, he's into winning championships. That put a smile on my face."

And the hope was exuded by Parcells, who, in a 50-minute Q & A with the media, explained that his final ambition as an NFL coach is to build the Jets into a championship-caliber team before riding off into a Jersey Shore sunset.

"I view this as the consummate challenge to hopefully revitalize this franchise to the point where we can compete for a championship," said Parcells, who signed a six-year, $19.5 million contract as coach/chief football operations officer. "Every place I've ever been, that's always been my goal."

Hess, who rarely reveals much of his private life, was so smitten with Parcells' arrival that he stepped out of character. He related stories of his youth, when he made up to 75 cents a day digging for clams in the waters off Asbury Park, N.J., not far from Parcells' new home in Sea Girt.

"Little did I think, 70 years later, eight miles away in Sea Girt, there could be a Tuna from the same ocean," said Hess, charming his audience. "Little did I think the good Lord would favor me in life and I could marry that Tuna."

Hess also used one of Parcells' favorite analogies, the one about shopping for groceries (picking players) and cooking the meal (coaching them).

"I just want to be that little boy that goes along with him and pushes the cart in the supermarket, and let him fill it up," Hess said.

The Jets' cart needs to be replenished. Parcells was widely criticized for some of his personnel moves in New England, but he defended his record.

"We were the worst team in the league when we took over, and we were in the Super Bowl four years later, so you can say what you want," he said.

Parcells, a law-and-order coach, will instill much-needed discipline. He will install a rigorous conditioning program, which should prevent injuries and fourth-quarter collapses. (The Jets lost seven games after leading at the half.) It will be his way or the highway.

"If you like football, you're going to like it," Parcells said. "If you're just picking up paychecks, you're not going to like it.

"We're going to find out who the bus drivers are," he added. "We'll see who's going to drive and who's going to ride or who's going to get off."

He declined to speculate on the prospects for the fall, except to say the team is "awfully thin at a couple of positions, and that scares me."

He did make one promise: This would be his final coaching job. He said the same thing four years ago in New England, but this time he means it.

"Unless," he said, "there's a senior flag-football league in Florida."

Jets Stay Perfect, Not Pretty

By Rich Cimini

The sound of Bill Parcells' voice was heard through the locker-room walls after last night's 15-9 overtime victory over the Buccaneers.

Parcells, who would say later that he was "exasperated" by the Jets' final performance of the preseason, ripped into the team after it escaped from a game it should have lost.

Parcells is in regular-season form. His team? That could be another story.

The Jets (4-0) completed the third perfect preseason in franchise history before only 21,342 at the Citrus Bowl, but their performance won't cause the Seahawks to alter their game plan for the season opener at the Kingdome a week from tomorrow.

Asked if he's ready for the season, Parcells said, "I'm as ready as I can get, because I couldn't possibly stand another preseason game like that."

It ended when rookie Leon Johnson scored on a 7-yard run with 10:23 remaining in overtime, capping a 70-yard drive that was highlighted by Glenn Foley's 48-yard pass to Wayne Chrebet. It was the last catch of a brilliant game for Chrebet, who had 10 receptions for 140 yards and a touchdown.

The Jets had the game wrapped up in regulation, but they surrendered a 37-yard completion from Scott Milanovich to Robb Thomas on a fourth-and-17 with 1:06 remaining. The Jets blitzed, and rookie cornerback Anthony Fogle was burned badly. On the next play, cornerback Ray Mickens was beaten on a 21-yard touchdown pass to wide receiver Brice Hunter.

It should have been over, but Michael Husted missed the extra point to force overtime, prolonging the tedium. The Jets did the same on their game-winning drive, going for the touchdown instead of opting for a quick field goal after Chrebet's catch.

As a result, rookie placekicker John Hall didn't get a chance to redeem himself after missing an extra point and having a 31-yard field goal attempt blocked by Marcus Jones. They were the first blemishes of Hall's preseason.

He had made six straight field goals, including a 27-yarder in the second quarter. Afterward, Parcells said he hasn't made a decision on the Hall-Joe Nedney battle, although all signs point to Hall. The Jets' starting offense, which had shown signs of explosiveness in previous games, performed like a damp firecracker, managing only a field goal in one half of work.

Neil O'Donnell, who had a solid preseason, didn't have one of his better games. He completed only 12-of-22 passes for 103 yards, and was guilty of six overthrows. He was sacked only once, but was under heavy pressure on several occasions.

Unlike last year's preseason totals (31 pass attempts), O'Donnell got plenty of work, completing 52-of-91 (57%) for 663 yards, four touchdowns and one interception.

"I'm ready to go," O'Donnell said. "Let's get the season going."

DAILY NEWS   Keith Torrie

Bill Parcells allows himself a smile after a regular-season win over the Tampa Bay Buccaneers. The Jets also defeated the Bucs in the preseason, which capped off only the third undefeated preseason in the history of the Jets' franchise.

Tuna's Trek to the Top

Parcells' long road began in Nebraska

By Rich Cimini

The incident occurred 33 years ago, when Bill Parcells was a neophyte in the coaching profession. It's too bad there weren't any television cameras around, because it must have been a priceless moment. After all, how often do you see Parcells, a legendary sideline screamer, on the receiving end of a stinging attack?

It happened to Parcells at Hastings College in Nebraska, the first stop in his circuitous coaching career. He was only 23, just out of college, but he thought he was hot stuff. Then came the sideline blowup, which had a profound effect on him as a coach.

Hastings, an NAIA school in the Nebraska College Conference, was playing Nebraska Wesleyan. Parcells, who coached the defense, had drilled his unit all week in preparation for Wesleyan's bootleg play. Wesleyan ran the bootleg every week, and scored with it every week.

But this was going to be different. Parcells wasn't going to let it happen to his defense.

Wesleyan got near the Hastings goal line, ran the bootleg and scored a touchdown, sparking a Parcells tirade. He chewed out his safety, a kid named Jack Giddings, who got caught out of position. Parcells was relentless, yelling at him in front of the whole team. Finally, the head coach, Dean Pryor, stepped in.

"Leave the guy alone," Pryor told his young assistant.

"But, coach, we worked on the damn play all week," Parcells said.

"Well," Pryor said, raising his voice, "you didn't work on it enough because they scored."

Parcells was stunned—and speechless.

"That was the first time I fussed on him," Pryor said the other day from his home in Jonesboro, Ark. "His jaw dropped."

The Jets' coach smiled when reminded of the story.

"That was a big lesson in my coaching career," said Parcells, who remembers it with amazing clarity. "It taught me about responsibility."

Parcells, 56, starts his 31st season in coaching Sunday at the Seattle Kingdome, where the Jets open against the Seahawks. For Parcells, it's the beginning of the end. After 10 coaching stops in three decades, he wants to finish his career with the Jets.

It has been a meandering journey, from small-college towns to the bright lights of Big Town, but Parcells will tell you it has been a constant learning experience. He has been like a tourist, accumulating trinkets of knowledge on a cross-country vacation. He has gone from the bootleg to the final leg.

He cherishes his short time at Hastings. It often crosses his mind, like that day in the Rose Bowl 10 years ago. In the waning seconds of Super Bowl XXI, when the Giants defeated the Broncos, Parcells' thoughts drifted back to the small school in Nebraska.

"I worked there just one year, but it was a good start," Parcells said. "It was a good introduction."

He accepted the Hastings job after being cut that summer by the Lions, who drafted Parcells in the seventh round from Wichita State.

He didn't harbor any fantasies about making it in the NFL.

"I had to survive," he said. "I needed to know what I was going to do. An opportunity came along that interested me, and that was to coach at Hastings. That sounds kind of funny, but I'm glad I took it."

It wasn't glamorous. In addition to coaching, he cut the grass, lined the field, washed the uniforms and helped build lockers for the players. He earned $3,000 for three months, less than half of what he makes per day in his $2.4 million-a-year job with the Jets.

It was a struggle. Parcells had a pregnant wife, Judy, and a daughter, Suzy, to support. They lived in a one-bedroom apartment underneath a dentist's office. There were no windows, just cinderblock walls. The rent was $62.50 a month. But he didn't mind. He was coaching.

Pryor, 66, described Parcells as "very, very intense. If he didn't have his work done before the afternoon practice, he wouldn't go to lunch. He showed a certain tenacity you wanted to see in young coaches.

"He still coaches like when I knew him," Pryor added, alluding to Parcells' blustery sideline demeanor.

Parcells' intensity spilled out after Hastings, nationally ranked in NAIA, lost a close game to its undefeated rival, Kearney State.

"My wife didn't think Bill would stay in coaching after the way he reacted to that game," Pryor said.

"It hurt him so bad to lose."

Pryor recognized the potential in Parcells, but "did I think a defensive coach at Hastings would go on to win two Super Bowls? Never in my wildest dreams did I think he'd have the opportunities he's had."

They still keep in touch. In fact, Pryor was Parcells' guest at Super Bowls XXI and XXXI. They also talked in February, when Parcells was entangled in the Jets-Patriots controversy.

The old coach is concerned about his former prodigy's health. Pryor is aware of Parcells' history of heart ailments, and he hopes the grueling lifestyle of the NFL doesn't cause a recurrence.

"I look at him and say, 'Bill gained another 10 pounds,'" Pryor said. "I worry about him even now. That job is a tough old grind."

In a way, so was the Hastings job. In coaching, it's all relative.

When Hastings' season was over, Parcells packed everything he owned into a 6-by-8 U-Haul trailer and drove to Wichita, where his in-laws lived. He flirted with the idea of applying to law school, but wound up taking a job on the Wichita State staff.

From there, he went to Army to Florida State to Vanderbilt to Texas Tech to the Air Force Academy to the Patriots to the Giants to the Patriots and to the Jets.

"I was told that, if you stay in one place too long as a young coach, you're going to get stagnant," Parcells said. "When you're going, you have no idea where it's going to end—or if."

It can't end yet, not when there are bootlegs to prepare for.

Tuna's Jets Kick Selves

By Rich Cimini

Bill Parcells returned last night to the stadium where he enjoyed one of his greatest coaching victories. This time, he went home with one of his most heartbreaking defeats.

It was a classic, a game that lived up to the extraordinary hype, but the Jets lost to the Patriots in overtime, 27-24, before a raucous crowd that had been frothing for weeks in anticipation of Parcells' return.

The Jets blew a chance to pull out a miracle in the waning seconds of the fourth quarter, when, in a span of 15 seconds, they tied it on a touchdown by Keyshawn Johnson, recovered a fumble on the ensuing kickoff and had a 29-yard field goal attempt by rookie John Hall blocked by Mike Jones. The Jets, staggered by a crushing blow, wilted in overtime. It ended with Adam Vinatieri's 34-yard field goal 8:03 into OT.

Afterward, Parcells, eight months removed from guiding the Patriots to the AFC championship here at Foxboro Stadium, was met at midfield by a throng of his former players, a touching moment that punctuated a night of roller-coaster emotions.

"I'm just disappointed we didn't win," a drained Parcells said. "We had the opportunity to win. . . . We couldn't concentrate enough on that last play (the blocked field goal). We hit the ball a little low. That's it. No excuses. They played better than we did in overtime."

One of Parcells' favorite former players, Curtis Martin, had an extraordinary game, rushing for a career-high 199 yards on 40 carries with a 2-yard touchdown run. He accounted for 40 yards on the Patriots' winning drive, which lasted nine plays for 62 yards.

A rivalry was hatched.

Nothing Is 'Free'

Tuna takes shot at Jets' ad-libbers

By Rich Cimini

Bill Parcells was in a sour mood yesterday. That was understandable, considering Sunday's blown opportunity against the Dolphins. But that wasn't the only reason for his consternation. It was how they lost that irked him most.

The Jets' coach blasted his team, which had several weaknesses exposed in the 31-20 loss. Parcells accused players of freelancing, straying from the framework of the scheme. He didn't name names, but he seemed to be most upset with the pass coverage, which surrendered 372 yards to Dan Marino.

"You tell someone to play a guy a certain way, and he plays the way he wants to," Parcells said disgustedly. "That (ticks) me off. They decide to play their own game, and it winds up costing us touchdowns."

Parcells, digging deep into his bag of psychological tricks, wasn't through. He also said certain players have "overinflated opinions" of themselves (again, no names), and he challenged the team's marquee players to take charge, starting with Sunday's critical home game against the first-place Patriots (5-1).

Nothing like a little Parcells venom to spice up Tuna Bowl II.

"We have to get our more talented players to step up a little bit more," he said. "That's the only way we're going to succeed."

The Jets (4-3) also must reduce their number of mental blunders. Parcells called them "technique" errors, subtle mistakes that can result in big plays. He gave the impression that he believes certain players knowingly disobeyed orders. Nothing irks him more than players who ad-lib.

"You try to be as adamant as you can, but pretty soon those freelance players can't fit into any system, and they can't play anymore," he said. "There's not a team in the league that plays a freelance defense. You can't be a street player."

Example: cornerback Otis Smith admittedly erred on Marino's 22-yard touchdown pass to Lamar Thomas. Smith was supposed to jam Thomas at the line of scrimmage, but he played off the receiver. The Jets also blew a coverage on Karim Abdul-Jabbar's 36-yard TD catch. A linebacker, believed to be Mo Lewis, missed the coverage.

Smith conceded some players deviated from the plan. "We had some mistakes where some of us tried to use a different technique. But I think you have to do that when you're playing against professional athletes. Sometimes when we changed up, it cost us. But you have to change up during the course of a game," Smith said.

Now Parcells is hoping for his best players to step up. He could be referring to Hugh Douglas, who has gone four straight games without a sack and three straight without so much as a solo tackle.

And to Adrian Murrell, who has rushed 36 times for only 85 yards in the last seven quarters. And to Aaron Glenn, who missed a couple of interception chances. And to Neil O'Donnell, who had a costly third-quarter fumble that annoyed Parcells.

Now here come the Patriots, who won Tuna Bowl I in OT, 27-24. This time, the stakes are greater.

"We have to beat New England to stay in the hunt," Smith said. "If we want to be competitors in our division, we have to win this game."

Said Glenn: "We're not going to put added pressure on ourselves, but this is a big game. A very big game."

Tuna's Switch Catch of Day

By Mike Lupica

You don't have to like Bill Parcells or the way he left the Giants once or the way he got to the Jets. You don't have to like the way he acts like a bully and a bouncer in the interview room sometimes. But you have to know Parcells is not afraid. It is one more reason why he is the best there is. He believes his job is to give his team the best chance to win the game, every single Sunday. It is why he benched Neil O'Donnell yesterday and went with Glenn Foley in the second half against the Patriots. All Foley was after that was the most exciting thing to happen for the Jets, in Giants Stadium, in 10 years.

After all the seasons before Parcells when the Jets had no chance to win the game.

"You gotta do something," Parcells would say after his team came back on the Patriots and finally beat them, 24-19. "You can't stay the same. That's what I aways tell the players. It can't stay the same. You can't live with it until Monday and then make a decision in your office."

The coach hasn't ever been a Monday-morning guy. He made his play for Foley exactly where he should have made it, where he is always at his best.

Middle of Sunday Afternoon.

Foley couldn't do him any good as his Monday-morning quarterback.

So he made his play before the Jets got further behind than 12-3, before they fell to 4-4. Before this started to feel like the season everybody expected. Parcells went up to Foley at halftime and said, "Get ready, you're gonna go."

O'Donnell's job status didn't matter, his salary didn't matter, his feelings didn't matter. Beating the Patriots mattered tremendously. Which is what Boston College's Foley did in grand style, the way he beat Notre Dame one time in South Bend, when Notre Dame was No. 1 in the country. He took the Jets down the field three straight times for touchdowns and completed 14 passes in a row at one time and ended up with 17-of-23 for 200 yards. By the end of it, they were chanting his name at Giants Stadium.

On November 5, 1995—in another terrible losing season for the Jets—Foley got a chance against the Patriots. Against Bill Parcells, Foley took the Jets 99 yards for a touchdown that day, another second half. But then he took a hit from a guy named Aaron Jones.

Jones busted Foley's shoulder and could have ruined his career.

"I went from being a guy people had some hopes for to someone whose career could have been over," Foley said.

Now two years later, almost two years exactly, he was a Boston kid from Boston College coming off the bench, beating the Super Bowl Patriots. If you have ever played the game the way Foley did for Tom Coughlin (now coach of the Jacksonville Jaguars) in college, you always believe you have days like this still inside you.

You never know it will be 14 in a row, pass after pass, a day out of your brightest imagination. But if you have ever been anything on Saturday afternoons in college, you always believe it all can travel to Sunday. Glenn Foley remembered it all yesterday, every bit of it.

Despite all the losing Sundays he had seen with the Jets.

"I've always looked at myself as a starter," Foley would say in front of his locker afterward. "I've always thought of myself as a guy who someday was going to be a starter."

Parcells wouldn't say if Foley is his starter now. O'Donnell said he expects to start two weeks from now, after a bye week for the Jets. Somebody asked Foley what his reaction would be if Parcells tells him he is a backup again and Foley said, "Then I'm the backup." Just like that. When he was asked about the last time he won a game as a quarterback and Foley grinned.

"Virginia," he said.

He was talking about the Carquest Bowl, Fort Lauderdale, at the end of his senior year at Boston College, the year he beat Notre Dame and some of Doug Flutie's passing records. He was always a winner there. Then he came to one of the great losers in sports, the Jets.

They were losing again yesterday, despite the fast start under Parcells. O'Donnell had thrown for just 59 yards in the first half. He moved his feet so much, so fast, in the pocket, you thought he had tap shoes. He threw the ball around as if he had David Cone's bum shoulder. Parcells told him to take a seat at the half.

"I thought we needed a spark," the coach said.

"You gotta do something," Parcells kept saying.

Foley missed with his first pass and then hit Wayne Chrebet for 20 yards on third-and-12, and from there it was one of those magic days a player has in sports sometimes. Like Livan Hernandez striking out 15 Atlanta Braves, pow, out of nowhere. That kind of day. Hernandez did it last Sunday in the playoffs. Before long Foley, off the bench, would complete 14 in a row at Giants Stadium.

He completed passes to Chrebet and Kyle Brady and Jeff Graham and Keyshawn Johnson. The Jets came back to 12-10, the Patriots stretched their lead to 19-10. Foley brought the Jets down and with 1:51 left in the third quarter it was 19-17. At the start of the fourth quarter, there was this dream drive for the Jets. Foley to Graham, twice. Foley to Adrian Murrell. Then Foley took a lateral from Murrell on a trick play, hit Johnson for 21 yards down the sideline.

Then Graham again. Brady again. Finally a touchdown pass to a kid named Lorenzo Neal in the right flat, Neal touching the ball for the first time this season on offense. Jets 24, Patriots 19. Alumni Stadium at BC is about half the size of Giants Stadium. Foley had never heard his name chanted like this. Football had sounded this big at Notre Dame that time, but for Notre Dame.

Never this big for him.

Football hadn't felt this big for the Jets, in this place, since the 1980s, when the Jets were 10-1 under Joe Walton one time, when Ken O'Brien was the quarterback. So much losing after that. So many Sundays when the Jets had no chance. The coach gives them a chance now. He gave Foley a chance yesterday. You can't stay the same, the coach said. You can't wait for Monday morning, with quarterbacks or anything else.

View from the Top

Jets' share of first is a 10-year first

By Rich Cimini

Now it's official: The Jets can say they've been to hell and back. Bill Parcells, who inherited a team that had spent 38 consecutive weeks in last place in the AFC East, has led the resurgent Jets into a three-way tie for first—the first time in a decade they've experienced first place this late in the season.

The unlikely ascension was completed early yesterday morning, when the Patriots and Dolphins lost to the Packers and Bears, respectively. The results of the rare Monday night doubleheader changed the look of the AFC East standings, with the Jets, Patriots and Dolphins now deadlocked at 5-3.

The Jets' new status made it easier for the players to return to work yesterday after a three-day bye weekend. The locker room was filled with a genuine excitement. And why not? The second half of the season, which begins Sunday against the Ravens (4-4), contains endless possibilities.

"We can compare ourselves to anyone now," defensive back Ray Mickens said. "It's real fun to be in this thing."

Parcells has been there, done that, many times, so he wasn't in a ga-ga mood about first place. He tried to keep it in perspective, telling the team that its potential dream season will dissolve unless it continues to improve on a weekly basis.

"I'm glad we're there—I'm not trying to diminish it—but I don't think it's that important right now," Parcells said.

Try telling that to the many long-suffering Jets fans. The last time their team owned at least a share of first place this late in the season was November 29, 1987, the strike-shortened year. The Jets were tied with the Bills and Colts at 6-5, but they faded out of contention, dropping the last four games.

It took 10 years to get back. Where were you in 1987? Ronald Reagan was president, Parcells was the Giants' coach and Hugh Douglas was a 16-year-old kid with a one-track mind.

"Back then, all I thought about was getting a girlfriend, not playing football," he said.

It's hard to believe, but the Jets have a real chance of winning the division. That would be a stunner, considering they're the only team—aside from the expansion Jaguars—which hasn't won a division title since the NFL-AFL merger in 1970.

"I don't know too much about the Jets' history, but I do know about the last two years, and I can say we've come a long way," Mickens said.

Can the Jets outlast the Patriots and Dolphins? The Jets have the softest schedule of the three, but their division record (2-3) could haunt them if tie-breakers are necessary. The Dolphins are perfect in the division (2-0) and the Patriots are 3-1, but they face each other twice, so something more has to give.

The way Parcells sees it, the division lacks a dominant team. He probably wouldn't have said that a month ago, but the Patriots, who have dropped three of their last four, don't seem to be as good as advertised.

"We can match up with anybody in the division," safety Victor Green said. "No one out there is dominant. We're in it for the long haul, and we have a good chance of winning this thing."

AFC East Standings as of October 29

TEAM	WINS	LOSSES
JETS	**5**	**3**
Dolphins	5	3
Patriots	5	3
Bills	4	4
Colts	0	8

Tuna: For Jets, Now Fun Begins

By Rich Cimini

Who can sleep at a time like this? Not Bill Parcells. Despite the Jets' lofty place in the AFC East standings—sole possession of first place—Parcells still experiences restless nights. He woke up at 1 a.m. yesterday, fretting over Jason Ferguson's shoulder injury and its potential roster implications. And to think, Ferguson is the backup nose tackle.

Parcells tossed and turned for 2 1/2 hours before dozing off again. By 5:50 a.m., he was at his Hofstra office, worrying about Ferguson and other problems—and loving it.

"That's what you do this time of year," Parcells said. "I'm ready to get to the next game. I'm looking forward to the challenge. Hey, I like this. This is fun."

Fun. Now there's a new word for the Jets' November/December vocabulary. Instead of counting the days to each paycheck and making off-season vacation plans, the Jets are battling for their first division title since 1969.

They're also challenging history. If the Jets (8-4) defeat the struggling Bills (5-7) Sunday at Rich Stadium, they will equal the biggest one-season turnaround in modern NFL history—an improvement of eight wins. It has been accomplished four times, most recently by the 1992 Colts, who went 9-7 after a 1-15 season.

Parcells wasn't eager to discuss the enormity of the Jets' turnaround. When asked about the team's "resurrection," Parcells responded as if he had just tasted a lemon.

"Hold it; you're too far down the road," he said. "If we're in the playoffs two or three years, then we're resurrected."

Parcells, trying to prevent the swelled-head syndrome from infiltrating his locker room, wouldn't even categorize the Jets as an "upstart" team. "I would say maybe upstarts or temporarily appearing like upstarts," he said.

Parcells won't admit it, but the turnaround has been remarkable. The Jets aren't dominant in any one particular area, but here they are, tied with the Jaguars and Steelers for the third-best record in the AFC.

"We're not talking about being some Rose Bowl team right now," Parcells said, "but the guys are hungry and they like this."

What's not to like? The Jets have proven they can beat upper-echelon teams—see Sunday's 23-21 victory over the Vikings—and they have demonstrated the ability to win tight games. In fact, the Jets are 5-1 in games decided by less than six points.

"It goes to show the difference from last year," said cornerback Aaron Glenn, alluding to the team's new fourth-quarter prowess. "Last year, we would lay down. This year, we play confidently for 60 minutes."

The Jets, enjoying a one-game lead over the Patriots and Dolphins (both 7-5), hope to parlay Sunday's dramatic, down-to-the-wire victory into a rousing stretch run. After Buffalo, the Jets are home to face the Colts (1-11) and Buccaneers (8-4) before closing on the road against the Lions (6-6).

"Hopefully, this (win) will catapult us for the rest of the season," said defensive end Rick Lyle, who made perhaps the biggest defensive play of the year, tackling running back Robert Smith on the two-point attempt with no time on the clock.

Now comes the tougher part for the Jets—staying in first place. "By and large, most people in the AFC East are just waiting for us to slip up," Parcells said. "They probably think we will slip up."

"Now," fullback Lorenzo Neal said, "is when you have to start separating from everyone. It's like you're running the 400. You've stepped a little ahead of the pack, and now it's down the homestretch. You're down to the last 100 meters."

This is no time to rest—or sleep, if you're the coach.

Jets, at Least, Get to Bill

Admits defeat has him at loss

By Rich Cimini

On the 300th day of his reign, Bill Parcells acknowledged his first case of the blues.

The Jets coach, still smarting from Sunday's 22-14 loss to the woeful Colts, conceded yesterday that the devastating defeat left his spirits at a season low.

"This is the first day I've been a little discouraged since I've been working here," said Parcells, who reported to work at sunrise to review the tapes of the playoff-crippling loss. "To have to look at what I looked at . . . "

It wasn't a pretty picture show. It was one of the ugliest—and most significant—losses in team history, draining the optimism out of a once-promising season.

"Even though we've lost some games, I was never discouraged," Parcells said. "But when you perform like we did (Sunday), you can't help but be a little discouraged, watching that. It's not down-and-out or despondent. I was just very disappointed. Extremely disappointed."

Welcome to the fraternity, Bill.

Sooner or later—usually sooner—every Jets coach reaches the point of aggravation. The bad coaches collapse under the pressure. The good ones . . . well, sorry, no recent examples.

Parcells, certainly the most accomplished coach in Jets history, vowed to stop the losing before it escalates into a full-fledged, honest-to-goodness December collapse. Repeating what he said after the game, the coach indicated that lineup changes might be forthcoming, although he refused to name names.

Thing is, it may not matter. The Jets (8-6), alone in first place two weeks ago, have been reduced to playoff longshots. They're one game behind the Dolphins and Patriots (both 9-5), who each own the tie-breaker advantage over the Jets.

To sneak in as a wild card, the Jets must win their final two games and hope for one of the following scenarios: either the Dolphins, Patriots or Jaguars (9-5) lose their remaining two games or the Jaguars lose one and tie the other. The Patriots and Dolphins play each other on December 22.

The Jets can be mathematically eliminated Sunday—even if they beat the Buccaneers (9-5) at Giants Stadium. The way they're playing, the Jets don't seem capable of beating anybody.

"I take responsibility for it," Parcells said of the Colts debacle, a game in which the Jets produced their lowest yardage total (126) in 20 years. "I'm embarrassed by it, I really am."

Parcells said the defeat was as "big a step backward as the Viking game was forward. I'm very disappointed because we were 8-4 and we had a chance."

Since then, the team has regressed. The Jets can't run the ball and they can't stop the run, a lethal combination of ineptitude. In the last two games they've been outrushed 390-63. The pass protection, ravaged by injuries to tackles Jumbo Elliott and David Williams, has disappeared. Neil O'Donnell was sacked eight times by the Colts.

"It was ugly to watch," O'Donnell said after reviewing a tape of the slaughter.

"Back to the same old thing again," receiver Keyshawn Johnson said. "I don't know where we go from here."

Cornerback Otis Smith said he felt the loss "from the top of my throat all the way down to the pit of my stomach . . . When we got hit by the Colts, we didn't fight back. It tells me we've got to start over."

Changes? With Glenn Foley (knee) still injured, O'Donnell will remain the starter. At other positions, younger players could emerge. Receivers Alex Van Dyke and Dedric Ward, fullback Gerald Sowell, cornerback Marcus Coleman and safety Raymond Austin could see increased playing time.

"The young guys have a chance to play better than some of the older guys did," Parcells said. "They can't play worse. I have nothing to lose. What are they going to get, nine sacks? Ten sacks? What difference does it make?"

On QB Question, Parcells Should Pass

By Gary Myers

It was pack-up-the-lockers day at Hofstra for the Jets, the depressing season-ending ritual when players say their goodbyes, exchange phone numbers and don't know if they will ever be teammates again.

By lunch time, the place had cleared out.

Bill Parcells finished up his final news conference, headed upstairs to his office/bunker to begin putting together the '98 Jets. And sometime in the next few weeks, he will have to make a crucial decision: what to do about the quarterbacks.

And we say: keep them both.

Neil O'Donnell is not his Phil Simms in green and white. Not when Parcells is taking the ball out of O'Donnell's hands and giving it to Ray Lucas and Leon Johnson, of all people, who are throwing crucial second-half interceptions in the season-ending game in Detroit.

Glenn Foley might be his guy, but he didn't stay on the field long enough to provide confidence he can make it through an entire season. Although O'Donnell has a suffocating $6.65 million salary-cap number that must be restructured and is due $2.75 million on February 20, Parcells should not get rid of him.

Not to bring in Vinny Testaverde, who could be gone in Baltimore if the Ravens sign Jim Kelly. Not to bring in Jim Harbaugh, who could be gone in Indy with the Colts owning the Peyton Manning pick. Not to bring in a free agent like Ty Detmer or Kent Graham. Not when O'Donnell played perhaps his best game in Detroit since the season opener when he threw five TDs in Seattle.

The play that had the biggest impact on next season came in Chicago when Foley tore up his knee in his second start. He had played well in his two relief appearances. He had played well in his first start in Miami and was moving the team in Chicago.

If Foley had finished out the season and established himself, then, fine, get rid of O'Donnell and clear out a good portion of his cap space. But until Foley proves he can avoid injury, the Jets' QB situation will be 1 and 1A.

Parcells acknowledged the difference between a quarterback doing it short-term and over the course of a season.

"Having to go week in, week out getting hit, executing 70 plays a week, 35 passes a week, to do that is much different than playing a couple of games," he said. "Some guys can't hold up to it mentally, some guys can't hold up to it physically. Some can't hold up to the scrutiny, the pressure of performing and leading a team every week. That's why there is such a premium paid for those who can."

Foley can handle the mental aspects. But two years ago, he dislocated his shoulder just as Rich Kotite was ready to hand him the job. This year, it was the knee.

Should the coaches be concerned? "There were two injuries," Foley said. "It doesn't matter what kind of quarterback you are, you're going to go down from it. I think it's more bad luck than anything. I started 50 straight games in college. That says something."

Foley wants the '98 starting job and this season showed signs of being a special player. He says he doesn't want anything handed to him, but "let's go out and duke it out."

In one sentence yesterday, Parcells said he "didn't see any reason why" O'Donnell would not be back next season, but then in the next he said, "I reserve the right to change my mind on Neil O'Donnell or anyone else on the team depending on the circumstances that come up."

For whatever reason, Parcells never gave O'Donnell the standard coachspeak vote of confidence, not even when it was clear that if the Jets were going to make the playoffs, O'Donnell was going to have to take them there, and a pat on the back might have helped get his game back together.

And as Parcells put '97 behind him yesterday and was pressed on his plans for '98, he remained noncommittal about what he would do at quarterback. He rejected the idea Foley would go into camp No. 1 because he was the starter before he was injured. "He was No. 1? I never said that," Parcells said. "He started a game. I never said he was the starting quarterback. Never once. I never told him that. I never told you that."

What he is telling us is that after a year of establishing credibility, it's time for the next step. And unless Parcells can pull off a trade for Peyton Manning, which would be quite a turn of events considering what happened last spring, the O'Donnell-Foley combo should remain intact.

CHAPTER 12

A CHAMPIONSHIP LOOK

Jets' 1998-1999 Season

Bill Parcells unveils the Jets' new retro look. Players (from left) Mo Lewis, Adrian Murrell, and Wayne Chrebet model the Jets' new uniforms.

AP/Wide World Photos

*I*t was going to be a new New York Jets team. From the new uniforms, reminiscent of the Jets' 1969 championship team, to a new quarterback, Vinny Testaverde from Long Island.

Parcells had shown that often-injured quarterback Glenn Foley was his first choice when high-priced Neil O'Donnell was released before training camp. But, when Foley was hurt, not to mention losing the first two games of the season, Testaverde stepped in. By the end of the season, Testaverde was the clear choice at quarterback. He led the Jets to first place in the AFC East with a 12-4 record and a first-round bye in the playoffs. A win over Jacksonville in the playoffs earned the Jets a place in the AFC championship game against the Denver Broncos, and a shot at their first Super Bowl in 30 years.

Look of a Champion

Jets' new uniforms are Super

By Rich Cimini

B efore he signed his first free agent, before he staged his first practice and before he chewed out his first player, Bill Parcells decided the Jets needed a new look—actually a new "old" look. He came to that conclusion in his second day on the job, almost one year ago.

His vision became a reality Tuesday at a Manhattan news conference, where Parcells—joined by former Jets great Joe Namath and several members of the Super Bowl III team—unveiled the new uniform and new logo.

Now they can be called the retro Jets.

Using a "Back to the Future" theme, the Jets returned to their original uniform and logo, first worn at the club's inception in 1963 and adorned by the Namath-led championship team in Super Bowl III.

The uniform represents "the pinnacle of the Jets era," Parcells said. "This is the identity of the Jets. I think each team needs an identity. When you think of the Jets, this is what we think of."

Said Namath: "We're all thrilled. It brings up all kinds of nostalgic feelings. It's more of a natural for me. This is more of what we know."

The Jets also will return to their original white helmet with their old green logo on the sides. The uniform differs slightly from the original version in that the green is a darker shade—hunter green, if you must know.

The logo also has been clarified, and a patch has been added to the front of the jersey for better identification. But some things don't change: The jersey still has white stripes and numbers on the sleeves.

The Jets wore their original uniforms from 1963 to 1977. They changed in 1978, going to green helmets and a new logo, with "Jets" spelled out.

Say goodbye to those threads. Say hello to the originals.

"I love them; it's a lot of tradition," said wide receiver Wayne Chrebet, who along with linebacker Mo Lewis and running back Adrian Murrell modeled the uniforms at the news conference. "It makes the will to succeed even greater, because we want to be part of that tradition."

People within the organization had been trying for years to make the change, but the movement always met opposition from the most recent head coaches. Not Parcells; just call him an old-fashioned kind of guy.

Actually, Parcells became smitten with the original uniforms in 1967, when as an assistant coach at West Point he often visited the Jets' training camp at the nearby Peekskill Military Academy.

"I always identified the Jets with those uniforms," he said.

Parcells wanted to make the switch for last season, but NFL Properties requires at least 12 months notice before the season. For marketing purposes, you understand. So they waited.

Owner Leon Hess applauded the move, saying in a statement, "I'm very happy we're going back to the uniforms and logo that we originated when we bought the team in 1963."

Hall of Fame coach Weeb Ewbank is particularly pleased that the white helmets are back. He said he had been trying for years to get the team to switch.

"The quarterback can pick out the white helmet better on the field," Ewbank said. "Paul Brown made sure the Browns and Bengals wore orange helmets so the quarterbacks could see the helmet. White is the next best color."

The Jets hoped a change in uniform would lead to a return of the winning ways of the '69 team.

School of Tuna

Parcells preaches to his coaching brethren

By Rich Cimini

There were no television lights in his face, no radio microphones beneath his chin. There was no game to dissect, no strategy to defend. This was simple and innocent: Bill Parcells, in a dimly lit school auditorium, talking football to his high-school brethren.

Parcells, unplugged.

The Jets' coach, who has maintained a low profile since the season ended two months ago, emerged from his Weeb Ewbank Hall bunker Friday night to speak at Uniondale High School, where the Nassau County High School Football Coaches Association held its annual two-day clinic.

Parcells was a hot ticket, drawing more than 400 coaches. They paid $40 for advance tickets—$50 at the door—to hear the Parcells doctrine. It was a rare appearance for the coach, who told his rapt audience it's been 10 years since his last high-school clinic.

He worked gratis—proceeds went to the association's scholarship fund—and spoke for 65 minutes, revealing a side of himself seldom seen in the 10-second sound bites that make the 11 o'clock news.

There was no sarcasm, no surliness. He was engaging, funny and insightful, illustrating his coaching theories with anecdotes about Lawrence Taylor, Harry Carson and Drew Bledsoe. (Sorry, no Neil O'Donnell stories.) Parcells was surrounded by his own kind, and the comfort level showed on his face.

"He loves football coaches," said Mickey Corcoran, Parcells' old high-school basketball coach and now one of his most trusted confidants. "He likes to be around football, and he likes to be around football guys."

Not newspaper guys, though. Parcells declined to be interviewed for this story.

No problem. With a few index cards at his fingertips and 34 years of coaching experience in his memory bank, Parcells said plenty in his address to his fraternity brothers. Many scribbled notes on legal pads, trying to sponge information the way aspiring actors would react listening to Pacino on Pacino.

"I can't wait to take some of this stuff back to my kids," Kevin McElroy, a coach at Mepham High, said afterward.

Parcells talked about integrating a philosophy, but also stressed the importance of being flexible within the framework of that philosophy. To make his point, he told a story about "No. 56 in a blue jersey. I think you know who he is."

The coaches nodded reverently.

Parcells, never mentioning Taylor by name, recalled the linebacker as a rookie in 1981. He said Taylor "didn't have a clue what he was doing. Like a dog chasing cars."

Example: Against the Cardinals, Taylor was assigned to cover receiver Mel Gray on a third-down pass, but he brain-locked and rushed the quarterback. Sacked him, too, but he still was scolded by Parcells—then the defensive coordinator—for making a potentially costly mistake. Won't happen again, LT promised.

It did. Same game, too. Taylor blew another coverage on Gray and sacked the quarterback again. This time, he forced a fumble, and it was returned for a touchdown by George Martin. Taylor had the rare speed to turn mistakes into big plays, but when he returned to the bench, he was greeted with an icy glare.

"Oh, I did it again, didn't I?" Taylor said, slapping his forehead.

"Don't you get it?" Parcells asked. "We don't even have what you're doing (in the playbook)."

Taylor replied: "Coach, we better put it in Monday."

Parcells did. The moral: Be flexible.

A coach also must demand "collective loyalty" Parcells told the coaches. He recalled a one-on-one showdown with his former Giants defensive captain, Carson, who once left training camp because of a contract dispute.

A livid Parcells ripped Carson in the media, questioning his leadership. When Carson returned two days later, he was challenged by Parcells in front of the team.

"What day you leaving next?" Parcells said, drilling holes through Carson with his pointed words.

Finally, after a few tense moments, Carson vowed to be a devoted captain. Crisis resolved.

A coach also must be accountable, Parcells said. Rewind to 1993, his first year with the Patriots. Inches from a last-minute, game-winning touchdown in Pittsburgh, Parcells instructed his rookie QB, Bledsoe, to run a fourth-down sneak. One problem:

"I didn't remind him to reach with the ball over the goal line," Parcells said. "I assumed that any idiot would know that."

Bledsoe didn't, and was stuffed.

"My fault," Parcells said. "I went to the player, said, 'I lost the game. I didn't have enough sense to tell you to put the ball over the goal line.'"

What about his legendary sideline explosions?

"They've been well-documented," said Parcells, perhaps alluding to his blow-up with O'Donnell in the season finale. "But what's never documented is the damage control.

"You beat 'em down, then find out where they are. Sometimes, when you go to them, it's not all that friendly, but at least you're there. They know you're thinking about them."

Interestingly, Parcells scarcely mentioned the Jets, except to say they had a "very poor self-image" when he took over last year, and that players were ashamed to wear Jets apparel in public.

He also mentioned the '97 Jets as an example of how a coach can rebuild a downtrodden program by building on one potential strength. For the Jets, it was special teams.

"Don't confuse us with being a good team—it wasn't a good team—but being decent in that one aspect allowed the team to maintain its competitiveness," Parcells said.

Parcells never was a high school coach, but he has a great affinity for them. He told about a legendary Texas coach named Gordon Wood, who "had as much influence on me as any single guy I've encountered in this profession."

They met only once, in the mid-1970s, when Parcells was an assistant at Texas Tech. Wood was a fixture at Tech's spring drills, commuting five hours every day to watch practice. Parcells was blown away by the man's dedication.

"Here's a guy who had 300 wins, and he's driving back and forth because he's trying to learn something," Parcells said. "I thought to myself, 'If you ever want to get anywhere in this business, you better start acting like this guy, because he's something special.' He really inspired me."

Twenty years later, Parcells left 400-plus coaches thinking the same thing about him.

O'Donnell Jet-tisoned

Vinny gets Tuna's call

By Rich Cimini

N eil O'Donnell is out, Vinny Testaverde is in. After months of speculation, Jets coach Bill Parcells yesterday ended his quarterback soap
opera, terminating his stormy relationship with O'Donnell and
replacing him with Testaverde.

Testaverde's contract is all but done and, barring a last-minute glitch in
negotiations, he will sign it today, according to several NFL sources. Testaverde,
in the area yesterday to participate in the Cadillac NFL Golf Classic in Clifton,
N.J., will be introduced at an afternoon news conference.

Testaverde, who is from Elmont, L.I., five miles from the Jets' Hempstead
base, will compete with Glenn Foley for the starting job. O'Donnell will be
released, probably today.

Parcells' interest in Testaverde, released June 2 by the Baltimore Ravens,
represents a stunning reversal. In February, Parcells said he had no interest in the
Heisman Trophy winner. But the coach, apparently frustrated by O'Donnell's
refusal to accept a substantial pay cut, had a change of heart about a week ago
and made contact with Testaverde's agent, Michael Azzarelli.

Yesterday, when the deal became imminent, Parcells notified O'Donnell's
agent, Leigh Steinberg, that he was planning to make a change. And so ended
the six-month staredown.

"Because of Neil's continued unwillingness to re-do his contract, Bill said
he's going in another quarterback direction, and that it might result in Neil's
release," Steinberg said.

O'Donnell's exit is a formality. He still will count as $2.4 million against
this year's cap (and $2.8 million in 1999), but his $4.25 million salary will be
cleared from the cap. He already has received $3.75 million in advances, but
that money must be returned to the team.

Details of Testaverde's contract weren't available last night, but it's believed he will count as more than $1 million against this season's cap, which means the Jets save roughly $3 million in the quarterback swap.

O'Donnell, hailed as the Jets' savior when he left the Pittsburgh Steelers to sign a five-year, $25 million free-agent contract two years ago, couldn't be reached for comment. Steinberg said he notified O'Donnell of Parcells' decision.

"Neil's reaction? He was aware there was a contractual dispute, and he knows the coach has a right to decide who he wants on the team," Steinberg said. "He would've liked to have stayed in New York. . . . It's a surprising development, but better now than in training camp."

O'Donnell was 8-12 as a starter in two star-crossed seasons, which were marred by injuries and his benching last October. The Atlanta Falcons are expected to contact O'Donnell within a day or two.

Steinberg said he last spoke with Parcells during the Jets' minicamp last month. At that time, the Jets still were trying to slash O'Donnell's salary to $2 million, with a chance to recoup it in incentives.

Testaverde, who also received offers from the Bengals, Seahawks and Chargers, leaked word of the Jets' interest in an interview with reporters at the golf tournament. Parcells confirmed through a team spokesman that "we've had some talks with Vinny Testaverde and his representatives."

It was the first time Parcells acknowledged an interest in another quarterback, an admission that all but confirmed O'Donnell's ouster.

"Me being from Long Island, I'd love to come home," Testaverde said.

Testaverde, a starter throughout most of his career, said he wouldn't be happy in a backup role, but would accept it "in the right situation." Assistant coach Bill Belichick is familiar with Testaverde, having coached him three seasons in Cleveland.

The interception-prone Testaverde would seem to be an odd choice for the turnover-intolerant Parcells, but he was the best available QB. Testaverde said he's willing to be salary-cap friendly.

"I'm not concerned about numbers and contracts," he said. "That stuff is behind me. I don't have too many years left . . . I just want to play for an organization that's focused on winning."

Keyshawn Catches on with Tuna

By Rich Cimini

It was supposed to be a bad marriage: Keyshawn Johnson, the brash Generation X poster boy, and Bill Parcells, the X's and O's disciplinarian.

But a funny thing happened on the way to divorce court—the pair clicked.

Now, after a year of Parcells, Johnson couldn't imagine himself playing for another coach.

"Like Michael (Jordan) feels about Phil Jackson, that's how I feel about Bill," the Jets' wide receiver said at training camp.

Parcells chuckled when told of Johnson's analogy.

"I don't know about that," the coach said, "but I do know this: I like having him on my team."

How did their relationship get so warm and fuzzy? By most accounts, Johnson has matured as a player. He seems to have distanced himself from his "Just-give-me-the-damn-ball" image, his rookie persona.

As for Parcells, he prides himself on being more patient than he was in his younger days.

He admitted that if he had coached Johnson years ago, they might have been like a pair of magnets—always repelling, unable to connect.

"He told me that if he had me when he was 25 years old, I probably wouldn't be on the team right now—or that he'd probably quit," Johnson said, smiling.

Johnson described Parcells as a savior. After his tumultuous rookie year, Johnson was so disgusted by the shenanigans of the Rich Kotite regime that he thought about requesting a one-way ticket out of New York.

If the Jets hadn't named Parcells to replace Kotite, he might have acted on his thoughts.

"There are certain coaches I could play for," Johnson said. "If Jimmy

Johnson were here coaching, I could play for Jimmy. But because of the sour taste from my rookie year, I probably would've tried to figure a way out; move me as quick as possible.

"If I didn't have Bill as a head coach right now," he added, "I don't know where the hell I'd be in terms of football."

Now in his third year, Johnson is a proven receiver, but still aspiring to reach the lofty expectations that came with being the No. 1 overall pick in the 1996 draft. In two seasons, he has 133 catches, 1,807 yards and 13 touchdowns. The numbers compare favorably with the first two years of Jerry Rice, who had 135 receptions and 18 touchdowns.

Despite his solid statistics, Johnson has lagged in the big-play department. He has produced only one 100-yard receiving game—a 104-yard effort against the Vikings last season.

This season, the Jets are counting on Johnson to be a cornerstone player in their offense.

"He's produced well, but there's more he can do, without question," Parcells said. "I think he can be a good, good player."

Parcells learned a lot about Johnson in the aftermath of the season-ending loss in Detroit, where he dropped two passes after boasting before the game that he always thrived in big games. Afterward, Johnson was crushed.

"That hurt him bad," Parcells said. "That bothered him a lot."

Parcells said he's convinced that Johnson, often described as a selfish player, cares deeply about winning. Those kind of players, Parcells likes to say, would show up for a game in an empty parking lot.

Is Johnson one of those players?

"He'd show up," Parcells said. "But he'd like people to be there watching."

Some things don't change.

Bill Gives Foley a Ribbing

Grins, bears poke & vote from coach

By Rich Cimini

Suggestion to Glenn Foley: Wear your flak jacket at all times. You never know when Bill Parcells will try another quarterback sneak attack.

Last week, the Jets' coach, perhaps trying to determine Foley's pain threshold, surprised his QB by walking up behind him and poking him in his tender ribs.

"He gave me a little rap on the side," Foley said yesterday. "I nearly collapsed. He said, 'You're not faking it. I guess you're not ready.'"

Call it hands-on coaching.

Parcells, who went to the bullpen for a four-touchdown performance from Vinny Testaverde in Sunday's 44-6 rout of the Colts, indicated he still has some questions about whether Foley (torn rib cartilage) will be ready to start against the Dolphins (3-0) in 12 days.

"I haven't gotten any indication that he's much closer," said Parcells, who will use the bye week to monitor Foley's condition. "I have to see for myself that everything is good with Foley. I can't just hear it; I've got to see it."

From all indications, Foley will start the game. The Jets (1-2) have seven practices before facing the Dolphins at home, giving him plenty of time to prove to Parcells he's capable of leading the team into a critical AFC East battle.

Foley, who vowed Sunday to be ready for Miami, was less adamant yesterday, although he may have been chided by Parcells about making bold predictions with regard to injuries. Parcells has lectured Foley in the past on that topic.

Nonetheless, Foley is confident about his chances of facing Miami's formidable defense, which has surrendered only 22 points.

"I still have a thing about worrying about getting hit there and maybe setting me back a little more," Foley said. "It was a painful injury to have, but that pain subsided over the last couple of days. It seems to get better every day."

Foley will share snaps with Testaverde this week in practice. Parcells reiterated that Foley still is the No. 1 quarterback, but he wondered how he will respond to contact.

"Can he take it or can't he take it? If not, he's not going to play," Parcells said. "I'll use him in spot duty."

Thing is, there's no way to simulate a high-speed shot to the ribs in practice. Or is there?

"I'll just sit there and let Bryan Cox run at me full speed," Foley cracked. "You don't know. It'll be one of those things where, 'Should I take the hit?' Then we'll find out.'"

As for his fill-in, Parcells offered only a lukewarm assessment of Testaverde's performance after the game but was in full-gush after reviewing the tapes.

"I feel good about what Vinny did," Parcells said. "That's what I was hoping for . . . He made good decisions. He didn't do anything to hurt us. I was very pleased with him. I'm glad I've got the guy."

Testaverde completed only 12 of 21 passes, but he threw for 203 yards and tied a career high with four touchdowns. Interestingly, the four scoring throws traveled a total of less than 20 yards in the air. A screen pass to Leon Johnson turned into an 82-yard touchdown.

Despite Testaverde's prolific day, Parcells squashed a potential controversy by making an immediate commitment to Foley—if healthy. Foley appreciated the vote of confidence.

Now Foley must beware of another Parcells attack. He's ready for anything.

"Karate kicks, karate chops," he said. "Whatever."

After starting quarterback Glenn Foley (right) went down with a rib injury the week before facing the Colts, Bill Parcells turned to Vinny Testaverde.

We'll See if Tuna Is Right Again

By Mark Kriegel

Bill Parcells picked Glenn Foley as his probable starter for Sunday's game against the St. Louis Rams. He gave no reason for this. He didn't have to. He is, after all, Bill Parcells.

But in choosing Foley, he goes against most conventional logic, including his own. Parcells' prime commandment, the cold-hearted ethos he reiterated yesterday: "This is a production business. If you don't produce, you're not going to be here."

So do the math yourself. Production is easy to quantify. Foley is 0-2 as a starter this season, 1-6 over the course of a career still lacking a complete-game victory. He has four touchdowns and as many interceptions. His quarterback rating is 77.2.

By contrast, Vinny Testaverde is 2-0 as a starter, having just led the Jets to a win over Miami, a division rival they hadn't beaten in three years. He has five touchdowns against a single interception, a Hail Mary pass thrown at the end of a half. His rating is 104.9.

All that, and Mr. Bottom Line is going with Mr. Foley. Yesterday, Testaverde was asked what he thought of this.

"What I thought doesn't really matter," he said.

He was asked if the decision was fair.

"Doesn't matter if it's fair," he said. "He's the head coach . . . I don't think Bill can make a wrong decision."

Of course not, he's Bill Parcells.

But here's the twist: For all Parcells' prickly imperiousness, his pigheaded belief in production and his convenient contradictions, there's something authentically endearing about his loyalty to Foley. Despite the numbers, against the inexorable logic of production, he believes in Foley. More than that, he likes him. He likes him even more than he disliked Neil O'Donnell.

Parcells went into this riff about "guys you just like." He spoke of Pepper Johnson and Keith Byars and Phil Simms. He likes older players whose talent has diminished with time, players who have survived long enough to love the game more than they did as rookies, players who know how precious playing time is.

And you have to figure Foley already thinks in those terms. He was the 208th pick in the 1994 draft. He spent four years as a backup, showing more toughness than talent those years. But none of that seems to hurt his chances with Parcells.

Maybe Parcells wants to think of Foley as he does of Johnson and Simms, as one of his guys.

Of course, Parcells frowns at the mere suggestion. "You can't tell," he says. "I've only been around him for a year. I don't know what the future is. I don't know how long I'm going to be around the guy." Then again, he concedes, "There's a chance that could happen."

There's also that chance Foley will be benched.

"If he can't function, he won't play," says Parcells.

Concerning these quarterbacks, the coach has contradicted himself before. But thanks in part to his infuriating, imperial sense of authority, there hasn't been any controversy. The team isn't divided. The players seem to know that the quarterback position is evolving. Most teams need two. Already, five weeks into the season, 10 backups have started.

Vinny Testaverde won't stay on the sidelines forever. At some point, Parcells goes back to his backup. And rest assured when he does, it won't be the wrong decision.

Tuna Admits Fumble

Rams butt in on Jet dream

By Rich Cimini

Minutes after absorbing the most lopsided defeat of his 21-game coaching tenure, Bill Parcells stood before his demoralized team and did something that surprised a few players: He accepted a heaping share of responsibility for yesterday's no-show performance against the Rams at the TransWorld Dome.

Parcells, humbled—a seldom seen event, several players admitted privately. That says everything about the 30-10 debacle. On this day, everyone was guilty by association. There was no place for alibis.

"I didn't do a good job getting the team ready to play," Parcells told reporters. "I tried as diligently as I could to forewarn them about the Rams' ability. Obviously, I didn't get through to them.

"That was as bad as we've played in a long, long time," he continued. "We had no chance to beat anybody today . . . We had 45 guys who dressed and 12 coaches who coached. Everybody stunk."

Shame on the Jets. Just when you think they've made progress, they pull out a clunker from their wretched past. So much for all that tough talk about growing up as a team. More than one season into the Parcells era, the Jets still need Pampers.

They underestimated the Rams, producing only 177 yards and committing five turnovers. The turnovers—three by quarterback Glenn Foley—led to 27 points, as the Rams (2-3) snapped an eight-game home losing streak.

Instead of bringing a three-game winning streak into next Monday night's showdown against the first-place Patriots (4-1), who beat the Chiefs, 40-10, the Jets (2-3) find themselves in a state of disarray.

Especially in the backfield. Curtis Martin, nursing a bruised thigh, didn't play. The quarterbacks are nursing bruised egos. Parcells declined to say which quarterback will start against New England, meaning Foley's job security is fading fast.

"It's as helpless as I've felt," said Foley, who started for the first time since September 13 and may have played himself out of a job. "Everything we tried seemed to be like driving right into a wall."

Foley, who had missed two games with a rib injury, was yanked with 3:13 remaining in the third quarter, with the Jets trailing, 23-3. He completed only five of 15 passes for 76 yards, threw two interceptions and had a fumble at his 14-yard line that set up the Rams' first touchdown.

Not that Vinny Testaverde (9-for-18, 96 yards) was much better. He fumbled once and was sacked three times, his only bright moment a 17-yard touchdown pass to Leon Johnson.

"It wouldn't have made any difference who was playing quarterback," Parcells said.

The key play came early. In the first quarter, Foley fumbled at the Jets' 14 after failing to protect the ball on a blind-side blitz by cornerback Todd Lyght. Foley saw the unblocked Lyght bearing down on him, but he had the ball slapped out of his hand as he tried to sidestep the blitzer.

Defensive end Mike D. Jones returned the fumble to the 11, setting up the Rams' first TD. Tony Banks, playing with a sore throwing shoulder, fired a seven-yard scoring pass to running back Derrick Harris, who was covered by linebacker Dwayne Gordon.

Foley admitted the offense wasn't prepared for the blitz. "They showed us something we weren't ready for," he said. "It was really a huge play in the game."

The Jets, coming off an emotional win over the Dolphins, proved they lack the maturity of a contending team. Several players admitted they may have taken the Rams too lightly.

"We heard all week, 'Don't let this happen,'" Gordon said. "Maybe we were too high from the Miami win."

Said Otis Smith, "Maybe we looked at their record and took them for granted."

Parcells, questioning the team's veteran leadership, said he thought they were "beyond a game like this, past this stage in the operation." Obviously, we're not.

"At this point, we have to re-evaluate what we're doing a little bit, because when you get beat like that, it really wakes you up."

Parcells Stuns Jets by Leaving Practice

By Rich Cimini

With his team facing a crucial game that could dictate the course of the Jets' season, coach Bill Parcells pulled one of the most extraordinary motivational stunts in his career.

Disturbed by the team's lethargic attitude in Friday's practice, Parcells walked off the field with his assistant coaches, according to team members.

Parcells stopped practice with over an hour remaining, gathered his assistants and the group walked in unison off the field, team members told the *Daily News*.

Picture this: 53 players—three days from a huge game tomorrow night against the Patriots at Foxboro Stadium—standing on the practice field, dumbfounded, wondering what to do.

According to team members, the rest of the practice session was coordinated by linebacker Pepper Johnson, the defensive co-captain. Players still were stunned even a day later.

"I guess this is one of his methods to create a sense of urgency," one player said yesterday. "It definitely gets everybody's attention. It just shows that he is not going to tolerate any BS."

Afterward, the team huddled in private and decided as a whole not to discuss the episode publicly. But there was an uneasy feeling yesterday in the locker room.

"Hopefully, it produces a positive result," one team member said. "We know what we have to do now. This was a huge wakeup call."

The Jets, coming off a 30-10 loss to the Rams, need a win against the first-place Patriots (4-1) to stay in the hunt for the AFC East title.

Parcells was in an edgy mood yesterday. His daily press briefing lasted less than a minute before he bolted and retreated to his office.

Clearly, Parcells is turning up the heat. This is personal for him, facing his old team on his old turf in a prime time game.

Instead of yelling at his players, Parcells showed them what he thought
by walking off the practice field.

No Reason to Get Upset

Vinny leads way as Jets fit the Bill

By Rich Cimini

Even if Bill Parcells pulls a Marv Levy and coaches into his 70s, he would be hard-pressed to produce a regular-season victory more satisfying than last night's 24-14 upset over the Patriots. It was sweet. It was huge. It was vintage Parcells.

Take that, Robert Kraft.

Three days after being abandoned on the practice field by an enraged Parcells, the Jets—in their first Monday night appearance since 1992—responded with their most emotional win in years.

Led by Vinny Testaverde, who threw for three touchdowns in his first game as the newly anointed starting quarterback, the Jets scored two fourth-quarter touchdowns to snap the Patriots' four-game winning streak at an electricity-filled Foxboro Stadium.

The Jets also received a boost from Curtis Martin, who in his ballyhooed return to New England, produced his third straight 100-yard game. Martin, who missed last week's loss to the Rams because of a thigh bruise, ran for 107 yards on 28 carries.

Afterward, a relieved Parcells, allowing a smile after a week of surliness, downplayed his nuts-and-bolt routine last Friday. The former Patriots coach insisted it "wasn't a factor" in his team's inspired performance.

"I don't know if it got anybody's attention," said the Jets' coach, who stunned players by storming off the practice field with more than an hour left in the session. "I was just sick to my stomach by what I saw, so I wanted to go somewhere to be alone."

Tight end Kyle Brady, who caught two one-yard touchdown passes in his best day as a pro, described Parcells' psychological ploy as "a rallying point. Guys said, 'Enough is enough. Let's get going.'"

Not only did the Jets make Parcells look like a motivational wizard, but they remained a factor in the AFC East race. They improved to 3-3, crawling within one game of the first-place Patriots and Dolphins. The Jets, who face the Falcons (5-1) Sunday at home, are 3-0 in division play.

The Patriots were stunned.

"Everyone is in awe," defensive tackle Chad Eaton said. "In this locker room it's quiet. I have no idea what went wrong."

After his Jets beat his previous employer, the Patriots, Bill Parcells could smile about storming off the practice field.

The Jets played a brilliant second half, shutting out the high-powered Patriots and scoring two touchdowns in a 5:26 span in the fourth quarter.

Testaverde (22-for-32, 294 yards) hit Brady (five catches for 40 yards) for a touchdown with 8:54 remaining, culminating their best drive of the season—17 plays, 80 yards in 8:35. Testaverde, cool under pressure, completed seven straight passes.

The touchdown drive was set up by the defense, as cornerback Aaron Glenn intercepted Drew Bledsoe (18-for-30, 206 yards, one touchdown) in the end zone.

Then, after a New England punt, the Jets attacked the NFL's fourth-ranked defense. Instead of milking the clock, Testaverde fired a 43-yard touchdown strike to Dedric Ward with 3:29 left to ice the game.

"We wanted to be aggressive," Parcells said. "We didn't want to give the ball back to Bledsoe, with three points."

Said Testaverde: "When that play came in, I said, 'I'm just going to lay it up for Dedric and let him run under it.'"

Testaverde, 3-0 as a starter, did a terrific job in what probably will be an extended run as the starter. Testaverde was sacked four times, but he didn't commit a turnover. The Jets came out in a spread offense and that seemed to surprise the Patriots.

Testaverde was at his best in the second half, orchestrating a brilliant 17-play drive to put the Jets ahead, 17-14. He hit passes of 17 yards to Ward, six yards to Wayne Chrebet on a third-and-3 and 19 yards to Keyshawn Johnson, who took a wicked shot to the back. Finally, at the 1, Testaverde found Brady.

The Jets' defense, which allowed a pair of first-half touchdowns, grew stronger in the second half. Rookie Robert Edwards, Martin's replacement, finished with 104 yards (including a one-yard TD run), but only 37 in the second half.

It made Parcells a happy man in his second return to New England, where he coached four seasons.

"I'm pleased to come in here and beat these guys, obviously," he said, adding that "we have to figure out if we want to be a yo-yo team" or a consistent squad.

Up, down. Good, bad. You never know with these Jets. But last night was one to remember.

Bit Less Pepper in Tuna Mix

By Michael James

I f you want to see Bill Parcells' blue eyes glaze over and hear him wax nostalgic, just talk about the good old days. Talk about the days when men were men who played on heart when their bodies gave out.

Or you can just mention linebacker Pepper Johnson.

Even on the worst of days when Parcells is feeling surly and not particularly talkative, Johnson's name can start rolling tales of a golden age. Over the years, Parcells has had many players he holds in esteem, the kind who will take over practice when the coach yanks his assistants off the field and leaves in disgust.

Pepper Johnson is that player, one whose days are numbered by time and cumulative collisions, a leader who never wants to leave the battlefield—even when it's in his best interest.

These days, it's Parcells who must decide if it's in Johnson's best interest to platoon him with Dwayne Gordon in order to preserve Johnson's body and possibly lengthen his career.

James Farrior's return Monday against New England afforded the Jets the luxury of spelling Johnson, who didn't like being pulled out of the game.

Before yesterday's practice to prepare for tomorrow's game against the Atlanta Falcons at the Meadowlands, Parcells said he's pacing Johnson for the linebacker's own good, trying to keep him from "getting killed."

But Johnson, 34, who began his career with Parcells and the Giants in 1986, defended his private complaints to teammates about being taken out.

"You've (the media) followed me long enough. You know I don't ever want to be taken out of a game," Johnson said, although he refused to question Parcells' decisions. Johnson, who has fought back from left knee surgery, added, "I feel like I'm 24. I don't know if that's good or bad."

But Parcells knows Johnson doesn't play like he's 24 anymore and is simply doing what he feels is best for the team. Deep down, Johnson knows Parcells is right.

"I don't ever try to con my team," Parcells said. "I just try to get them to see things the way I see them. When you've had guys who've been with you six or seven years, they know because you've been through these situations six or seven times."

Even with the possible added motivation Johnson might feel going against Falcons and ex-Giants coach Dan Reeves, who waived Johnson just before the '93 season, Parcells will platoon his aging star. And Johnson, who said he feels he has two or three more years left in him, will have to go along with it. After all these years with Parcells—who made Johnson his first unrestricted free agent signing when he took over the Jets—Pepper Johnson will go along with his coach.

DAILY NEWS Linda Cataffo

Bill Parcells knew Pepper Johnson would play an important role on his Jets defense. But Parcells knew he'd have to use Pepper sparingly.

Parcells Is Hot Stuff in Cold Weather

In November, his teams win

By Rich Cimini

The pressure is mounting, the temperature is dipping and his team is getting stronger. That can mean only one thing: November, Bill Parcells' favorite month on the football calendar, is almost here.

The Jets' coach, who owns a 32-21 career record in November, believes now is the time to establish position for the stretch run. Evidently, he knows how to convey the message, because his teams are 12-5 in the last four Novembers.

Now here come the Jets (4-3), riding a two-game winning streak and preparing to face the battle-tested Chiefs Sunday at Arrowhead Stadium—the first day of a potential make-or-break month.

"We have to distinguish ourselves," fullback Keith Byars said yesterday. "If you want to be in the playoffs, you have to win the games now. You can't lay goose eggs and then in December you say, 'Okay, let's try to make a playoff run.' That's not a healthy situation to be in."

Two weeks ago, the Jets, reeling from a dreadful loss to the Rams, were the picture of bad health. But thanks to Vinny Testaverde, Curtis Martin and an emerging defense, they beat the Patriots and Falcons, who have a combined record of 9-5.

Now look at the Jets: After an 0-2 start, they have won four out of five. They're tied with the Patriots and Bills for second place in the AFC East, one game behind the Dolphins.

After facing the Chiefs, who fell to 4-3 with last night's loss to the Steelers, the Jets finish November with the Bills, Colts, Oilers and Panthers. Combined record: 8-20. Suddenly, things are looking bright.

Parcells, still savoring Sunday's 28-3 win over the Falcons, acknowledged the impressive turnaround but he wasn't about to let himself get too giddy.

"It showed me they're capable of doing something," he said, describing the way the Jets rebounded from the stinker in St. Louis, "but you have to show the will to sustain it."

Despite having seven starters over 30, the Jets remain an immature team, according to Parcells and several players. The immaturity surfaced before Sunday's game, as Byars and linebacker Bryan Cox sensed a lack of intensity in the locker room.

"There were a lot of glassy stares," said Byars.

Parcells continued to bemoan the lack of fire, especially among some of the younger players.

"It's always prod, prod, getting them to do stuff," he said. "You run out of energy. In the end, it never really works. You can push that sled so far, and then someone has to start pulling it."

Cox is starting to pull. The once-volatile linebacker, enjoying a rebirth with the Jets at age 30, has emerged as a voice of reason. Parcells praised him for his leadership.

"He'll talk to some of the young guys pretty quick, which is good," he said.

Then, with a half smile, Parcells added, "They need some talking to—with a board."

The Jets now face what Cox called "the biggest challenge of the year." The Chiefs will be looking to recover after ending their 11-game regular-season winning streak at Arrowhead, where the Jets haven't played since 1988.

"New England was a hostile environment because of the Parcells and Curtis Martin thing, but Kansas City may have the absolute loudest fans in the league," Cox said. "These people, they come from out of the sticks, from way out in the woods, to see the Chiefs play."

The Jets also have come out of nowhere—from 0-2 to a November that still matters. Could this turn into something special?

"Yeah, I can sense it," linebacker Mo Lewis said. "Now it has to be on a consistent basis. It can't be one of those flukes."

Tuna's Timely Lesson

By Michael James

When Bill Parcells benched free safety Kevin Williams last Sunday against Atlanta for being late to a team meeting the night before, the coach was giving his rookie a dose of the same medicine Parcells' dad gave him when he was growing up.

Parcells said his dad mandated he keep his grades up if he wanted to play football, and made good on his promise to buy Parcells a car if his son graduated from college. "I did the same thing for my three daughters," said Parcells, who rewarded each with a new automobile after their graduations. He said benching and fining Williams was a way to make the rookie more responsible.

"I thought it was a good chance for him to understand that other people are depending on him," Parcells said. "Like I told you, somebody's got to make these guys accountable. Once they learn to be accountable in this business, a lot of times that's the first step to succeeding."

Williams, who was late due to a traffic accident on the George Washington Bridge, said he learned that he needs to leave a little earlier.

"I'm usually on time for everything. That just happened to me that time," he said. "I don't look forward to being late ever again. They knew I was going to be late because I called and told somebody where I was at when I was stuck on the highway."

But Williams found few sympathetic teammates.

"There's no excuse for being late for anything, to me. This is your job," said cornerback Otis Smith, who said he's never been late for a practice, game or team meeting in his nine years in the league. "If you're stuck in traffic, hey, you should have left earlier. This is New York, you've got to know your surroundings. I don't see a reason to be late. What could be more important than your job?"

November 2, 1998

FG Makes It First & Jets

Hall's kick stuns K.C., forges 4-way tie at top

By Rich Cimini

Minutes after John Hall kicked the Jets into a four-way tie for first place in the East, Pepper Johnson stood in the middle of the locker room and punctuated the team prayer—and yesterday's 20-17 victory—with a musical tweak directed at the Chiefs.

Mimicking an Arrowhead Stadium tradition, in which the fans finish the final line of the national anthem by screaming Chiefs!, the Jets' defensive leader sang aloud. And his teammates responded on cue.

Johnson: "And the home of the . . . "

Thunderous reply: "JETS!"

The Jets had a right to be giddy. Aesthetically, their performance wasn't a K.C. Masterpiece—Curtis Martin ran 30 times for 42 yards—but they outslugged and outslogged one of the NFL's most dominating home teams.

Finally, after 59 minutes, 58 seconds of wet-and-wild drama, Hall—in the face of swirling winds and a driving rain—made a 32-yard field goal to lift the Jets to their third straight victory.

It's OK to believe now. The Jets (5-3), who have won five of their last six games, aren't a fluke. They reached the midpoint of the season atop the division, tied with the Dolphins, Patriots and Bills, who they face Sunday at Giants Stadium.

Vinny Mania vs. Flutie Magic.

"We're stacked up like club sandwiches," a rain-soaked Bill Parcells said of the AFC East.

"It doesn't get much more exciting than this," he added. "It gives the players confidence. That's what you have to do. You have to go to New England and win, and you have to come in here and win to be a really good team."

Said wide receiver Keyshawn Johnson: "Coming in this hostile environment and beating these guys, it's huge. You have to be excited."

An Exercise in Flutility

By Rich Cimini

Flutie Flakes aren't just for breakfast anymore. At the Jets' defensive meeting Saturday night at the team hotel in New Jersey, coordinator Bill Belichick delighted his players by unveiling a box of Western New York's hottest cereal.

They sampled the sugary concoction as they reviewed the game plan on how to stop the Bills' magical quarterback. Subliminal motivation?

"Somebody was saying they wanted to get the real Flutie, that they didn't want the flakes," Jets defensive back Corwin Brown said last night at Giants Stadium, recalling the snack-and-scheme session. "They wanted the real deal."

So they had him for lunch.

Belichick's ravenous defense, continuing its rapid ascent, chewed up Flutie and his merry band of miracle workers, lifting the Jets to a 34-12 victory. Flutie, replaced by Vinny Testaverde as the darling of the AFC, said it had been "a good five years since I've had to deal with one of these kind of beatings."

On this day, the diminutive quarterback was dwarfed by Testaverde, who maintained his perfect record as a starter (6-0) by throwing for 258 yards and three touchdowns.

Led by Testaverde, wide receiver Keyshawn Johnson (seven catches for 95 yards) and the cereal-killing defense, the Jets (6-3) overcame three first-half turnovers to win their fourth straight, their longest winning streak since 1993 and only the second time since 1986 they have won four in a row.

More important, the Jets, having won six out of seven, remained atop the AFC East. They're tied with the Dolphins, and one game ahead of the Bills and Patriots (both 5-4), who also lost yesterday. The Jets next face the Colts (1-8) in Indianapolis.

This is getting serious.

"The possibilities are endless," fullback Keith Byars said. "One of my goals is to get in the playoffs before Week 16. We could be the No. 1 or No. 2 seed. Hey, there's no rule written that says Denver can't go 5-3 in the second half."

Predictably, coach Bill Parcells downplayed the streak, which includes a 4-0 record in the division—the first time since 1978 they won their first four division games.

"I've been down this road before," Parcells said. "They're not sending any two dozen roses over here today. If they do, I'm sending them back."

His defense deserved a bouquet, stifling Flutie (12-for-30, 154 yards), running back Antowain Smith (37 yards) and holding the Bills to four field goals. This was the same Buffalo offense that had been averaging 27 points over a five-game winning streak.

The 36-year-old Flutie, who began the day as the highest-rated passer in the AFC, was intercepted twice (by Otis Smith and Ray Mickens) and sacked twice.

How did the Jets do it? The secondary played more man-to-man coverage than usual, the front seven did a terrific job of keeping the slippery Flutie in the pocket and reserve linebacker James Farrior was deployed at times as a "spy" in a newfangled 4-4-3 scheme.

"It wasn't easy shutting down that guy," linebacker Bryan Cox said of the 5-9 Flutie. "That little son of a buck is tough."

"Compliments to our defense," said Curtis Martin, who had another frustrating day (21 carries for 54 yards), save for a 6-yard TD run in the fourth quarter. "Usually, when you turn it over three times, you don't finish the day like we did."

Testaverde (22-for-31) was intercepted on his first pass, and Jerald Sowell, who replaced Martin for two series, lost two fumbles. But the Bills were able to convert the three turnovers into only three points.

"Our defense responded very well to quite a bit of adversity," Parcells said.

Then Testaverde took over, hitting three different receivers for touchdowns—Johnson (25 yards), Dedric Ward (36) and Wayne Chrebet (12). Johnson delivered in the clutch, with four third-down receptions and one fourth-down grab.

"The first play was a little rough, but I thought he did a terrific job," Parcells said of Testaverde, who now has 15 TD passes and only three interceptions. "Everything we asked him to do, he did well."

The passing attack offset another sluggish performance on the ground, although the Jets did manage 78 yards in the second half to milk the clock. The offensive line, meanwhile, surrendered only one sack to Bruce Smith & Co.

In the end, the Jets had their Flutie Flakes—and ate 'em, too.

"They're kind of sweet, but they tasted pretty good," Otis Smith said, grinning. Not as good as the taste of victory.

Colts' Jolt Cools Jets

Strike Pey-dirt with 24 ticks left

By Rich Cimini

Fifteen minutes after the Jets lost a game they couldn't lose, Bill Parcells stood at a podium outside the locker room, trying to explain the unexplainable. His flushed face was covered with streams of sweat, and his words were doused with venom. He took "hot and bothered" to a new level.

"This is as disappointed as I've been since I've been here," the Jets coach said after yesterday's stunning and embarrassing 24-23 loss to the previously 1-8 Colts at the RCA Dome. "It damn makes me sick."

Moments earlier, Parcells expressed the same sentiment to the team, with a postgame speech that was described by one player as "quick and violent."

This game was supposed to be quick and painless for the Jets, another win on their march toward the postseason. The Colts had lost 21 of their last 25 games, including a 44-6 defeat to the Jets in Week 3.

But this time, the Jets came in reeking of overconfidence. In the end, they just plain reeked, completing a no-show second half by allowing a 14-yard touchdown pass to Marcus Pollard with 24 seconds left and fumbling away their last chance in the final seconds.

End of four-game winning streak. End of Vinny Testaverde's undefeated run as the starting quarterback. End of the giddiness.

The Jets (6-4) dropped one game behind the first-place Dolphins in the AFC East, and they fell into a second-place tie with the Bills. The Patriots (5-5), who lost to the Bills, slid into fourth. The Jets now face the red-hot Oilers (6-4) on the road.

"It's a big blow," linebacker Mo Lewis said. "We continue to make things hard for ourselves. I thought we put these type of games behind us. It's obvious we didn't."

Said Parcells: "That's a big step back. We had a chance to put ourselves in pretty good position. Now we're back in a little bit of trouble."

It was an emotional win for the Colts, who dedicated the game to their hospitalized teammate, Craig (Ironhead) Heyward, who underwent 12 hours of brain surgery on Thursday. Afterward, the Colts chanted his name: "Iron-head! Iron-head!"

Conversely, the Jets should've been yelling "Bone-head! Bone-head!" at themselves. The mistakes were plentiful.

Fred Baxter, Keyshawn Johnson and Wayne Chrebet dropped key passes. Baxter blew a wide-open touchdown when he failed to get both feet down in the back of the end zone. Baryshnikov, he's not.

Want more ugliness? The defense tackled like jayvee players, including a blatant miss by safety Corwin Brown on a fourth-and-15 pass to Marshall Faulk—an 18-yard gain that kept alive the Colts' 15-play, 80-yard drive in crunch time.

"All we have to do is make one play, and we couldn't," Parcells said of the Colts' final drive.

More ugliness: Testaverde (12-for-28, 249 yards), in his worst game as a Jet, threw an interception, lost a fumble and was sacked four times. Not even one of the longest plays in NFL history—Aaron Glenn's 104-yard touchdown on a field-goal return—saved the Jets, who blew a 23-10 intermission lead.

"This is embarrassing for a team that considers itself a playoff contender," guard Todd Burger said.

Essentially, the Jets made only two plays—Chrebet's 63-yard, game-tying TD catch in the second quarter and Glenn's run for the ages to end the first half. The latter came on a 63-yard field goal attempt by Mike Vanderjagt. The kick was short, but Glenn went long, buzzing through the Colts' napping field-goal team.

"After a play like that, it's easy to think, It's not meant to be," said rookie QB Peyton Manning, who threw for three touchdowns and 276 yards. "But we never thought that way."

Before leaving the locker room at halftime, Parcells warned the team, "How would you feel if this team comes back to beat you?" It didn't listen, as the offense produced only 125 second-half yards against the NFL's 28th-ranked defense.

Manning took over at his 20 with 3:04 left, and, overcoming three penalties, hit eight of 13 passes for 93 yards and found Pollard, who dragged cornerback Otis Smith the final three yards into the end zone. Begin, misery.

"If we want to be a championship team, if we want to be a division winner and go to the playoffs, these are games we have to win," Kyle Brady said.

Fullback Keith Byars blamed the team for failing to heed Parcells' urgent warnings about the Colts.

"If he tells you there's cheese on the top of the mountain, you'd better bring crackers," Byars said. "He's not a crazy old man."

Except crazy with anger.

Tuna's Not off the Hook

By Rich Cimini

Contrary to a weekend television report, the Patriots haven't filed tampering charges against Bill Parcells, an NFL spokesman confirmed yesterday. But that doesn't mean the Jets coach is off the hook.

The league still is investigating a recent phone conversation between Parcells and Patriots quarterback Drew Bledsoe, the spokesman said. But the investigation was initiated by NFL commissioner Paul Tagliabue, not the Patriots, according to the league.

CBS reported Sunday that the Patriots had filed a complaint alleging that Parcells shared information about injured Patriots receiver Terry Glenn with Dolphins coach Jimmy Johnson the week of Miami's game against New England last month.

Both Parcells and Johnson denied the report.

"I have no idea what they're talking about," Johnson said yesterday. "I've got better things to do than worry about phone calls and he-said, she-said."

NFL spokesman Greg Aiello said the alleged Parcells-Johnson conversation is "not an issue as far as we're concerned." The league is focusing on the Parcells-Bledsoe talk, which occurred two days after the Jets' 24-14 win over the Patriots on Oct. 19. It could be a violation of league rules.

Parcells said he called his former quarterback as a friendly gesture, a response to Bledsoe seeking him out after the game. In their conversation, Bledsoe mentioned that Glenn was unlikely to play against the Dolphins.

League policy says any contact between members of one organization with players of another organization could potentially interfere with employer-employee relationships.

Sunday's Best

By Mike Lupica

I have never been able to see Bill Parcells coaching the Jets after January of 2000, which means after he takes them to Super Bowl XXXIV. But you have to know this as you watch him build something that will outlast him at Giants Stadium: Since Vince Lombardi there has been no one better at this kind of work. He is made for Sunday afternoons more than any of his players. He gets another today against Seattle.

Joe Torre deserves all the credit in the world for the job he has done with the Yankees. Torre started with a playoff team. Parcells was handed 1-15, and one of the most famous and lasting losing cultures in the last quarter-century of pro sports in this country.

Parcells has earned all the money Leon Hess has paid him already and will pay him down the road; he is worth all the trouble it took to get him. He is a bargain. If he made as much as the top player makes, no one would argue. He turned the Jets around in a year. It does not mean they are a lock to finish first in the AFC East. There are still holes all over the place, on both sides of the ball. They are 8-4 going for 9-4 and if they get there today, it means Parcells is 18-11 with the Jets. This is the shot their fans have waited for since Namath. Anybody still looking for reasons to take shots at Parcells has to really want to.

With it all, you don't know how long he will be around. He means it when he decides after every season if he wants to come back. He gets into the big car, pops in the doo-wop tapes, drives from Jersey to Jupiter, Fla.

Last year, my sons and I went over and watched the New Year's Day football games with him. When the Cotton Bowl was on, he said, "You know what this is?"

What?

"A day off," he said. He looked as if he needed a month of them, as if the whole season, one that had ended with that bad loss to the Lions, was still sitting right there on his chest.

Enjoy these Sundays. Parcells has brought his gift for Sundays, for shaping a team and inspiring its players, making them all better, back to Giants Stadium where it belongs and where he belongs. Enjoy the run, for as long as it lasts, whether it ends at a Super Bowl or not.

Tuna Can't Hide from Spotlight

By Filip Bondy

Why do they go and put his unfashionable mug on the cover of magazines? Why do they stick the sideline cameras in his face?

Like Garbo, like Salinger, like any genius at work, he only wants to be alone. Give Bill Parcells his personal space. Is that too much to ask?

"I use profanity on the sidelines," Parcells was saying yesterday at Hofstra, a plaintive cry to the network paparazzi. "I'm portrayed in a profane, aggressive way. People make judgments. They read your lips.

"I'm ashamed of some things I say. But that's not me at home. I don't use that language. I never did it when I was raising my daughters—though there were times when I probably should have."

The cameras create a distorted image. The mikes take the words out of context. We are not seeing the real Parcells, Parcells keeps saying. And even if we are, it's none of our business. Focus on the field. The players are more important than the coaches.

Sunday in Miami is more than the Parcellulites versus the Jimmys. "It isn't about Bill Parcells and Jimmy Johnson," Parcells said.

That is the theory. But the more he talks, the more that Parcells grumps and moans and wins, the more news he makes and the less his players seem to matter. If these particular guys in green weren't around, then surely some others would take their place.

And they would win, too. They would better win.

"He can have all the attention he wants," Jumbo Elliott said yesterday about his coach. "I don't think we really worry about who symbolizes the Jets. We just know the preparation is here, the coaching staff knows what it's doing, and the guys will work hard."

Nobody worries, yet everybody knows. Parcells is the Jets. He is the SST, the 747, the flying Tuna. Not Vinny Testaverde. Not Keyshawn Johnson. Not

Wayne Chrebet. Not the cast of faceless heroes who make the tackle, then endure the coach's grimaces and scoldings.

Yes, he talked to *Sports Illustrated*. Yes, he posed for the photo. He asked to be inside SI, though, not outside. Somebody promised him.

Then he was betrayed, again.

"I'm not surprised," Parcells said. "Every time I expect more, I'm disappointed.

"It can be an advantage in that it takes the pressure off the players," Parcells said about the publicity. "It can be a disadvantage, because you're scrutinized more than you should be."

He doesn't seek the headlines, he says. He doesn't read them. And then, there they are again. The news finds Parcells like a Scotland Yard bloodhound. He is escaping New England, at war with the Patriots' owner. He is going head to head with his quarterback, Neil O'Donnell. He is chatting on the phone with Drew Bledsoe. He is taking game-day gambles, every week, that don't just beg debate.

They demand it.

We can't stop watching Parcells, or the scrunching, sneering mouth. If we look closely enough, we can almost make out the pea under his mattress, the one that is torturing him at any given moment.

We listen, too. Parcells happens to speak English instead of footballese. When reporters carry a self-important statistic to his throne, he tosses the offering back in their faces. Sacks? Don't matter. He'd rather have consistent pressure on the quarterback. Total rushing yards? Deceptive, because a single long gainer often disguises game-long futility.

"You tell me numbers I don't even know about most of the time," Parcells said. "They get so distorted. I just look at my team. I use my eyes. Sometimes there's no sacks, but my quarterback is close to getting killed. What most people think is irrelevant to what I think."

Right now, he is on the brink of something special, maybe the Jets' first division title in 30 seasons. We would never know. He says such an achievement is meaningless unless he gets a No. 2 playoff seeding. If he can avoid a wild-card game, that would be nice.

"That's a 33% advantage in the playoffs, one less game to win," he said. "Otherwise, it's pretty much the same." Did he just use a number? News, again.

"There's no less pressure," Elliott said about the way Parcells deflects, attracts, siphons publicity. "With him, there's always more pressure."

On Sunday, Parcells will scream more profanities, take more gambles, make more headlines. His sideline is not for the squeamish.

Jets Call Him Jolly St. Tuna

By Michael James

Forget what you hear about big, bad Bill Parcells. In the week leading up to the most important game of the season for the Jets thus far— tomorrow night's showdown against Miami for sole possession of the AFC East lead, a locked-up playoff spot and possibly a division title—it was learned Parcells went a little soft on his crew. All this week he had them practice without pads.

Surely no true hard-driving, win-at-all-costs, drag-the-injured-to-the-sidelines madman head coach would dare put away the whip with so much on the line. But Parcells, who has a reputation for driving his horses harder at the end of a season, admitted going light to get ready for the Dolphins.

The Jets' field commander said he did it for a reason.

"I haven't pushed them hard this week," said Parcells, who had worked the team in pads Wednesday, Thursday and Friday each of the last three weeks and got three wins.

"I'm trying to refresh them physically . . . I'm trying to get my team to the best energy level phase they can be in . . . I'm just trying to get everybody the best they can feel for this game. Emotionally, we're going to be ready to play. If they're not, there's nothing I could've done about it anyway, with what's on the line."

According to Parcells, by practicing at full speed without pads, they get more repetitions in at practice. On a typical Wednesday, the Jets run 46-48 plays. Without pads they go in the high 50s, he said. Over the course of a week, that means 30 extra plays. It also means the group should have fewer nicks and be fresher for the game.

Linebacker Bryan Cox, whom Parcells presented with a gift of a gas can (half-filled with water)—suggesting the fiery ex-Dolphin was running out of gas—said the move was personally beneficial.

"I certainly feel a lot fresher," said Cox, who added he'll treasure his container and accompanying note:

"To Bryan Cox. From Bill Parcells. Merry Christmas."

"I'm going to keep that forever," Cox said. "I knew who it was from right away. It's getting late in the season and he wanted to know how my gas can was doing."

Gifts. Light workouts. Bill Parcells? Doesn't seem to quite fit in the same sentence. But maybe these are hints that Parcells knows he's got something special going on with these here Jets. Maybe he really, gasp, believes in them.

At any rate, Parcells' kind gestures are a hit with the team. Wide receiver Keyshawn Johnson, however, said he wouldn't have minded going full-out with the combat gear this week.

"I'm always ready to go without pads, but because I like to play the game, it doesn't affect me one way or the other," Johnson said. "I like to play."

Johnson even said he wasn't sure the Jets gained an advantage by staying out of pads this week.

"I don't think we're looking for an edge, we're just looking to freshen our minds up, our bodies a little bit because there's been a tough road in the past," he said. "This kind of just freshens us up a little bit mentally and physically."

The way Bill Parcells seems to be softening up, should the Jets emerge victorious tomorrow night, the big guy may just let them stay in the land of sun and fun for the rest of the week.

But they shouldn't count on it.

You'd have to be living in exile not to know the Jets will be playing their biggest game in a long while when they take on the Miami Dolphins tomorrow night at Pro Player Stadium in Miami.

Jets Hook the Big Fish

Clinch playoff spot, alone in first in East

By Rich Cimini

In a long-ago fairy tale, the Jets came to this city and won a game that changed the landscape of professional football. They won another big game here last night—not nearly as significant as Super Bowl III—but a victory that elevated the Jets to a status they have achieved only six times since that magical day in 1969.

The Jets are going to the playoffs. The Same Old Jets are dead.

Only two years removed from the humiliation of a 1-15 record, the Jets secured a postseason berth and moved into sole possession of first place in the AFC East with a high-voltage, 21-16 victory over the Dolphins at Pro Player Stadium.

With their fourth straight win, the Jets (10-4) moved within one victory of clinching their first divisional title since the NFL-AFL merger in 1970. They can lock it up Saturday, when they face the Bills at Rich Stadium.

Afterward, the players in the Jets' locker room, still energized from a frantic fourth quarter in which they won a staredown with the incomparable Dan Marino, talked of bigger goals.

"The party has just begun," Keyshawn Johnson said.

Mo Lewis, the longest-tenured Jet, said: "I'm happy it happened, but for all the years of going home early, I want more. I'm not satisfied. . . . I want the Super Bowl."

Indeed, Bill Parcells, who will become the third coach in history to take three different teams to the playoffs, congratulated the team on making "the show." But in his next breath, he told the players, "Don't be satisfied."

The Jets could wind up with the No. 2 seed in the AFC playoffs. They're tied with the Jaguars but own the tiebreaker advantage.

"I feel good about it," Parcells said of the team's dramatic turnaround. "It's one of the reasons why I'm in coaching. I enjoy that. It's very satisfying."

Bill Parcells betrayed his tough image by giving his players a light week. It worked, as they defeated Jimmy Johnson's Miami Dolphins, 21-16.

The Jets, in the playoffs for the first time since 1991—a wild-card berth captured on this very field—scratched their seven-year itch with an inspired performance. They hit Marino like never before, sacking him five times—the most in 28 games against the Miami quarterback. Fittingly, it was a defensive play that secured the win.

With under two minutes to play and the ball in the magical hands of Marino, defensive tackle Ernie Logan sacked him and stripped the ball. It was scooped up and returned 23 yards for a touchdown by linebacker Chad Cascadden with 1:51 left.

"I was running scared, but I put some coal in the furnace and picked up steam," said Cascadden, barely able to restrain his excitement.

Cascadden's play punctuated a wild final quarter in which the Jets almost squandered the game with three huge mistakes:

Vinny Testaverde threw an end-zone interception, which was returned 61 yards by Terrell Buckley to set up Marino's 3-yard touchdown pass to O.J. McDuffie. That made it 14-10 with 6:25 to play. Testaverde (17-for-29, 232 yards, one touchdown) made "a really bad throw" to Johnson, Parcells said.

On the ensuing kickoff, the Jets fell asleep, and the Dolphins recovered an onside kick. Fortunately for the Jets, they escaped without any damage.

With 2:25 left, Curtis Martin fumbled and the Dolphins took over at their 30.

"When that happened, I thought we were in trouble," Parcells said.

But the Jets, continuing to swarm Marino (30-for-57, 321 yards, one interception), mugged him on the second play. No Marino miracle. Not this time. The Dolphins scored with three seconds on a 1-yard run by Stanley Pritchett, but the ensuing kickoff was handled by the Jets. Game over.

"I'm extremely upset and frustrated with the fact that we're playing at home and we should have won this game," said Marino, who was held to only two TD passes in two games against the Jets.

The Jets won the war of the league's stingiest defenses, befuddling Marino with an array of blitzes and disguised coverages. In the not-so-old days, the Jets wilted at the sight of Marino.

The Dolphins' vaunted defense had allowed only 40 points in its six previous home games, but the Jets struck with a 12-yard touchdown pass to Wayne Chrebet (five catches for 105 yards) and a 9-yard touchdown run by Martin (70 yards on 19 carries).

"For some reason, I'm not happy with this," Chrebet said of the win. "I want to try to get a good seed, but I'm happy to be in the show."

Said Otis Smith: "This puts us in the upper, elite class, as opposed to everybody looking down on us. We'll get a lot of respect now."

Tuna's Tears for a Crown

By Filip Bondy

B obby Hamilton and Wayne Chrebet poured a bucket of ice water over Bill Parcells, but still nobody woke up from the dream at Ralph C. Wilson Stadium. The NFL's best coach, the man who performs magical turnarounds with a system and a sneer, was smiling and hugging people along the sideline. Parcells, just a Christmas teddy bear after all, lumbered up the rampway back to his locker room.

Parcells walked past Bryan Cox, who greeted each teammate with a chest bump. Everybody was roaring. "Thank you, Jesus," screamed Mo Lewis, who had endured too many bad seasons in green. Cox wanted to bump chests with Parcells, too, but the coach looked too tired for that, now.

Parcells kept walking, tapped a couple of assistants on the back near the locker room door. Then he walked inside and waited for his team to enter, champions of the AFC East. Champions of something, of anything, for the first time in 29 years. Richard Nixon hadn't heard of the Watergate Hotel when this sort of thing last happened.

"You hear same old Jets, same old Jets," Parcells told his players behind the closed door, choking up trying to get the words out, going speechless for long seconds, even minutes. "Well, now you're the champs and nobody can take that away from you. You have a responsibility to keep playing that way."

Another tight victory yesterday, 17-10 over the Bills, their third escape in a row. Same new Jets. Parcells' Jets.

"Our guys, they just try hard for me all the time," Parcells said. "They're not the greatest team. But mentally, they're really tough now. I'm proud and happy.

"It's pretty emotional for me today," Parcells said. "I can't even recount much of this game."

The game he couldn't recall wasn't all that memorable, really, except for a big, 71-yard touchdown pass from Vinny Testaverde to Dedric Ward in the third quarter and another uncanny job of containment by the defense. The Impeachment Bowl was a game filled with mistakes, more by the Bills than by the Jets. It was marred by yet more questionable officiating, by gusty winds that warped passes and curled kicks.

The story wasn't the game, though, or how Bill Belichick owns Doug Flutie. The story was the season. It was the whole, amazing 11-4 season.

Parcells had told the players this could happen when he came stomping into Hempstead, L.I., in the summer of 1997. The younger guys believed him then. A few of the veterans surely had doubts. It had been so long, and too many coaches had tried too many things.

Still, they listened. They tried. "I figured it would come," said Kyle Brady, one of the converts. "There was a lot of talent and it was just a matter of the right organization. But I don't think anyone expected it would come this fast."

Not two years. Not two years from 1-15 to a title, and probably to a bye in the first round of the playoffs.

"Chumps to champs," said Keyshawn Johnson, already wearing an AFC East champions cap. "We all endured a lot around here."

They had, until they found their savior, their organizer. Parcells had led them from the darkness, as promised. Then, taken aback by his own success, Parcells finally found himself humbled yesterday before his own feat.

Maybe he hadn't been so sure of himself, after all. "It was the first time he was at a loss for words, the first time we'd ever seen that," Cox said.

"Bill broke down on us," Chrebet said, disbelieving.

In the locker room, Parcells had lost his bellow. The players filled in the blanks. They laughed. They cheered.

Soon, he would pull himself together, making plans. The coach was tying up the loose ends.

Parcells wanted to make sure of a few things. The players would get two days off, a reward. He would set up a conference call with reporters. The game ball would go to Leon Hess. Definitely, to Hess.

"When we were 0-and-2 this year, I didn't know if we'd ever win a game," Parcells said. "There's still a lot to do. I don't think we're done."

The players felt the same way. They'd won the game yesterday that Republicans tried to keep you from watching. They could keep winning, until the next Congress meets.

By then, Parcells should have his voice back.

Passing or Chasing, It's His Day of Vin-dication

By Mike Lupica

When it was over, when he was finally in the AFC championship game, Vinny Testaverde ran underneath the goal posts with the game ball under his right arm, ran through the green-and-white confetti that came from the upper deck at Giants Stadium and underneath the sign that read "www.newyorkjets.com." This was more than a Web site, of course. This was Testaverde's dream, a huge chunk of it anyway, Giants Stadium looking this way, the day sounding this way, the Jets on their way to Denver, their shot at the Broncos with a Super Bowl on the line. Vinny, who grew up with Namath's picture on the wall in Elmont, finally gets Namath's kind of action, against the odds the rest of the way.

"You know, I was sitting with Vinny the other day and I said, 'Hey, if we win, this is as close as you've ever been, isn't it?'" David Meggett was saying after the Jets beat the Jaguars, 34-24, yesterday. "And he looks at me and he says, 'Yeah it is.'"

Meggett, who has won a Super Bowl with Bill Parcells' Giants and played in another with Parcells' Pats, smiled now.

"I said, 'Vinny, how does it feel?' And he said, 'Dave, it feels goooood.'"

Once you get past the coach, the quarterback is the star of this Jets team the way Namath was the star of the team. Vinny Testaverde was not the only star against the Jaguars. Namath wasn't the only star in '69. He had Matt Snell to run and Don Maynard and George Sauer to catch the ball. Curtis Martin gained 124 yards yesterday and scored a touchdown and Keyshawn Johnson caught nine balls for 121 yards and scored two touchdowns, one of them on a reverse. At the end, Parcells had Keyshawn on the field when Jacksonville's Mark Brunell threw a desperation pass, and Johnson even got himself an interception.

If he is anywhere between the tunnels, the ball will find Johnson, the way the spotlight finds him, and microphones always find his great big mouth.

Touchdown reception for Keyshawn yesterday. Rushing touchdown on an end-around. Fumble recovery after a Jets fumble. Interception. There hasn't been a performance like this since before two-platoon football.

The Jets made their mistakes, for sure, in a game they should have won by four touchdowns and if they make mistakes like this against the Broncos they will lose by four touchdowns. Martin dropped the ball. Testaverde threw an interception in the fourth quarter that gave the Jaguars their last chance. The Jets let Brunell throw a touchdown bomb on the last play of the first half, when the game should have been over already. And they nearly gave up a touchdown to Reggie Barlow on a kickoff return.

The game should have been over at 17-0 for the Jets and 24-7 for the Jets and 31-14 for the Jets and never was, no matter how many amazingly stupid plays the Jaguars made. But every time the Jaguars would come back, either Testaverde would make another third-down throw or Martin would make a big run or Johnson would do something, and the Jets would still have enough room, on their way to Mile High Stadium and a fight with the champ.

And the crowd at Giants Stadium, the biggest sports crowd in the history of the place—only the Pope can outdraw Parcells in Jersey—would rock the place a little more, making it rumble like an elevated subway platform. Then everybody would get up for one more standing ovation, on an afternoon when it seemed there were a hundred of those, on the afternoon when the Jets made it back to their sport's final four for the first time in 16 years.

"The crowd got going pretty good, didn't it?" Parcells said on the way to his office. He had heard Giants Stadium get going this way for his Giants, never for the Jets.

On the other side of the room, Testaverde was asked if he was surprised the way everything has worked out for him since he came home to the Jets, after all the years when his career ran into dead ends, in Tampa and Cleveland and Baltimore, when he never got to make the kind of run out of Sunday afternoon he made yesterday.

"I'm not surprised," he said, after 24-of-36 passing and 284 yards. "And I'm excited. But I'm not satisfied. Not yet."

Tuna's Rocky Mountain Low

Looks back on career as Broncos tailgater

By Rich Cimini

When Bill Parcells walks on the field Sunday at Mile High Stadium, he can revisit perhaps the most unusual chapter in his career. All he has to do is look up at the end-zone seats at the open end of the stadium, and he will see where he spent eight Sundays in the fall of 1979.

Bill Parcells, Broncos season-ticket holder. Can you picture that?

Two decades ago, long before anyone in New York knew his name, Parcells spent two years in Colorado—one as the head coach at Air Force, the other as an unemployed coach/businessman who didn't know which direction his career was headed.

Now he's coming back as a two-time Super Bowl champion, looking to beat the Broncos in his quest for a third ring. How's that for symmetry?

"At that point in time, it was different for me because I was trying to decide what I was going to do for the future," the Jets' coach said this week, recalling his Colorado experience. "I was in business there. I met some friends there. I liked Colorado, living there. But, you know, I still had a pretty strong feeling for coaching."

It drove him crazy, being away from football. To support his family, he worked as a real-estate salesman at the Country Club of Colorado, making $45,000 a year. He also served as recreation coordinator at the club, organizing swimming and tennis programs for the members and their children.

Not an easy thing to envision, is it?

"I was Julie from 'The Love Boat,' only bigger," Parcells says in his autobiography, *Parcells: The Biggest Giant of Them All.*

After a 3-8 season with Air Force, Parcells resigned to become the linebackers coach with the Giants. Ray Perkins was the head coach. Shortly after accepting the job, Parcells quit because his family was reluctant to leave Colorado Springs.

So he returned to Colorado, became a 9-to-5 family man and bought season tickets to the Broncos.

"They had a great team, guys like Craig Morton, Haven Moses, Tom Jackson and Randy Gradishar," said Parcells, who tailgated before the games and sat with his wife, Judy.

Was it torture to be so close to football, yet so far?

"You get acclimated, so I wasn't really worried about that too much," Parcells said. "I was just enjoying what I was seeing—studiously."

But in his book, Parcells paints a different picture, saying he was miserable away from the sidelines. Every time he went to Mile High, he would "die a little more."

Parcells stayed close to football by announcing high-school games on KRDO radio in Colorado Springs. His salary: $25 per game. His play-by-play man, Jeff Thomas, could tell Parcells was hurting.

"We'd go to the games together, and he was always very quiet in the car," Thomas said yesterday. "Once we got to the game, I could see the sparkle in his eye and the life in his face."

On one particular day, Parcells, staring out the car window on the drive to a game, lamented the opportunity he missed by walking away from the Giants, the team he rooted for as a kid in New Jersey. According to Thomas, who remembers it vividly, Parcells said: "Who knows, one day I might have been the head coach of the Giants." Who knew?

Parcells, with the blessing of his family, returned to coaching the following year as an assistant with the Patriots. But on those days at Mile High, he was facing the unknown.

"You never know when you're going to get another opportunity," he said. "But it turned out OK."

Super-stition Fills This Bill

By Rich Cimini

J ets coach Bill Parcells wasn't happy last month when he appeared on the cover of *Sports Illustrated*. Parcells insisted that his feelings had nothing to do with the so-called *Sports Illustrated* cover jinx, but that's exactly why he made such a stink about it, according to people close to the coach.

You see, Parcells is extremely superstitious. Here's a rundown of his superstitious and quirky habits over the years:

- Earlier this season, Parcells visited his dentist every Tuesday morning during a winning streak. He continued to go even when the dental work had been completed. When the Jets lost to the Colts, he stopped going. Wonder how the insurance company handled that one?
- In his office, Parcells has a display of elephant figurines. The trunks absolutely must point toward the ceiling—for good luck, you understand.
- He never wears a hat during games.
- He rides in the cockpit on team charter flights.
- He asks friends to call him at the exact same time every week if the team is on a winning streak. One longtime friend calls him every Tuesday at 8 a.m.
- Before leaving for Super Bowl XXV in Tampa, Parcells demanded the same airplane and same pilot that flew the Giants to Super Bowl XXI four years earlier. One problem: The pilot had retired.

Parcells insisted, so the pilot came out of retirement, which meant he had to be re-certified. If the Jets beat the Broncos, that same pilot may have another assignment.

Jets Find Positives in Defeat

By Rich Cimini

It was the second-biggest defeat of Bill Parcells' career—next to the Patriots' loss in Super Bowl XXXI, of course—but there were traces of pride shining through his disappointment.

"It's always disappointing, but not one person in this whole arena thought we could be doing what we did today," the Jets coach said after the 23-10 loss to the Broncos yesterday in the AFC championship game at Mile High Stadium.

Two years ago, on this very field, the Jets began a 1-15 season with a 25-point loss to the Broncos.

Out went Rich Kotite, and in came Parcells.

The Jets improved to 9-7 in 1997, falling short of the playoffs, and they followed that with a 13-5 record this season and a trip to the AFC title game.

"This wasn't baby steps," Parcells said, referring to the Jets' dramatic climb this season.

"This was a quantum leap for this team, about as far as you can jump.

"You can compare that with any team in history over a two-year period. I'm not saying that from an egotistical standpoint, but from an accomplishment standpoint on the players' part."

Days from now, maybe weeks, the Jets will appreciate what they accomplished this season, which came unraveled in a six-turnover performance against the defending Super Bowl champions.

Parcells, hurt by the loss but hardly disconsolate, addressed the team after the game.

"I told them that I was proud of a lot of things they accomplished this year," said Parcells, who lost his first conference-title game in four tries. "I thought they did a good job in many areas."

Indeed, the Jets captured their first division title since 1969, and they set a team record for most wins in a season. They reached the title game for the first time since the 1982 season.

Not many players wanted to dwell on the positives, not after blowing a 10-point lead in the third quarter, but there were a couple of rose-colored views.

"It's not demoralizing," said safety Victor Green, who was beaten on Ed McCaffrey's 47-yard, game-turning reception in the third quarter. "Things happen. We had a great season. A lot of people didn't think we'd get this far. It was fun while it lasted."

Linebacker Mo Lewis, one of the survivors of the 1-15 disaster, said: "We came a long way, but it's not a good feeling to lose."

Others took the bottom-line view.

"We're still trying to get to the big game, and that's all that matters," cornerback Otis Smith said.

Said guard Todd Burger: "Maybe in a week or so I'll say, 'Hey, we had a great season.' Right now, I feel miserable."

DAILY NEWS Linda Cataffo

Bill Parcells and Bill Belichick (right) look on as the Jets fall,
23-10, to the Denver Broncos in the AFC championship game.

CHAPTER 13

ONE
LAST
SEASON

With free agents like Steve Atwater on board, Parcells raised speculation that he was making one final push for a fourth Super Bowl.

*I*n just two seasons, Bill Parcells had taken the Jets from 1-15 to the AFC championship game—and just one half of a football game away from going to the Super Bowl. The Jets' resurgence surprised some, but now the Jets wouldn't surprise anyone, as they had become the favorites in the AFC.

As teams geared up for the last season of the century, Parcells picked up a few key free agents, kept his coaching staff together, and made it look like he had all the pieces in place to win the whole thing. That would secure his place in history as not only the first coach to take three different teams to the Super Bowl, but also the first to win the Super Bowl with two different teams.

But one unfortunate step exposed the Jets' Achilles' heel.

Tuna Already Back in Swim

Looks at next step as upstream battle

By Rich Cimini

Life after Bill Parcells won't begin for at least another year. The Jets' coach, still lamenting Sunday's loss to the Broncos but already plotting for the off-season, doused speculation about his future yesterday by declaring that he will return for the 1999 season.

"Oh, yeah, my intention is to coach next year," Parcells said 24 hours after losing the AFC championship game, 23-10, in Denver. "I know in my heart what I'm going to do, and I'm going to make every effort to be back here, doing a good job.

"I want to try to do this," he continued. "I like the players. I like this team. I like coaching this team. I do. It's not an easy job, but I like it."

The 57-year-old Parcells, who inherited a 1-15 team two years ago and led it to the brink of Super Bowl XXXIII, claimed he would have returned even if the Jets had gone all the way. But he admitted he was "very tired" from the 18-game season. The last six weeks were especially draining, he said.

But Parcells' competitive fire still seemed to be burning, even as he sat before the media, running down his lengthy off-season agenda.

"I told the players I won't rest," said Parcells, who addressed the team in the morning and spoke individually with the potential free agents. "My whole idea is to try to improve this team each year. We'll see what we can do to do that."

Parcells reached the Super Bowl in his first two incarnations, with the Giants and Patriots, and he came agonizingly close on Sunday, holding a 10-0 lead with 27 minutes of football left. But the Jets, who committed six turnovers, suffered a third-quarter meltdown against the defending Super Bowl champions.

As the clock wound down, Parcells already was starting to think of the off-season and the task of trying to build another championship-caliber team.

There was a sense of déjà vu. He said the circumstances reminded him of the Giants' 21-0 loss to the famed '85 Bears in the NFC semifinals at wind-swept Soldier Field.

"I felt exactly the same way," Parcells said. "It was the same kind of setting, the same kind of game, the same kind of opportunities for our team. A couple of freak things happened, too."

On the flight home from the Chicago loss, a disconsolate Parcells received a biting piece of advice from his mentor, Mickey Corcoran, who said: "You gotta find a way to beat those guys." That remark made an impact on Parcells, who won the Super Bowl the following year.

Thirteen years later, the mission is the same: The Jets must find a way to beat the Broncos, the two-time AFC champs. The Jets' roster is in good shape, with 18 of 22 starters under contract, but they still have seven or eight needs, according to Parcells.

Still, the Jets (13-5) had the Broncos on the ropes.

"We were probably one more play from separating to 17-0, and then the whole game changes," Parcells said. "The pressure totally falls to Denver."

Didn't happen. The Jets, with big mistakes by playoff-tested veterans such as Curtis Martin, Keith Byars and David Meggett, cracked. There also was the game-turning defensive lapse by safety Victor Green on Ed McCaffrey's 47-yard catch.

Parcells vowed to keep plugging. He recalled his messy departure from the Patriots, saying it was "the saddest thing" to leave that team with so much promising young talent. And that was coming off an AFC title, no less.

"I'm not going to do that here without giving it my best shot," Parcells said. "Last year I gave it my best, this year I gave it my best and next year I'll give it my best shot."

Jets' Signs Say Tuna to Can It

By Gary Myers

Bill Parcells always says he decides his coaching future year-to-year. Judging by his free-agent personnel moves and the way he maneuvered to keep his staff intact in January, this could be the year.

Is Parcells loading up for one last run for the Super Bowl? There's plenty of circumstantial evidence—and when you add it all up, it strongly suggests he's going for it now and getting out after the '99 season.

The Jets came within a game of the Super Bowl two months ago—they should have beaten Denver—and if John Elway announces his retirement, then the Jets immediately become the AFC favorites to get to Atlanta in January.

Here's why this season could be Parcells' last, regardless if he gets another ring:

He was tired after the Jets' surprising run. It was the hardest he's coached in over a decade and it wiped him out. He got a doctor's note to excuse him from going to the Pro Bowl. "I know for a fact he was fatigued," one NFL source said. "Coupled with the fact Dan Reeves just had his deal (heart surgery), it spooked the hell out of him. That was his life revisited. He was genuinely tired."

Parcells will be 58 by the time the season opens and summers at Saratoga may start to look pretty good.

In January, three things happened with the Jets coaching staff that indicated a desire to keep them together for one last run. Bill Belichick, who has been promised he will succeed Parcells, interviewed a year ago for the Raiders job, but this year turned down the opportunity to interview in Chicago and Kansas City. His reluctance to leave could mean his elevation to Jets head coach is imminent—meaning after this season.

Browns coach Chris Palmer wanted to hire Jets DL coach Romeo Crennel as his defensive coordinator. A nice promotion. But Palmer, who worked for Parcells in New England and received a strong recommendation from Parcells that helped him get the Cleveland job, never offered the job. Why? Sources say after Parcells helped him get him the job, Palmer wasn't about to turn around and raid his staff.

Panthers coach George Seifert has no such loyalty to Parcells, but was blocked from hiring Jets LB coach Al Groh as his defensive coordinator because Parcells slapped the supervisor's tag on Groh, preventing a move. If Parcells was going to be here for more than a season, you would think he would have helped a couple of loyal assistants, with no immediate opportunity to advance on his staff, get well-deserved promotions with other clubs.

The Jets upgraded with their free-agent signings, but most are short-term moves with backloaded contracts, meaning serious salary cap ramifications down the road, when Parcells could be gone. Instead of developing Scott Frost at their troubled free safety spot, Parcells signed Steve Atwater, 32, at the tail end of his career. Roman Phifer is a tackling machine at weakside linebacker, but he's 31, and it probably means the end for James Farrior, who was Parcells' No. 1 pick just two years ago. Tight end Eric Green is an excellent blocker and a more accomplished receiver than Kyle Brady, who signed with Jacksonville, but at nearly 32, he's five years older, and his injury history suggests this is a short-term move, too. And Parcells made sure he got Tom Tupa by giving him $1.8 million to sign, a record for a punter, although he could wind up as the No. 2 QB if Glenn Foley is traded or cut.

Is Parcells gone after this year? Add it all up and it sure looks that way.

Parcells Makes One More Run

By Rich Cimini

When the Jets check into their Hofstra dorms Thursday for the start of training camp, there will inevitably be a widespread sense of déjà vu. For many players, even some coaches, it'll feel like the start of senior year in college.

Remember those emotions? You're gung-ho, prepared to have the time of your life, but you have no idea what lies beyond graduation. So much promise, yet so much uncertainty.

Welcome to the post-Hess era.

Next year, the Jets will be under new ownership, coach Bill Parcells probably will be summering in Saratoga and defensive coordinator/heir apparent Bill Belichick could be coaching elsewhere.

Change is coming; the players can sense it.

Parcells, who turns 58 next month, was near exhaustion after last season's dramatic playoff run. That concerned him. Another factor could be the ownership situation. Parcells, who was treated like a king by the beloved Hess, may not want to work for another owner.

If this is the last hurrah, the ultimate finish would be a trip to Super Bowl XXXIV in Atlanta, giving Parcells the chance to go out on top, à la Elway.

Las Vegas oddsmakers list the Jets as the AFC favorites, slightly ahead of the two-time Super Bowl champion Broncos. Mention this to Parcells, and he looks like he just tasted a bad clam.

"It's all B.S.," he said of the preseason expectations.

Unlike some of his counterparts, Parcells has no use for rose-colored glasses. The most he allows is, "I'm looking forward to the season very much."

Parcells' battery is recharged, thanks to a long vacation and an off-season workout program. He couldn't remember the last time he lifted weights—the last thing he hoisted was the Lombardi Trophy after the Giants' Super Bowl win in 1991—but there he was, pumping iron with his players.

There was concern about Parcells' health after last season, which taxed him physically and mentally. Now, according to friends, he seems reborn, even looking forward to the grind of training camp.

"You just can't help but anticipate it when you've been doing it this long," said Parcells, preparing for his 17th NFL camp. "I don't say, 'Oh, gee, I have all this work in front of me.' I've never, ever had that feeling.

"There are times during the season when you say, 'Jeez, just give me a break for 48 hours.' But I enjoy (camp). This sounds corny, but I like being outside in the summer."

If Parcells seems relaxed, it could be because he doesn't have to worry about the season being disrupted by the sale of the team. The club has been on the market for two months, but those running Hess' estate, perhaps in deference to Parcells, are moving at a glacial pace.

The Jets haven't faced expectations this high since 1983, the year after they lost to the Dolphins in the muddy AFC championship game. They under-achieved in '83, falling to 7-9 under rookie coach Joe Walton.

Now, perhaps, they can take the last step, giving Parcells a chance to write an Elway-like ending to his magnificent career.

"I sure hope so, because we can both get something out of it," cornerback Aaron Glenn said, smiling. "I'd get a Super Bowl ring and he'd get to retire with one."

Let the last fling begin.

Super Expectations

By Rich Cimini

The most eagerly awaited season in Jets history starts today with Tuna Bowl V. If it lives up to the hype, the season will end four months from now with another Roman-numeral game.

Amazing, huh? Three years ago, the Jets won a game. Now they're talking about winning *the* game. The defending AFC East champions, supremely confident after last season's Super Bowl flirtation, intend to be a Y2K bug for the rest of the AFC.

"I expect big things from this team; everybody does," safety Victor Green said. "We got stuck last year in the championship game—came up a little short —but at least we know what it takes to get there. Now we're going to try to make that run for the Super Bowl."

What better way to get it started than a game against their blood rival, the Patriots? That it is being played at Giants Stadium—the Jets' first season opener at home since 1993, and only the 10th in their 40-year history—should create enough electricity to light the top of the Empire State Building.

Even Bill Parcells, 58, beginning his 15th and probably final season as a head coach, suspected he will have a case of pregame butterflies. And, no, not because he's facing his former team and an old boss who fought him in divorce court. "It's the time of year where there's always a lot of apprehension," said Parcells, who, coincidentally, is reading a book about worrying. "We're not in ideal condition. We had a couple of things we had to adjust to very late in the preseason, so that's a little worrisome."

He was referring, of course, to the Wayne Chrebet injury, a blow to the Jets' high-powered offense. His replacement, Dedric Ward, is quicker than a thought, but he has very little experience in two-receiver sets. In fact, 48 of his 49 career catches have come with three receivers on the field, the Jets' most popular formation last season.

"I'm confident he can do it," Parcells said, "but I'm not certain he can." The Jets' coaching staff is very good at making adjustments, and they should be able to devise a few wrinkles to exploit Ward's strengths. Don't forget, the Jets still have Johnson, quarterback Vinny Testaverde and running back Curtis Martin, each coming off a Pro Bowl season. The offense includes two newcomers, both potential impact players—athletic right guard Randy Thomas, the first rookie guard to start a Jets opener since Randy Rasmussen in 1967, and tight end Eric Green, who has wide-receiver hands and offensive-tackle blocking power. Unfortunately, he also has middle-aged knees. Defensively, the Jets will open in a 3-4 scheme, attacking with waves of linebackers. Their most prominent newcomer, 32-year-old safety Steve Atwater, will be tested immediately by the Patriots' explosive passing attack, featuring quarterback Drew Bledsoe and his cadre of receivers.

As far as the Jets are concerned, this is the start of something special. How special?

"It's going to be difficult—everybody will be after us—but if we play together," Victor Green said, "I think we can make it."

To the big game in January, he meant. Bigger than any Tuna Bowl.

DAILY NEWS Mike Albans

With the sale of the Jets moving slowly, Bill Parcells had carte blanche to try and take the Jets to the Super Bowl.

Vinny, Jets Down and Out

Testaverde out for season

By Rich Cimini

The most animated reaction came from Keyshawn Johnson, who was so exasperated after yesterday's season-opening and season-turning loss to the Patriots that he slammed his fists on the podium and bolted the interview room at Giants Stadium.

On the other side of the Jets' somber locker room, Curtis Martin offered a calmer, yet no less powerful response to Vinny Testaverde's devastating Achilles injury.

"It was one of those days," the always-philosophical Martin said, "where you want to look to the sky—and I found myself doing it—and ask, 'Why?'"

Why Testaverde? Why this season?

The Jets strutted into 1999 and Tuna Bowl V with Super Bowl dreams, and no player symbolized the hope more than Testaverde. Less than one hour into the season, the big green balloon had been burst.

With 7:12 left in the second quarter, the Jets' franchise quarterback, writhing in pain, was carted off the field. He was loaded into an ambulance, accompanied by the previously injured Wayne Chrebet, a close friend. They were taken to Lenox Hill Hospital in Manhattan, where Testaverde was prepped for season-ending surgery to repair his ruptured left Achilles tendon.

That the Jets lost to the Patriots, 30-28, was secondary. The real matter was Testaverde. It did not help that the Jets also lost all-purpose back Leon Johnson, who suffered a season-ending knee injury, and that nose tackle Jason Ferguson, with a sprained knee and ankle, also will be gone for an undetermined length of time.

Wait 'til next year?

Vinny Testaverde's blown Achilles tendon all but ended the Jets' hopes for the Super Bowl.

"God is playing sometimes," said Bill Parcells, who may not have a next year. "That's all you can really say."

Parcells, not wanting to show any signs of panic, didn't even mention the injuries in his postgame address to the team. He focused strictly on the game, a not-so-pretty affair in which the Jets allowed Drew Bledsoe to have a 340-yard passing day.

"A couple of guys got hurt," Parcells said.

"That's life in the big city," the Jets coach said later, trying to put on a brave face. "That's the way it goes. It's a humbling game, a game that can turn very quickly. We've got 15 games to go and we've got to figure out a way to approach those."

The season was forever changed when Testaverde went down. Martin fumbled and the ball went backward to the 25, where there was a scramble. Testaverde, about five yards behind the pileup, started toward the loose ball. He never made it.

"Vinny is such a leader that, for that moment when he was laying there, a piece of everyone on the team was laying there with him," said Martin, who rushed for 85 yards.

Testaverde was carried to the sideline and placed on a golf cart. And off he went, carted out of the stadium and the season.

First-Win Rally Great

Jets drop Broncs to 0-4 in 'rematch'

By Rich Cimini

This time, there wasn't a trophy presentation on the field. There wasn't a champagne-soaked victory celebration. The Jets-Broncos rematch yesterday at Mile High Stadium wasn't about a championship. It was about survival.

Someone had to be 0-4, and when it became apparent that it was going to be the Broncos, Bryan Cox enjoyed the moment by taunting the two-time-defending Super Bowl champions. Late in the Jets' 21-13 victory, the fiery linebacker turned to the Denver sideline and waved goodbye. Over and over, he waved.

"I was saying good riddance," a smiling Cox said later in an upbeat Jets locker room.

The Broncos, who lost star running back Terrell Davis to a likely season-ending knee injury, are as good as done. Only one team in history—the '92 Chargers—has made the playoffs after an 0-4 start.

As for the Jets (1-3), they felt reborn. Suddenly, there's hope again.

"It seems like we've been holding our breath for three weeks," said cornerback Ray Mickens, who went from last week's goat to one of yesterday's heroes. "We can exhale now."

Keyshawn Johnson, a dominant force again, managed a small smile. It was a smile of relief.

"We were one of those teams at 0-3, on the ledge, strangling ourselves," said Johnson, who had eight catches for 98 yards and a touchdown. "But we put some slack back in the rope, and now we can move forward."

They will enter next week's game against Jacksonville (3-1) with a little of their old swagger. Finally, the Jets are a confident team, having survived a heated fourth quarter that included trash-talking, near-brawls and several huge plays by the Jets' maligned defense, which racked up six turnovers. That's three more than the combined total from the first three games.

"This wasn't artistic or anything, but we just played a lot better defensively," Bill Parcells said.

Tuna, Jets Keep Playoffs on Menu

Beat Bills, feed playoff hunger

By Rich Cimini

S ay this for the Jets: Even as postseason long shots, they haven't lost their appetite. That would've been easy to do, considering their plight, but the Jets proved again yesterday they still have the hunger of a playoff hopeful, as they handled the Bills, 17-7, for their third straight win.

Anything for a free meal, courtesy of Bill Parcells.

The Jets coach, tickled by the mini-resurgence, was in such a giddy mood last week that he provided food for thought. He promised to treat the players to dinner if they defeated the favored Bills at Giants Stadium.

You can almost hear the maître d' now: Parcells, party of 53.

He will make good on the promise. Minutes after the win, spearheaded by a blitz-oriented defense that forced three turnovers and scored on a fumble recovery by Eric Ogbogu, Parcells assigned linebacker Mo Lewis to organize the affair.

"I'm really proud of them, about as proud as I've been in the team in a long time," said Parcells, who shared those thoughts with the players.

Three weeks ago, the Jets (4-6) were left for road kill. That was after they blew a 17-point lead to the Raiders. Now they have rebounded to put themselves on the outskirts of the playoff race.

The Jets have a new and exciting quarterback, Ray Lucas, and they have rediscovered their once-formidable defense, which munched on Doug Flutie (22-for-40, 220 yards) and held the Bills to 60 yards on the ground. In the first meeting, the Bills ran up 224 rushing yards.

Did someone say playoff push?

"We still have playoff hopes in this locker room," center Kevin Mawae said. "We got a taste of it last year, and we want to get back. We're not here to die. We're here to fight the rest of it out."

Parcells crunched a few numbers. The Jets, who face the Colts (8-2) Sunday on the road, are only two games behind the Bills. Hmmm.

"I'm not that good in math," he said, "but it's possible. Not probable, but possible."

Credit the defense, which has surrendered only 31 points in the last three games. Bill Belichick designed an impressive scheme for Flutie & Co., surprising the Bills with the variety of blitzes.

The biggest play of the game came on a blitz, as nickel back Ray Mickens raced in from the slot and stripped Flutie in the end zone. Ogbogu pounced on the ball for a touchdown, giving the Jets a 14-0 lead in the second quarter.

"Vintage D.T.," joked Mickens, referring to Chiefs sack artist Derrick Thomas.

Earlier, Mickens was unblocked on the same blitz, but he didn't get the sack because Flutie unloaded the ball. Mickens was hoping for another chance.

"I was happy Belichick made the call when he did," Mickens said, smiling.

So was Ogbogu, who scored his first touchdown since his days at Stepinac High School.

"The ball looked as big as the moon," said Ogbogu, who replaced Bryan Cox as a dime rusher after not dressing the last two games.

It was a banner day for young defensive linemen. Jason Wiltz, a seldom-used rookie, squashed the Bills' last hope by intercepting a pass at the Jets' 15, a ball that was batted at the line by Ernie Logan. It was the Jets' second red-zone interception. The first came from Victor Green, who had a second-quarter interception at the 9.

"We figured they were going to do something different," Bills center Jerry Ostroski said of the Jets' defense. "It seems like they have a trademark for that every game. They pick something different every week. They came at us, and made the big plays."

The Jets' opportunistic defense complemented a conservative but turnover-free offense. Curtis Martin (64 yards on 23 carries) saw his streak of four straight 100-yard games come to an end, and the Jets didn't have a play longer than 20 yards, but they got by.

Lucas (16-for-20, 142 yards) was efficient, if not prolific. Mostly, he dumped off to Martin, who had a team-high seven catches. But Lucas did score on a 9-yard scramble, his first career touchdown.

"There's no quit in this team," said Lucas, now 2-1 as a starter. "The record doesn't show it, but we have the heart of a champion."

At least the heart still is beating.

Jets Can See Hopes Wayne

Chrebet drops last gasp of '99

By Rich Cimini

The ball was in Wayne Chrebet's hands, and then it wasn't. In a nanosecond, the Jets' season went from hope to history, and the emotions of the 13-6 loss yesterday to the Colts spilled out on the carpet of the RCA Dome.

Chrebet, who dropped the potential game-tying touchdown pass with 1:39 remaining in the fourth quarter, was flat on his back in the end zone, staring at the puffy white ceiling and the dark cloud that was quickly forming above him.

"It's a catch I've made thousands of times in practice and games throughout the course of my career," he would say later, gamely facing the media not 30 minutes after that fateful pass smacked him in the kisser and bounced away.

Ray Lucas, who made his best throw of the day, was on his knees at the 26-yard line, pounding the turf—a display eerily reminiscent of the Vinny Testaverde injury scene in Week 1.

It was that type of defeat, the "worst loss of the season, even worse than the Raiders because I know it should've been better," said Bill Parcells, referring to the game last month in which they blew a 17-point lead.

"You can't help but feel crushed," said Curtis Martin, who rushed for 83 yards to become the fourth back in history to reach 1,000 in each of his first five seasons.

The Jets' season, unofficially, is over. At 4-7, they have virtually no shot at the playoffs. In fact, several players made concession speeches. So much for a meaningful Jets-Giants showdown Sunday at Giants Stadium.

The gritty Jets had made the season interesting, taking a three-game winning streak into yesterday, but they blew a 6-0 lead and self-destructed with a spate of errors against the first-place Colts (9-2), who have won seven straight for the first time since 1975.

But they came tantalizingly close to pulling off the upset, holding the ball for 7:21 in the fourth quarter and setting up the last gasp to Chrebet on a fourth-and-19 play from the 26. In fact, Chrebet suggested the play, asking for the ball because he thought he could get open against the soft middle of the Colts' defense.

The Colts covered it well—defensive back Billy Austin was right there in the end zone—but Lucas' laser shot was on the money.

"It was the perfect chance and he made a hell of a throw," Parcells said. "It hit him in the hands, didn't it?"

Chrebet, owning up to his drop, said: "Anytime you get your hands on the ball and don't bring it in, it's disappointing. I pride myself on third- and fourth-down plays, when the team needs a big play. I fully expect to come up with those."

He was asked if the play typified the Jets' season.

"I don't know if one play can sum up a whole season," Chrebet said. "It's just been one of those seasons."

The loss to the Colts was just one of many disappointments of the 1999 season.

Emotion Not Part of Tuna's Game Plan

By Rich Cimini

B ill Parcells, Jersey guy, started rooting for the Giants when he was 8 years old. He still remembers the first time he saw them play at Yankee Stadium. It was against the Steelers in 1956, and Ted Marchibroda was the Pittsburgh quarterback.

Two years later, when the Giants faced the Colts in the celebrated NFL championship game, Parcells, only 17, listened on a radio at Lake Hopatcong. His friends were outside, ice skating. He was inside, dying with the Giants in overtime.

Today, Parcells faces the Giants, the team he coached to two Super Bowls, for only the second time. The first meeting was the 1996 finale, when his New England team overcame a 22-0 deficit and won, 23-22, to clinch the homefield advantage throughout the AFC playoffs. Afterward, Parcells was choked up.

"I remember that last game was very emotional," said Jets punter Tom Tupa, who played for the Patriots. "The players knew all about it. You could tell when we got to the stadium it meant a lot to him."

Not this time, according to Parcells, who insisted that Jets vs. Giants has no special meaning for him. Of course, that's hard to believe. Wouldn't your heart flutter if you encountered your first love at a high school reunion?

"I'm past that," said Parcells, nine years removed from the Giants. "So much time has expired. I'm not nostalgic like that too much." Then, adding another pearl to his anti-sentimental philosophy, he added: "It's not the places, it's always the people you have the feeling for."

Suffering Jet Lag

Parcells ashamed of disaster

By Rich Cimini

It was so humiliating that Bill Parcells said it was the first time as the Jets' coach that he felt "ashamed" by the team's effort.

It was so bad that strong safety Victor Green said it was worse than anything he experienced during the 1-15 season in 1996.

It was so one-sided that the combustible Keyshawn Johnson was too drained to throw another postgame tirade on the way to the locker room. The star wide receiver's famous mouth was defaced by a fat lip, and there had to be something symbolic in that.

The Jets' 41-28 loss to the Giants yesterday at Giants Stadium was a microcosm of their season: They were out of it from the start.

"We were outplayed, outprepared, outcoached, out-everything, and I'm ashamed," said Parcells, calling it one of the most embarrassing losses of his career. "This is the first time in three years I've been ashamed."

Parcells took responsibility for the loss, easily the Jets' poorest performance since the Week 5 debacle last season in St. Louis, but he made it clear they weren't surprised by anything the Giants threw at them. That's another way of saying the players messed up.

And they did. This is all you need to know: The Giants produced 264 yards on six big plays. The Jets finished with 291 yards—in total.

The Jets (4-8), losers of two straight, were ill-prepared and ill-motivated. Just plain ill. They fell behind, 17-0, after three possessions, looking every bit like a team that had quit on its season. That it came against the Giants, who began the day with a three-game losing streak and internal strife, made it tougher to comprehend.

"This is one of those games you want to destroy your opponent," said Curtis Martin, who rushed six times for a career-low 4 yards (not a misprint). "But we came out and we got destroyed."

Jets Make Parcells Proud

Curtis, defense wing Seahawks

By Rich Cimini

As the final seconds ticked away yesterday at Giants Stadium, the crowd rose to its feet and delivered a collective appeal to Bill Parcells. "One more year!" the fans chanted as the Jets concluded maybe the best 8-8 season in their history.

Minutes later, an emotional Parcells stood before his team, 19-9 winners over the Seahawks, and fought back tears as he commended the players on their stunning 7-2 finish. The Jets coach told them they "played like champions" over the second half of the season, and that's when he choked up. Later, there were handshakes and hugs for players and assistant coaches.

This was either an emotional farewell to football or a proud coach simply caught up in the moment.

Parcells, his future the subject of intense speculation, revealed in his postgame news conference that he will declare his intentions "very, very quickly."

In recent days, Parcells had seen saying he wanted to huddle with the new owner before making a decision. Curiously, he amended that timetable, claiming he has to "get on with business."

"I'm going to think this over real quick," said Parcells, who would shock many of his players if he retired. "We've got imminent changes here in the organization. I have a responsibility to the organization and I will adhere to that all the way."

Parcells was truly touched by the turnaround, marking the Jets' third straight non-losing season—a feat they hadn't accomplished since 1967-1969.

"I really think they played like champions in the second half (of the season)," he said. "Not that it makes any difference, because we're 8-8, but they showed a lot of guts."

Parcells talked about a carryover to next season. He didn't say if he would be there to witness it.

CHAPTER 14

OFF THE
SIDELINES

Bill Parcells said he knew it was time to go. But staying gone wouldn't be easy.

W hen Bill Parcells told the players that he was retiring, he didn't give a fiery speech. He simply read a poem, *The Man in the Glass*, then left the room.

"The Man in the Glass"

When you get what you want in your struggle for Self
And the world makes you king for a day
Just go to the mirror and look at yourself
And see what "the man" has to say

For it isn't your parents, your children, or wife
Whose judgment upon you must pass
The Fellow whose verdict counts most in your life
Is the one staring back from the Glass

Some people may think you a straight-shooting chum
And call you a wonderful guy
But the Man in the Glass says you're only a bum
If you can't look him straight in the eye

He's the fellow to please, NEVER MIND THE REST
For he's with you clear up to the end
And you've passed your most dangerous, difficult test
If the Man in the Glass is your friend

You may fool the whole world down the pathway of Life
And get pats on the back as you pass
But your final reward will be heartaches and tears
If you've cheated the Man in the Glass.

— Dale Wimbrow

Parcells Sez He's Finished

Jets coach is tired of 365-day grind; will stay as top exec

By Kenny Lucas and Bill Hutchinson

Legendary sidelines master Bill Parcells rocked football fans yesterday, resigning as Jets head coach after transforming Gang Green from perennial pretenders into contenders.

With a bit of poetry and "a little sadness," the man who led the Giants to two Super Bowl victories tearfully exited a day after chanting Jets fans begged for him to try his championship magic "One more year!"

"There won't be any coaching rumors about Bill Parcells, because I coached my last game," he said at a noon news conference. "This is the end of my coaching career."

The burly bear, who snarled and stomped along the gridiron for three seasons with the team, became teary-eyed as he told his players he was passing the coaching reins to defensive coordinator Bill Belichick.

Parcells, 58, who will stay on as the team's chief operating officer, said he was stepping down after more than three decades in coaching because "I can't give it the way I know I have to to be successful 365 days a year."

Instead of a fiery pep talk, Parcells chose to read his players a poem that he said summed up his feelings—Dale Wimbrow's "The Man in the Glass." He choked up and paused halfway through the verse.

"It basically says that you can't fool yourself," Parcells explained. "I knew it was time. The important thing for me is that the players who played for me thought I was trying to win every game we played."

"A lot of people were just stunned and didn't know what to think," said running back Curtis Martin.

Field Leader in a League of His Own

By Mike Lupica

He talked yesterday about taking the ride Sunday to Giants Stadium from the hotel where the Jets stay on Saturday nights before home games. Bill Parcells talked about Jersey streets he knows as well as his playbook, driving past landmarks like his first house, his first school, his mother Ida's house in Hasbrouck Heights, just up the hill from where the Jets would play Seattle in the afternoon.

Parcells said it was the same route he always takes, past the same memories. But it was all different this time, because it was the last time. Parcells would coach this game against Seattle and then walk away from coaching for good. The Jets won, 19-9. Yesterday they lost as great a coach or manager as any New York sports team has ever had.

"It was such a nice day, Sunday," he said. "I couldn't believe what I was seeing on the second day of January. ... It was a wonderful day to play."

There have been other football coaches in Parcells' time, in other cities, some who won more than he did. Parcells was the biggest star of them all. He was the kind of star Vince Lombardi once was with the Green Bay Packers. Maybe it figures they both came out of Jersey.

Parcells made the Giants matter again. Then he did the exact same thing with the Jets. He came back to Giants Stadium and put it all on the line and leaves bigger than ever. This is the way big guys are supposed to do it.

"I'm not gonna coach any more football games," he said yesterday.

He does not deliver a Super Bowl trophy to the Jets the way he did twice with the Giants. He does not even get the Jets to the Super Bowl. But he gave Jets fans a run. He delivered hope to them after all the seasons when they had none.

At the end on Sunday, Jets fans chanted "one more year" at him. They begged for one more season even as Parcells had already decided that 15 seasons as a head coach in the NFL were enough, that there had been enough Sundays like this, that he was 58 and it was finally time to get on with the rest of his life.

You don't have to like him or his style or the way he could sound like a bully sometimes, even on "60 Minutes" on Sunday, when he said his wife, Judy, didn't know whether a football was blown up or stuffed with feathers. He walked away from contracts with both the Giants and Patriots and didn't win any class awards from either one of them.

But in the end, his last Sunday, he was at Giants Stadium where he belonged, winning one more game. The Jets are better off today than at any time since Joe Namath. Whatever money Parcells was making, it wasn't enough.

The Jets, in the process of being sold, are worth plenty more today than they were three years ago when Leon Hess hired Parcells away from the Patriots. More importantly, Jets tickets feel like gold again to the people who have them in their pockets. There is no way to measure the value of a feeling like that in sports.

The two years before Parcells got here, the Jets won three games. Under Parcells, the team averaged 10 wins a season, came within a game of the Super Bowl last year and would've gone this year if Vinny Testaverde, their quarterback, hadn't blown an Achilles tendon one hour into this season. The Giants have always been the bigger game in town. That changed as soon as Parcells got the Jets.

Parcells said yesterday that "if I did go somewhere, when I left there it was a better operation."

Everybody thought he would come back because the Jets will be one of the favorites to win it all next season, with Testaverde back and an exciting kid like Ray Lucas backing him up. But after all the years and all the jobs in college and the pros, after bringing this Jets team back from 1-6 to 8-8, Parcells decided he didn't have to prove anything to anybody.

"I think it's time," he said. Then he corrected himself and said, "I know it's time."

Jets Can't Find Rhyme or Reason to Move

By Rich Cimini

S tunned silence. That's how the Jets reacted yesterday upon hearing from Bill Parcells that he was stepping down as head coach.

Parcells, in a 10-minute address to the players in the second-floor auditorium at Weeb Ewbank Hall, made a few general remarks about the season, then dropped the bombshell about his coaching retirement. Before leaving, he read a 65-year-old poem entitled "The Guy in the Glass."

After the last line—"But your final reward will be heartaches and tears if you've cheated the man in the glass"—Parcells walked out of the room.

"He dropped the mike and left teary-eyed," said linebacker Dwayne Gordon, one of 13 original Parcells Jets who was asked by the outgoing coach to stand at the meeting. "We all stood there and you could hear a pin drop. It was quiet for a little while. Everybody was looking at each other like 'What do we do now?'"

It was a theatrical goodbye for a coach who always had a flair for the dramatic.

"We were pretty stunned," said running back Curtis Martin, who, in four of his five seasons, has played under Parcells. "A lot of people were just stunned, and we didn't know what to think. A lot of people sat there for a second, looking very confused."

A few players said they suspected Parcells might quit, but the overwhelming majority admitted they were surprised by his decision. There was a sense of disappointment, maybe even traces of resentment, among players who were counting on Parcells to return in 2000 with the hope of building on this season's strong finish.

"Bill Parcells at 75% is better than most coaches in the league," defensive back Ray Mickens said. "For him to go out in this way, it sort of hurts because you enjoy playing for a coach like that. But, looking at the upside, you see (Bill) Belichick, and he's going to be a great coach, and I know he's been waiting for this moment for a long time."

Keyshawn Johnson figured Parcells was a goner after observing his emotional demeanor following Sunday's season-ending win over the Seahawks. Yet the star wide receiver said he was "still kind of numb" by the sudden turn of events.

Disappointed?

"It's not so much a disappointment, but you would've just hoped he had stayed on and continued to coach us the way he did in the last nine games," Johnson said. "But it's time for a new coach. Coach Belichick is an insider, not an outsider, so we pretty much have everything intact."

Quarterback Vinny Testaverde, who considered Parcells a father figure, said, "Selfishly, I'm sad, but I'm happy for coach Parcells. In my opinion, he's the best coach who ever coached the game."

Most players said they understood Parcells' sentiment about not being able to give 100% to the job.

"It's his time and you have to respect that," safety Victor Green said. "Just like when Michael (Jordan) retired, it was his time. You have to respect it, no matter how much more you can still bring to the game."

After Parcells walked out of the meeting room for the final time, there were about 15 seconds of dead silence. Finally, the tension was shattered when defensive line coach Romeo Crennel hollered, "D-line, I need to see you."

And life without Parcells went on.

Jets' Coach Lasts One Day

Belichick walks out on contract

By Bill Hutchinson

Bill Belichick blindsided the Jets yesterday, throwing the team into chaos and stunning fans by abruptly quitting as head coach one day after Bill Parcells anointed him with the job.

With Gang Green reeling from Parcells' sudden resignation Monday, Belichick said he decided that uncertainty about who would buy the team would keep him from leading with "100% conviction."

"As of today, I'm resigning from the New York Jets," Belichick, 47, told reporters yesterday at the team's Hempstead, L.I., training facility. "This is the only way to be fair to me, the organization and everyone else in the organization."

The bombshell announcement came amid a bidding war between two moguls for the franchise, which Parcells and his longtime assistant Belichick had spent the last three seasons trying to turn around.

The Tennessee native's decision could spark a legal battle between him and Jets brass, who vowed to prevent the defensive guru from coaching for the New England Patriots or any other National Football League team.

Belichick, who has toiled for years in Parcells' shadow, said they spoke briefly before his news conference.

Parcells, whose relationship with Belichick was strained during the Jets' 8-8 season, declined comment.

NFL officials said the Jets cannot make Belichick coach against his will. But under his contract, they can block him from taking another coaching job— unless the team compensates the Jets with such incentives as draft picks.

Belichick said that without new ownership in place, he would be unable to make "the strong, hard, fast, tough decisions that you need to make as a head coach."

As Jet Coach, Tuna Fin-ished

By Rich Cimini

Two weeks ago, Bill Parcells walked away from coaching, claiming it was "definitely the end of my football career." He apparently wasn't kidding. The Jets' director of football operations, in a lengthy meeting on Friday with Woody Johnson, told the owner-in-waiting he doesn't want to return to the sideline, a person familiar with the meeting said last night.

Johnson, who would like nothing better than to have Parcells lead his $635 million team on the field, told the former Super Bowl coach to take the weekend off before making a final decision, the source said.

As of last night, there was no word on the resolution. But, barring a last-minute change of heart, Parcells has coached his last game. He apparently told Johnson that, at 58, he wants to get on with a life after coaching.

During two weeks of tantalizing speculation, it has been reported that Johnson is prepared to make Parcells the richest coach in league history with a salary of at least $5 million a year. But for Parcells, who made $2.5 million last season as the coach/director of operations, this apparently isn't a money issue.

Parcells is famous for changing his mind, but he left Johnson with the "distinct impression" that his intention was to stay retired, the source said.

That would open the door for Al Groh, a career assistant who has emerged as Parcells' choice for the head-coaching job. Groh has coached 13 years with Parcells, the last three as the Jets' linebackers coach. Parcells' objective is to maintain continuity, trying to build on the success of his three-year reign.

Parcells, out of loyalty to the late Leon Hess, is expected to remain with the club in a front-office capacity.

The outcome of the two-week coaching puzzle should become public in the next day or two as other pending issues surrounding the team are resolved.

Once those matters are settled, the Parcells-Groh tandem can move on to other, more pressing matters.

Tuna Will Swim Straight into Hall

By Gary Myers

W hen one of his players had a breakout game, former Giants, Patriots and Jets coach Bill Parcells always liked to say, "Don't put him in Canton yet."

Well, a year from now, Parcells, who announced his retirement from coaching Jan. 3—and confirmed it when he didn't return after Bill Belichick resigned—is a lock himself to be on his way to Canton in his first year of eligibility.

Joe Horrigan, a VP of the Pro Football Hall of Fame, said yesterday Parcells is immediately eligible to be on the list of about 70 candidates for the class of 2001.

Players have to wait five seasons before they are eligible, but coaches don't. Horrigan said the 38 voters will be given the list of candidates at the end of the October. They reduce it to 15 finalists and they are announced two weeks before the Super Bowl. The new enshrinees are named the day before the Super Bowl.

"I think he is the Joe Montana of next year," said one voter, Geoff Hobson of the *Cincinnati Enquirer*. "Don't even have a discussion. If you want to take a bathroom break, take it then."

Parcells has the credentials: He won two Super Bowls with the Giants and took the Patriots to one. Parcells, Don Shula, Dick Vermeil and Dan Reeves are the only coaches in NFL history to take two different teams to the Super Bowl.

Go ahead, put him in Canton.

APPENDIX:

Bill Parcells' NFL Head Coaching Record

*Away game

1999 NEW YORK JETS:
8-8   5th in AFC East

Sept. 12	New England	L	28-30
Sept. 19	Buffalo*	L	3-17
Sept. 26	Washington	L	20-27
Oct. 3	Denver*	W	21-13
Oct. 11	Jacksonville	L	6-16
Oct. 17	Indianapolis	L	13-16
Oct. 24	Oakland*	L	23-24
Nov. 7	Arizona	W	12-7
Nov. 15	New England*	W	24-17
Nov. 21	Buffalo	W	17-7
Nov. 28	Indianapolis*	L	6-13
Dec. 5	NY Giants*	L	28-41
Dec. 12	Miami	W	28-20
Dec. 19	Dallas*	W	22-21
Dec. 27	Miami*	W	38-31
Jan. 2	Seattle	W	19-9

1998 NEW YORK JETS:
12-4   1st in AFC East

Sept. 6	San Francisco*	L	30-36
Sept. 13	Baltimore	L	10-24
Sept. 20	Indianapolis	W	44-6
Oct. 4	Miami	W	20-9
Oct. 11	St. Louis*	L	10-30
Oct. 19	New England*	W	24-14
Oct. 25	Atlanta	W	28-3
Nov. 1	Kansas City*	W	20-17
Nov. 8	Buffalo	W	34-12
Nov. 15	Indianapolis*	L	23-24
Nov. 22	Tennessee*	W	24-3
Nov. 29	Carolina	W	48-21
Dec. 6	Seattle	W	32-31
Dec. 13	Miami*	W	21-16
Dec. 19	Buffalo*	W	17-10
Dec. 27	New England	W	31-10

AFC Playoff Game:

Jan. 10	Jacksonville	W	34-24

AFC Championship:

Jan. 17	Denver*	L	10-23

1997 NEW YORK JETS:
9-7   3rd in AFC East

Aug. 31	Seattle*	W	41-3
Sept. 7	Buffalo	L	22-28
Sept. 14	New England (OT)*	L	24-27
Sept. 21	Oakland	W	23-22
Sept. 28	Cincinnati*	W	31-14
Oct. 5	Indianapolis*	W	16-12
Oct. 12	Miami	L	20-31
Oct. 19	New England	W	24-19
Nov. 2	Baltimore (OT)	W	19-16
Nov. 9	Miami *	L	17-24
Nov. 16	Chicago*	W	23-15
Nov. 23	Minnesota	W	23-21
Nov. 30	Buffalo*	L	10-20
Dec. 7	Indianapolis	L	14-22
Dec. 14	Tampa Bay	W	31-0
Dec. 21	Detroit*	L	10-13

1996 NEW ENGLAND PATRIOTS:
11-5   1st in AFC East

Sept. 1	Miami*	L	10-24
Sept. 8	Buffalo*	L	10-17
Sept. 15	Arizona	W	31-0
Sept. 22	Jacksonville (OT)	W	28-25
Oct. 6	Baltimore*	W	46-38
Oct. 13	Washington	L	22-27
Oct. 20	Indianapolis*	W	27-9
Oct. 27	Buffalo	W	28-25
Nov. 3	Miami	W	42-23
Nov. 10	NY Jets*	W	31-27
Nov. 17	Denver	L	8-34
Nov. 24	Indianapolis	W	27-13
Dec. 1	San Diego*	W	45-7
Dec. 8	NY Jets	W	34-10
Dec. 15	Dallas*	L	6-12
Dec. 21	NY Giants*	W	23-22

1996 CONTINUED:

AFC Playoff Game:

Jan. 5	Pittsburgh	W	28-3

AFC Championship:

Jan. 12	Jacksonville	W	20-6

Super Bowl XXXI (New Orleans):

Jan. 26,	Green Bay	L	21-35

1995 NEW ENGLAND PATRIOTS:
6-10   4th in AFC East

Sept. 3	Cleveland	W	17-14
Sept. 10	Miami	L	3-20
Sept. 17	San Francisco*	L	3-28
Oct. 1	Atlanta*	L	17-30
Oct. 8	Denver	L	3-37
Oct. 15	Kansas City*	L	26-31
Oct. 23	Buffalo	W	27-14
Oct. 29	Carolina (OT)	L	17-20
Nov. 5	NY Jets*	W	20-7
Nov. 12	Miami*	W	34-17
Nov. 19	Indianapolis	L	10-24
Nov. 26	Buffalo*	W	35-25
Dec. 3	New Orleans	L	17-31
Dec. 10	NY Jets	W	31-28
Dec. 16	Pittsburgh*	L	27-41
Dec. 23	Indianapolis*	L	7-10

1994 NEW ENGLAND PATRIOTS:
10-6   2nd in AFC East

Sept. 4	Miami*	L	35-39
Sept. 11	Buffalo	L	35-38
Sept. 18	Cincinnati*	W	31-28
Sept. 25	Detroit*	W	23-17
Oct. 2	Green Bay	W	17-16
Oct. 9	LA Raiders	L	17-21
Oct. 16	NY Jets*	L	17-24
Oct. 30	Miami	L	3-23
Nov. 6	Cleveland*	L	6-13
Nov. 13	Minnesota (OT)	W	26-20
Nov. 20	San Diego	W	23-17
Nov. 27	Indianapolis*	W	12-10
Dec. 4	NY Jets	W	24-13
Dec. 11	Indianapolis	W	28-13
Dec. 18	Buffalo*	W	41-17
Dec. 24	Chicago*	W	13-3

AFC Playoff Game:

Jan. 1	Cleveland*	L	13-20

1993 NEW ENGLAND PATRIOTS:
5-11   4th in AFC East

Sept. 5	Buffalo*	L	14-38
Sept. 12	Detroit (OT)	L	16-19
Sept. 19	Seattle	L	14-17
Sept. 26	NY Jets*	L	7-45
Oct. 10	Phoenix*	W	23-21
Oct. 17	Houston	L	14-28
Oct. 24	Seattle*	L	9-10
Oct. 31	Indianapolis*	L	6-9
Nov. 7	Buffalo (OT)	L	10-13
Nov. 21	Miami*	L	13-17
Nov. 28	NY Jets	L	0-6
Dec. 5	Pittsburgh*	L	14-17
Dec. 12	Cincinnati	W	7-2
Dec. 19	Cleveland*	W	20-17
Dec. 26	Indianapolis	W	38-0
Jan. 2	Miami (OT)	W	33-27

1990 NEW YORK GIANTS:
13-3   1st in NFC East

Sept. 9	Philadelphia	W	27-20
Sept. 16	Dallas*	W	28-7
Sept. 23	Miami	W	20-3
Sept. 20	Dallas	W	31-17
Oct. 14	Washington*	W	24-20
Oct. 21	Phoenix	W	20-19
Oct. 28	Washington	W	21-10
Nov. 5	Indianapolis*	W	24-7
Nov. 11	LA Rams*	W	31-7
Nov. 18	Detroit	W	20-0
Nov. 25	Philadelphia*	L	13-31
Dec. 3	San Francisco*	L	3-7
Dec. 9	Minnesota	W	23-15
Dec. 15	Buffalo	L	13-17
Dec. 23	Phoenix*	W	24-21
Dec. 30	New England*	W	13-10

NFC Playoff Game:

Jan. 13	Chicago	W	31-3

NFC Championship:

Jan. 20	San Francisco*	W	15-13

Super Bowl XXV (Tampa, Fla.):

Jan. 27	Buffalo	W	20-19

1989 NEW YORK GIANTS:
12-4   1st in NFC East

Sept. 11	Washington*	W	27-24
Sept. 17	Detroit	W	24-14
Sept. 24	Phoenix	W	35-7

Oct. 1	Dallas*	W	30-13
Oct. 8	Philadelphia*	L	19-21
Oct. 15	Washington	W	20-17
Oct. 22	San Diego*	W	20-13
Oct. 30	Minnesota	W	24-14
Nov. 5	Phoenix*	W	20-13
Nov. 12	LA Rams*	L	10-31
Nov. 19	Seattle	W	15-3
Nov. 27	San Francisco*	L	24-34
Dec. 3	Philadelphia	L	17-24
Dec. 10	Denver*	W	14-7
Dec. 16	Dallas	W	15-0
Dec. 24	LA Raiders	W	34-17

NFC Playoff Game:

| Jan. 7 | LA Rams (OT) | L | 13-19 |

1988 NEW YORK GIANTS:
10-6   2nd in NFC East

Sept. 5	Washington	W	27-20
Sept. 11	San Francisco	L	17-20
Sept. 18	Dallas*	W	12-10
Sept. 25	LA Rams	L	31-45
Oct. 2	Washington*	W	24-23
Oct. 10	Philadelphia*	L	13-24
Oct. 16	Detroit	W	30-10
Oct. 23	Atlanta*	W	23-16
Oct. 30	Detroit*	W	13-10
Nov. 6	Dallas	W	29-21
Nov. 13	Phoenix*	L	17-24
Nov. 20	Philadelphia (OT)	L	17-23
Nov. 27	New Orleans*	W	13-12
Dec. 4	Phoenix	W	44-7
Dec. 11	Kansas City	W	28-12
Dec. 18	NY Jets*	L	21-27

1987 NEW YORK GIANTS:
6-9   5th in NFC East

Sept. 14	Chicago*	L	19-34
Sept. 20	Dallas	L	14-16
Sept. 27	Miami*		Strike
Oct. 5	San Francisco	L	21-41
Oct. 11	Washington	L	12-38
Oct. 18	Buffalo (OT)*	L	3-6
Oct. 25	St. Louis	W	30-7
Nov. 2	Dallas*	L	24-33
Nov. 8	New England	W	17-10
Nov. 15	Philadelphia*	W	20-17
Nov. 22	New Orleans*	L	14-23
Nov. 29	Washington*	L	19-23

Dec. 6	Philadelphia (OT)	W	23-20
Dec. 13	At St. Louis	L	24-27
Dec. 19	Green Bay	W	20-10
Dec. 27	NY Jets	W	20-7

1986 NEW YORK GIANTS:
14-2   1st in NFC East

Sept. 8	Dallas*	L	28-31
Sept. 14	San Diego	W	20-7
Sept. 21	LA Rams*	W	14-9
Sept. 28	New Orleans	W	20-17
Oct. 5	St. Louis*	W	13-6
Oct. 12	Philadelphia	W	35-3
Oct. 19	Seattle*	L	12-17
Oct. 27	Washington	W	27-20
Nov. 2	Dallas	W	17-14
Nov. 9	Philadelphia*	W	17-14
Nov. 16	Minnesota*	W	22-20
Nov. 23	Denver	W	19-16
Dec. 1	San Francisco*	W	21-17
Dec. 7	Washington*	W	24-14
Dec. 14	St. Louis	W	27-7
Dec. 20	Green Bay	W	55-24

NFC Playoff Game:

| Jan. 4 | San Francisco | W | 49-3 |

NFC Championship:

| Jan. 11 | Washington | W | 17-0 |

Super Bowl XXI (Pasadena, Calif.):

| Jan. 25 | Denver | W | 39-20 |

1985 NEW YORK GIANTS:
10-6   2nd in NFC East

Sept. 8	Philadelphia	W	21-0
Sept. 15	Green Bay*	L	20-23
Sept. 22	St. Louis	W	27-17
Sept. 29	Philadelphia (OT)*	W	16-10
Oct. 6	Dallas	L	29-30
Oct. 13	Cincinnati*	L	30-35
Oct. 20	Washington	W	17-3
Oct. 27	New Orleans*	W	21-13
Nov. 3	Tampa Bay	W	22-20
Nov. 10	LA Rams	W	24-19
Nov. 18	Washington*	L	21-23
Nov. 24	St. Louis*	W	34-3
Dec. 1	Cleveland	L	33-35
Dec. 8	Houston*	W	35-14
Dec. 15	Dallas*	L	21-28

1985 CONTINUED:

DEc. 21	Pittsburgh	W	28-10
NFC Wild Card Game:			
Dec. 29	San Francisco	W	17-3
NFC Playoff Game:			
Jan. 5	Chicago*	L	0-21

1984 NEW YORK GIANTS:
9-7   2nd in NFC East

Sept. 2	Philadelphia	W	28-27
Sept. 9	Dallas	W	28-7
Sept. 16	Washington*	L	14-30
Sept. 23	Tampa Bay	W	17-14
Sept. 30	LA Rams*	L	12-33
Oct. 8	San Francisco	L	10-31
Oct. 14	Atlanta*	W	19-7
Oct. 21	Philadelphia*	L	10-24
Oct. 28	Washington	W	37-13
Nov. 4	Dallas*	W	19-7
Nov. 11	Tampa Bay*	L	17-20
Nov. 18	St. Louis	W	16-10
Nov. 25	Kansas City	W	28-27
Dec. 2	NY Jets*	W	20-10
Dec. 9	St. Louis*	L	21-31
Dec. 15	New Orleans	L	3-10
NFC Wild Card Game:			
Dec. 23	LA Rams*	W	16-13
NFC Playoff Game:			
Dec. 29	San Francisco*	L	10-21

1983 NEW YORK GIANTS:
3-12-1   5th in NFC East

Sept. 4	LA Rams	L	6-16
Sept. 11	Atlanta (OT)*	W	16-13
Sept. 18	Dallas*	L	13-28
Sept. 26	Green Bay	W	27-3
Oct. 2	San Diego	L	34-41
Oct. 9	Philadelphia	L	13-17
Oct. 16	Kansas*	L	17-38
Oct. 24	St. Louis (OT)*	T	20-20
Oct. 30	Dallas	L	20-38
Nov. 7	Detroit*	L	9-15
Nov. 13	Washington	L	17-33
Nov. 20	Philadelphia*	W	23-0
Nov. 27	LA Raiders*	L	12-27
Dec. 4	St. Louis	L	6-10
Dec. 11	Seattle	L	12-17
Dec. 17	Washington*	L	22-31

WINNING TRADITIONS...

Bill Parcells
and the
United States
Postal Service

UNITED STATES
POSTAL SERVICE.